Tudor Portraits
Success and Failure of an Age

Tudor Portraits
Success and Failure of an Age

MICHAEL FOSS

HARRAP  *LONDON*

First published in Great Britain 1973 *by*
GEORGE G. HARRAP & CO. LTD
182–184 High Holborn, London WC1V 7AX

© Michael Foss 1973

ISBN 0 245 50887 2

Composed in Intertype Baskerville type and
printed by The Anchor Press Ltd, Tiptree, Essex
MADE IN GREAT BRITAIN

FOREWORD

Restless and energetic times are often hard on the citizen. The triumphs of the Tudor age are well known; less apparent is the pain that went hand-in-hand with success. One of the purposes of this book is to consider the cost of great achievement, and therefore several of the people portrayed here were, in effect, the victims of the times. Thomas More is an obvious case; but Mary Tudor, Kett, Gilbert and Greene, none of them evil and all with talent and feeling, were all undone by the stern course of the century. Even Walsingham was made poor and hurried to the grave by the laborious demands of Elizabeth's administration, and the resplendent Philip Sidney found no place for his chivalrous idealism in the faithless world of contemporary polity.

Concerned with the plight of the individual, I take an 'old-fashioned' view of enclosures. The use of enclosures, as modern historians have pointed out, brought prosperity to the land owners, helped to make farming more rational, and eventually raised the standard of agriculture. The denunciations of enclosures by such men as More, Hugh Latimer and John Hales were exaggerated. Good men usually do decry social injustice too passionately. But they were honest witnesses (among the best men of their time), and they saw that the prosperity of the rapacious caused the suffering of the poor; depopulation, dispossession, starvation, vagabondage and crime were among the immediate consequences of sixteenth-century agrarian changes. The historian, writes a wise member of the profession, 'sees the problem of the sixteenth century as a temporary crisis only'. But the peasant, distracted by poverty and hounded by authority, 'saw rich farmers taking up more and more land but giving less employment than ever before to the labourer. . . . It was difficult to keep a balanced outlook when one's own livelihood was at stake.'[1] The pains of the

[1] Joan Thirsk, *Tudor Enclosures* (Historical Assoc. 1959), p. 21.

5

weak and the unfortunate, crushed by impersonal social and economic forces, are relevant facts of history to be set against the aggrandizement of nations and the successes of the strong.

M.F.

CONTENTS

ILLUSTRATIONS

1
Tudor Monarchs

THE ENGLISH MONARCHY sank low in the fifteenth century. Philippe de Commines saw the Duke of Exeter, brother-in-law of Edward IV, trudging barefoot in the retinue of the Duke of Burgundy; the members of the House of Lancaster, Commines wrote, were poorer than street beggars. Never was the crown so disregarded, so despised, so bullied; never was the king in such danger of deposition and murder. In 1485 Henry VII, from an obscure family with only the slightest tinge of royal blood, came to the throne in the manner of the century, by force of arms, and in one reign raised the crown from impotent beggary to settled and prosperous power. 'From the time of William the Conqueror to the present', wrote an Italian envoy in 1498, 'no king has reigned more peaceably than he has, his great prudence causing him to be universally feared.'

Within fifteen years the wounds of the feudal discord were healed. The astute *Relation of the Island of England,* which the Venetian envoy wrote as a guide for his fellow countrymen to this far northern realm, pictured a well-favoured land. The fields were rich and gave forth with great abundance so that the people lived easily enough, cultivating just sufficient for their needs. The country was forested with a great variety of trees, and the envoy noted 'all our fruit trees' with the exception of the olive and the orange. Animals, both domestic and wild, were plentiful and well-grown so that 'stags, goats, fallow-deer, hares, rabbits, pigs, and an infinity of oxen' were available for meat. The rivers and the coastal waters provided good fishing, and various fowl were highly regarded, in particular pea-fowl, partridges, pheasants and swans 'which are eaten by the English like ducks and geese'.[1] Tilling the

---

[1] The swan was a royal bird. Only persons with freehold property to the value of five marks a year or more were allowed to own them; all other swans were for the use of the King. Peasants were also excluded, under severe penalties, from the deer-parks of the rich landowners.

fields was the chief occupation of the people, but the most notable feature of the countryside was the 'enormous number of sheep'. The wool trade was already the greatest source of England's wealth, and the lamentable policy of enclosure, which later caused such rural misery, was much practised. Besides the weaving of the wool, there was little industry, though iron and silver were produced and valuable mines existed for tin and lead.

The envoy noted that the countryside was very thinly populated while London was crowded and vigorous. The domestic architecture was not distinguished and the streets were a mess; ravens, kites and crows, far from being birds of ill-omen, as they were in Italy, were encouraged by the English to clear the offal and the garbage from the streets. The townsmen lived comfortably but not too fastidiously; Erasmus commented on the dirt and carelessness of the English household. If the houses were poor, the churches were grand. The greater monasteries were 'more like baronial palaces than religious houses', and the shrines of the saints were resplendent. The envoy wondered especially at the tomb of St Thomas Becket at Canterbury, 'entirely covered over with plates of pure gold' studded with sapphires, diamonds, rubies and emeralds.

Indeed, luxurious richness was apparent everywhere. 'The riches of England', wrote the envoy, 'are greater than those of any other country in Europe.' A small innkeeper might well have silver drinking-cups; a modest householder might have silver-plate to the value of £100. In the parish churches the crucifixes, candlesticks, patens, censers and cups were usually silver, and the quantity of wrought silver was 'the most remarkable thing in London'. In one street by St Paul's 'there are fifty-two goldsmith's shops, so rich and full of silver vessels, great and small, that in all the shops of Milan, Rome, Venice, and Florence put together, I do not think there would be found so many of the magnificence that are to be seen in London'.

The citizens, whom the envoy found 'handsome and well-proportioned', dressed well, ate well and drank well; they were polite and quick-witted, but not learned. They went through the forms of piety, going to Mass often and distributing alms, but the Venetian thought that they had 'various opinions concerning religion'. He thought the reputation of English soldiers was well earned 'from the great fear the French entertain of them'. But he agreed with an older authority that the English were liable to break off the battle for a good feast, and to ride to war loaded with wine and cheeses rather than armour and lances. The chief characteristic of Englishmen, however, was nationalism. 'The English', said the envoy, 'are great lovers of themselves, and of everything belonging to them; they think that there are no other men than themselves, and no other world but England.' And consequently they disliked all foreigners, suspecting that 'they never come into their island, but to make themselves masters of it, and to usurp their goods'. An insular, rugged, proud race, children of a beneficent land, kept from greatness, perhaps, by ignorance and lack of confidence.

The qualities of Henry VII, the man who raised England to such prosperity in so few years, were not those that make a man loved. Francis Bacon, who admired him, called Henry 'sad, serious and full of thoughts'; he was also cold, suspicious and avaricious. He supported justice in the State but overrode it in his own interests. He was not cruel, 'but the less blood he drew the more he took of treasure'. He had, however, the patience and sagacity to overcome all the disadvantages of a cold nature. From the first he showed a remarkable political wisdom, what the Venetian envoy called his 'prudence'. As he had won the throne on the battlefield, he did not disguise the source of his power. He had his battle standards laid in state at St Paul's, and would not marry Elizabeth of York, whose hand would give him some title to the crown, until after the coronation and confirmation of his place by Parliament. He chose, said Bacon, 'rather to keep state and strike a reverence into the people than to fawn upon them'. The sanction of power was a recognized reality; as a later writer put it, 'the sword hath always been better than half the title to get, establish or maintain a kingdom'. In the lawless age of the fifteenth century very little divinity surrounded the King, and Henry was not thought any the worse because he came to the throne by force of arms. He made his title good, not by doubtful claims or fraudulent pedigrees, but by his care of the country. Wise observers noted how he drove himself in the work of government. Ayala, the Spanish envoy, called him 'old for his years, but young for the sorrowful life he has led'. His chilly calculations were what good sense recommended for the well-being of the land. Bacon imputed his actions 'to nature, age, peace, and a mind fixed upon no other ambition or pursuit'.

Henry VII saw a strong monarchy as the most secure bulwark against the anarchy which had weakened England for so many years. During the wanderings of his exile in France he had seen the advantages of a centralized royal administration, and he was determined to try the same system in England. Monarchs, who before had been very often the pawns of circumstance, became by the deliberate policy of the Tudors the majestic and all-powerful governors of the State. To impress both countrymen and strangers with the glory of the English crown, Henry, who relentlessly extracted every last penny from the pockets of his poor subjects and hated war as a consumer of treasure, was prepared to spend lavishly on the upkeep of the royal family and the court. His own clothes were the most expensive that could be found and his tailors scoured Europe for jewels and precious metals, cloth of gold, silks, satins, furs and velvets. The Queen and the royal children were also radiantly dressed, and even the royal buckhounds went in silks of eight different colours 'garnished with crowns, roses, fleurs-de-lis, and other our badges'. Entertainments at court were done with the maximum of show and the greatest cost. The Venetion noted that six or seven hundred people might sit down to dinner at court and be regaled with a vast array of food. For the feast of Henry's nuptials with Elizabeth, in 1487, there were some fifty different dishes, from lampreys to sturgeon, from swans to plovers, from 'jelly hippocras' to 'custard royal'. The Venetian envoy wrote that Henry, 'though frugal to excess in his own person', spent £14,000 a year on his table. 'There is no country in the world', a Spanish traveller commented, 'where queens live with greater pomp than in England, where kings have as many court officers.'

Not only feasting, but also patronage of the arts became a duty for Renaissance kings seeking grandeur. Henry himself was not a learned man; Bacon called him studious rather than cultivated. His knowledge of French was good from his years in exile, and his Latin was adequate. But with his usual practical wisdom he knew what was wanted in his northern kingdom for so long ravaged by war and starved of thought and wit, and he set out to encourage the arts and sciences. His mother, the redoubtable Lady Margaret, was a great friend of scholarship, and perhaps under her influence he ensured that his children were educated up to the standard of princes. At the age of eleven, Arthur, the eldest son, impressed the Milanese ambassador with his learning; in 1494 Henry, the second son, was given John Skelton, poet and 'laureate' of Oxford, Cambridge and Louvain, as his tutor. At a time when England was noted for music, the royal family was musical. The children had the best training and the King maintained vocal and instrumental musicians, to sing in the Chapels Royal and to provide the entertainment at his interludes; he also, as his meticulous account books reveal, made many payments to trumpeters, fiddlers, organists, harpists, and even bagpipers.

Having seen to the education of his own household, Henry tried to increase the stock of public knowledge. Foreign scholars such as Pietro Carmeliano and Barnard Andre were welcomed. The printers Wynkin de Worde and Pynson were encouraged; Peter Artois was licensed to import books and manuscripts, and to sell them free of customs duties. The Italian Polydore Vergil was commissioned to write the history of England, which he wrote in Latin and finished in 1507. Henry was also a great builder. In his reign additions were made to the palace of Westminster, to the Tower of London, and to several of the royal manors. In 1503 the foundations were laid for the Henry VII Chapel at Westminster Abbey, the finest example of late perpendicular architecture in England.

Since Henry did most things by calculation it is hard to say what joy he got from his own magnificence. Perhaps his only real recreation was in sports and hunting which, like all the Tudors, he followed enthusiastically. The chief business of his reign was neither pleasure nor the fostering of the arts, but the accumulation of money, which he did with single-minded purpose. Again, he did this not so much from personal greed or ambition, but because his understanding of the condition of the country taught him that this was the best thing for England. 'There may no realm prosper', wrote Sir John Fortescue in the chaotic days of the Wars of the Roses, 'or be worshipful under a poor king.' The trading part of the nation, growing in importance under the new economic climate of capitalism and with the potential riches of the wool trade before their eyes, were tired of the disrupting anarchy of feudal war and supported a king who understood their interests. Henry, wrote Bacon, 'could not endure to have trade sick'; he husbanded the resources of the crown as carefully as any merchant. He was a trader himself, hired out his ships, and loaned money on interest. He preserved and improved all the means of raising revenue. He demanded excessive fines for the slightest wrongdoing and under the colour of the law extracted very large sums from towns, noblemen, mayors, aldermen and private citizens. He wrung from Parliament large grants to wage his minor, cautious and inexpensive campaigns, on all of which he made a profit. And he persuaded the French King to grant him a pension as the price of peace. By this ruthless economy he cleared off the debts of the crown in the first seven years of his reign. He then began to save and for the rest of his reign grew richer and richer. When he died it was estimated that he left over a million pounds in currency, jewels, plate, bonds and notes.

The wealth of the crown went hand-in-hand with a new prosperity in the country. At the start of the reign a Spanish ambassador had written that 'Henry likes to be much spoken of, and to be highly appreciated by the whole world. He fails in this because he is not a great man'. The Spaniard missed Henry's strength. Despite his disagreeable personality, his lack of humanity, generosity and warmth, Henry made England an important power. He had conserved her resources by avoiding war; he had fostered her commerce; he had prepared the ground for an efficient administration. No wonder England looked so strong to a later observer. In the midst of contending nations, wrote the Milanese envoy, the English King 'can stand like one at the top of a tower looking on at what is passing in the plain'.

In most ways Henry VII was a conventional man who followed the habits of his predecessors. He made no great innovations, even in his favourite field of taxation. What he achieved came from efficient practicality rather than new theory—as Bacon wrote, 'what he minded he compassed'. But the inheritance he left his son was the sure basis for the future success of his dynasty. A most brilliant foreign policy made a peaceful country respected abroad. Careful management, a ruthless will and canny self-advertisement gave the crown a new authority and prestige. Commercial success and the sense of power that comes from riches left a people united in an ever-rising nationalism.

Henry VIII, unlike his father, was royally bred and given every advantage of the Renaissance prince. The grace and the accom-

1a HENRY VII

1b HENRY VIII

2 EDWARD VI

plishments of his early years were stunning. His learning, his abilities in poetry and music, his bodily prowess, his charm made him seem by right the first man in the kingdom. Whereas his father wore the kingship like a disguise, Henry VIII wore it like a natural part of the body. His qualities and his training invested the kingship with a new radiance, and his speculative mind formed a theory of majesty which made explicit the despotism that had been present, but still hidden in the conduct of his father. In former times the king had been addressed as 'Your Grace'; Henry VIII was the first to be called 'Your Majesty', a title which was soon expanded into 'Your Sacred Majesty'.

The new title clothed a real new power; the king became, in the words of the French ambassador, 'a statue for idolatry'. Englishmen imagined themselves to be sturdy freemen while most continentals were slaves, but foreigners were astonished by the servility that Henry demanded from all his subjects. Even the princesses knelt before their father, never speaking 'but in adoration and kneeling'. And Marillac, the French ambassador, was amazed by the fawning of church dignitaries in the royal presence. The authority, almost the divinity, that Henry claimed for himself was something quite new in English history. The best minds of the Middle Ages had derived sovereignty from the people. They agreed that all dominion came ultimately from God, but between God and the ruler they interposed the community whose interests were paramount. In Henry's view, however, the prince was divinely ordained to be the shepherd of his people, and was the image of God in his own realm. He referred to the 'kingly power given him by God', and so plain was his authority that soon the idea of his divine right became the dogma of the age. Though a few bold spirits such as the Catholic Sir Thomas More and the Protestant Hugh Latimer contested this pretension, most Englishmen fell into line and echoed to some degree the cringing opinion of the lawyer Richard Crompton who declared that subjects must submit to all royal orders, even those against the word of God. The notion of the king's divinity became a commonplace of the drama. 'He that condemneth a King', said the old play *King John*, 'condemneth God without doubt.' Shakespeare wrote in *Hamlet* of the divinity that 'doth hedge a king', while Marlowe, always infatuated with power, put into the mouth of his Queen Dido a statement that did justice to the Tudor view of kingship:

> Shall vulgar peasants storm at what I do?
> The ground is mine that gives them sustenance,
> The air wherein they breathe, the water, fire,
> All that they have, their lands, their goods, their lives.

But the strange thing was that Henry VIII gave himself these semi-divine and despotic powers with the active consent of the people. All his revolutionary steps were incorporated in Acts of Parliament; his additions to the statute book take up more space than all the earlier Acts together. Before his time the influence of Parliament had been declining; when he had finished his critics could complain bitterly at 'this new-found article of our creed, that Parliament cannot err'. Like all Tudors he was quite prepared to bully Parliament and pack it with his supporters, but hardly found it necessary. Parliament was made up of property owners only—the landlords, the squires, the merchants, the lawyers, the burgesses—and Henry very quickly discerned that their interests coincided with his own. He made this self-seeking body the major instrument of his reform, and from the Reform Parliament in 1529 until the end of his reign he relied on Parliament to support his legislation. 'He has', the ambassador of the Emperor admitted, 'always fortified himself by the consent of Parliament.'

What Henry had done by his legislation was to put himself at the head of a unified and independent state that answered the national aspirations of most Englishmen. The country gave him the deference he demanded because he had won freedom from foreigners, and had made Englishmen the sole governors of English life. Faith was never an issue in Henry's mind; in his own opinion he was an orthodox Catholic until he died. His vast conceit helped him to maintain this opinion, but he never did regard his recasting of the English Church as anything more than a rational step in English policy. And with this peculiar blindness he was surprised that his actions had led to such bitter religious controversy. In his last speech to Parliament he denounced Catholics for calling Protestants heretics, and Protestants for calling Catholics papists and hypocrites. He was 'sorry to hear how unreverently that most precious jewel, the word of God, is disputed, rhymed, and jangled in every alehouse and tavern'. In his own opinion he had not created a merely secular state. With the blasphemy of one who felt he could do no wrong, he took himself seriously as Head of the Church, and saw no reason why his theology should not be as authoritative as his policy. But his political sense never deserted him for a moment. Everything he did was done with legal form; he never acted as the king alone, but always as the king through Parliament, the king through his Council, or the king through Convocation. His sure grasp of the instinctive desires of his countrymen usually enabled him to please the influential parts of society; and those he could not please he could usually intimidate. The relentless and pitiless extermination of those he feared, like the Duke of Buckingham, or those who would not obey him, like Sir Thomas More, soon cowed opposition. For the rest, he was the symbol of a proud and self-sufficient land. So long as a child of Henry lived, even the sickly youth Edward VI and the fanatical Catholic Mary, no other person or family could think of ruling in England.

The State became the mother of all. That loyalty which in feudal times was owed by person to person, by the underling to his protector, was now given by the citizen to his country. Making good use of that strong national feeling and insularity which the Venetian envoy had remarked on in 1498, Henry VIII encouraged a spirit of patriotism that seemed to override all other considerations. The duty to the country was universally stressed, by government, by constitutional lawyers, by writers, and by ordinary citizens. 'My king, my country I seek for whom I live', wrote the poet and diplomat Sir Thomas Wyatt on his return from Spain. The name of Machiavelli was an abomination to Englishmen, but the mentality of sixteenth-century England was an ironic confirmation of his cynical realism. 'Where the welfare of the country is at stake', he wrote in a *Discourse on Livy,* 'no consideration can intervene of justice or injustice, mercy or cruelty, commendable or ignominious, but putting all else aside, one must adopt whatever cause will save its existence and preserve its liberty.' It was the resolution born of this patriotism that saved the country from the Spanish Armada in 1588.

It is not too much to say that most Englishmen were Christians by unthinking habit, became Protestants by order of the government, but were patriots by faith and conviction. Few things are sadder or more touching than the victims of religious persecution, both Catholic and Puritan, still protesting on the scaffold the love of the country which had condemned them to death. The priests Campion and Sherwin prayed for Elizabeth with their heads on the block; the Puritan Stubbs, with his hand chopped off, waved the bleeding stump crying 'Long live the Queen'. Even Cardinal Allen, the most implacable and outspoken enemy of England's religion, protested that the one desire of himself and his fellow Catholics in exile was to serve 'our beloved country'. In the many Catholic ballads to the memory of the executed there is much courage and humility and resignation to the will of God, but almost no rage or hatred for England. The ballads ask for peace and the strength to meet death, but they seek no revenge :

> O God above, relent,
>   and listen to our cry;
> O Christ, our woes prevent,
>   let not thy children die.

Elizabeth, who knew her people so well, always judged a man by his patriotism and not his religion. Her faithful secretary Walsingham was a strong Puritan, yet he never lost her favour. She appointed the Catholic Lord Howard to be her admiral, and he had command of the fleet against the Armada.

The concentration of the people into a single family with the sovereign at the head brought a new unity to English life. When the division between Church and State was abolished by Henry VIII, much of the traditional discord between the spiritual realm and the temporal realm was also done away with. The clergy, because of their especial exemptions, were no longer able to lord it over the laity. The objectionable ecclesiastical courts could no longer charge a man with heresy merely for a refusal to pay the church fee demanded on an infant's death. In most matters, all men now stood on equal footing before the same courts. This unity of the people under the crown made England, in a century notorious for change, revolt and bloodshed, comparatively peaceful. There was less religious strife than in most other European countries, and fewer people died for their faith. Revolt was always a possibility from the ambitious, the conservatives, or the poor oppressed by social and economic changes; and the Tudors were always on the watch for the first sign of rebellion which they usually put down with the greatest severity. But rebels in England had harder work to do and less chance of success than in continental lands. The interests of the majority of the people agreed with the interests of the crown, as the brilliant and popular Essex found to his cost when he tried to steal the power from Elizabeth in her declining and embittered years.

When the national consciousness, fostered by the monarchy, was allied to old native energy and new inquisitiveness, great things were achieved in England. Henry VII and his son had encouraged shipbuilding, and most men were greedy for the riches of the New World; but England's age of exploration did not begin until patriotism was blended with the greed in the seamen's minds. The heroic tales of Hakluyt's *Principal Navigations* are the record of attempts to serve the country, and Hakluyt also had service in mind when he laboriously collected their stories. And the navigators, whatever their crimes, had the honour of their country in mind. The piratical Drake at his first sight of the Pacific, without hypocrisy prayed God 'to give him life and leave to sail an English ship upon that sea'. The navigator John Davis had such a high sense of England's destiny that he wrote : 'We of England are this saved people, by the eternal and infallible presence of the Lord pre-destinated to be sent into these gentiles in the sea, to those isles and famous kingdoms, there to preach the peace of the Lord.' To a large extent it was this sense of national purpose that transformed the English sailor from merely a good seaman to the commander of the ocean. 'They are victorious, stout and valiant,' wrote the Dutchman van Linschoten; 'and all their enterprises do take so good effect that they are thereby become lords and masters of the sea.'

The same national fervour helped the arts to flourish. So much life centred round the exalted figure of the monarch; and monarchs as able and learned as the Tudors could not but help the progress of the arts, which were throughout the sixteenth century under the particular patronage of the sovereign. This influence of the prince was described by Marlow in *Edward II* :

> Music and poetry are his delight;
> Therefore I'll have Italian masques by night,
> Sweet speeches, comedies, and pleasing shows.

The new learning of the Renaissance came to England with the royal stamp of approval. Despite the English dislike for foreigners, the great minds of the continent were welcomed at court, from

Erasmus in the reign of Henry VII to Giordano Bruno in the reign of Elizabeth. The Tudors were the supporters of the universities, and the learned repaid them with the compliments of their art. For the sovereign and the court, poems and plays were written, music was performed, and pictures were painted. Encouraged by the nationalism of the prince, writers began to take a pride in English language and history. The humanists had called for a pure and chaste Latin, but the need was also recognized for an elegant and vigorous English. The great classical scholar Sir John Cheke called for an English 'unsullied and unmangled with borrowings of other tongues'. Such scholarly essayists as Roger Ascham and Gabriel Harvey preferred English to the ancient languages; Harvey hoped that the English would soon cease to care what happened in 'ruinous Athens or decayed Rome'. In the same spirit men began to discover their island. Holinshed, Camden, Stow and others investigated antiquities, local history and customs. The *Description of England,* by the Elizabethan country clergyman William Harrison, was a novel attempt to give a full picture of the social life of the time. The poets, too, recognized the glorious resources of their language. Spenser was commended for his labours to find an English vocabulary fit for his poetry, and Gascoigne urged writers to use short, English words rather than 'inkhorn' terms. Sidney, Spenser, Marlowe, Shakespeare were all recognized in their day for their mastery of the English tongue, and their virtues favourably compared with those of the ancient classics.

Whatever the sudden triumphs of Tudor nationalism, perhaps the final account showed questionable gains. An 'island race', hedged by its exclusiveness, breeds pride, ignorance and contempt for others. The dangers were not apparent to Henry VIII. His purpose was to have the whole management of the country vested in his hands, so that an Englishman was the master of English fate. He succeeded and has had the applause of history for doing so, but it was not done without great pain. The despotic power of the sovereign was liable to have terrible consequences, and the Tudors were quite ruthless in furthering their policies. One of the first acts of Henry VII was to date his reign, by a legal fiction, from 21st August 1485 so that all those who fought against him at Bosworth could be attainted with high treason. The three chief Tudors practised a judicious cruelty for political ends which would have done credit to any Italian follower of Machiavelli. Henry VIII was bloodthirsty even by the standard of his age; his use of the axe seemed the more terrible because of his remorseless, dispassionate pursuit of the victims; those of high rank or noble quality were the most certain to fall, as examples to lesser beings. Elizabeth has been rightly commended for the comparative leniency of her religious persecution. But the same grace was not extended to her political opponents. After the Catholic uprisings in the North, in 1569–70, by deliberate policy a few were taken from each village that had supported the rebels and were executed; 800 died in this way. Mary alone refrained from political terrorism. It is ironical that the fanatical persecutor of Protestants should have been so gentle with rebels. If Northumberland's revolt, the most serious attack on the throne in the Tudor age, had happened in the reigns of Mary's father or sister, streets would have run with blood.

Nor did the safeguards of Parliament and the judiciary check the royal despotism. The Tudors used the legislature and the courts when they could gain something by doing so, but otherwise ignored or intimidated them. Elizabeth ruled by royal prerogative and only summoned Parliament with reluctance. The Tudors had the political wisdom to give their actions legal form, but they relied on a cowed and venal judiciary that did not dare to try the temper of the monarch. The probity of Sir Thomas More was exceptional; more typical was the man who accused him, the servile Rich, perjuring himself to please a king. Nor did the Tudor reforms of English life improve the justice and humanity of government. Tyrannical, unscrupulous sovereigns infected their officials. Cromwell, the 'new man' who carried out the policies of Henry VIII, was no less insolent and high-handed in office than his proud predecessor Cardinal Wolsey. Spies and informers had been a feature of life at least since the time of Edward IV, but the Tudors greatly increased the number and the scope of their operations. Cromwell relied on their information to impose Henry's settlement in Church and State. It was said that Walsingham's 'secret service' was so extensive, it consumed most of his large wealth. The common people were still oppressed by those in power. The dissolution of the monasteries put an end to many church abuses; but the corrupt dealings over the division of the spoils among the wealthy imposed as many more on the poor. Neither conscience nor justice checked the greed for riches. The peers who condemned the Duke of Buckingham to please the King, afterwards divided the Duke's huge estates among themselves. A statesman, wrote a Tudor essayist, could hardly resist the temptations of vice, who 'assaults with the weapons of power, self-love, ambition, corruption, revenge, and fear'.

The worst aspect of the nationalistic policy of the Tudor despots was the way in which it pandered to the acquisitive selfishness of the age. At the end of the changes by which Henry VIII set up the omnipotent state, the poor were the sufferers. Without Parliament Henry could hardly have forced his reforms upon the country. He bought the goodwill of the propertied classes who sat in Parliament by allowing them the spoils of the Church and the countryside. The powerful centralized State was born at the expense of rural depopulation and misery; this rising gentry prospered at the expense of the peasant. The bankruptcy of the arable farmer, the decay of villages, the notable increase in crime and vagrancy were the price exacted from the countryside to make Henry the supreme head of the State. It was no accident that the champions of the poor were the greatest opponents of Henry's State and his extreme pretensions. The opposition of Sir Thomas More, 'the best friend the poor e'er had', is well known; but the Protestant Latimer also defended the poor and criticized the Tudor theory of majesty. The *Dialogue* by Thomas Starkey stated that the rule of one man was the 'gate to all tyranny' and condemned the English kings who 'judged all things pertaining to our realm to hang only upon their will and fantasy'.

But the opposition made little noise. The poor had no voice, and their champions were either silenced or went unheeded. The Tudor revolution in the State had been so successful with the influential parts of society that hardly anyone questioned the royal claim to absolute power. The young Edward VI, in his *Discourse about the Reformation of Many Abuses,* expressed the conventional opinion when he wrote that not less royal authority, but more was needed for good order and peace in the land. He thought England could thrive only if a paternal crown kept each citizen in his or her appointed place working industriously for the good of the State.

That, too, was the opinion of Elizabeth, though she was never so innocent as to set it down and give her enemies a club to beat her. Reformed by the prudence of Henry VII and the national fervour of Henry VIII, England had won a place in the world. It was Elizabeth's hard task to prove the reputation of an independent, Protestant island against the enmity of the powerful continental kingdoms. The practice of her ancestors was the only light she needed to guide her on this perilous way. From her grandfather she learnt caution and practicality, and from her father a profound understanding of the mind and the heart of her people.

She began with the typical Tudor advantages of natural ability trained by a rigorous education. Since the succession was a preoccupation of the Tudor dynasty, and since no one knew where fate might place the crown, all the Tudor children were educated up to the standard of the Renaissance prince. It was said of Elizabeth that 'her sweet tongue could speak distinctively Greek, Latin, Tuscan, Spanish, French, and Dutch'. Bacon wrote after her death, when there was no longer any reason for flattery, that all her life she set aside certain hours for study. She regarded even the dangers of her early life as a lesson in the arts of government. The execution of her mother Anne Boleyn and her own consequent disfavour, her trials in the reign of her Catholic sister, taught her both the wilful power of the sovereign and also the need for cunning, dissembling and political flexibility. She was prepared to rule, and the wasteful, destructive years of Mary's reign gave her, on accession, the unlimited goodwill of the country.

> Lady, this long space
> Have I loved thy grace,
> More than I durst well say;
> Hoping, at the last,
> When all storms were past,
> For to see this joyful day.

That, in the words of the ballad, was the popular sentiment on her coronation. No one knew better than she the value of popularity. She was an adept publicist; by means of pageants, visitations and 'progresses' she kept herself in the eye of the people. Her regal presence and her wit enabled her to carry off these occasions in great style. When the time was right she was capable of an impressive democratic rhetoric, as in her famous speech at Tilbury before the attack of the Armada. More than any other English sovereign, she kept the good opinion of most of her people throughout a long and difficult reign. To her poets she was 'Eternal Virgin, Goddess true', 'Blessed Astraea', 'Fair Eliza, Queen of Shepherds all', 'Cynthia, the Lady of the sea', their great Gloriana. Staid men in Parliament were as giddy about her as the poets. 'If I might prolong her Majesty's life but for one year,' one said in 1585, 'I protest I would be content to suffer death with the most exquisite torments that might be devised.' The common people continued to love her. In 1600 the ballad-maker wrote :

> The noblest queen
> That ever was seen
> In England doth reign this day.

She became eventually a talisman for the people. Bishop Goodman described how, as a boy in 1588, he was swept along by a rumour that the Queen was to be seen going to Whitehall. After an hour Elizabeth emerged. 'Then we cried "God save your Majesty! God save your Majesty!" Then the Queen turned unto us and said, "God save you all, my good people! . . . You may well have a greater prince, but you shall never have a more loving prince".' The reply was admirably calculated. No wonder the crowd 'did nothing but talk what an admirable queen she was, and how we would adventure our lives to do her service'.

This adulation, and the need to cultivate it, left marks on her character. Those who live by popularity learn conceit and eccentricity. Elizabeth, like her father, was extremely egotistical. The German traveller Hentzer noted that she expected the court to fall to their knees before her. Though she was not handsome, she was surprisingly coquettish. The professions of love from ambitious young courtiers, which her wisdom recognized for the flattery they were, still puffed up her tough old heart. As age advanced she covered her plainness with fantastic eccentricity. When de Maisse, the French ambassador, met her for the first time in 1597, she seemed a grotesque fright. Above her thin face, with pinched nose and crooked yellow teeth, she wore a vast red wig, spangled with gold and silver, and with two great curls hanging down to her shoulders. She was much encrusted with jewels, and wore a kind of nightgown of silver gauze cut so low that her breasts were easily seen. This indecorous dress she would from time to time open at the front as if she were too hot. And in their conversation, where the ambassador found her gracious and sharp-witted, she still

expected compliments. An old harridan deceived by wilfulness and
embittered by sexual frustration.

No triumph of personality would have compensated for a failed
policy. Elizabeth's command of the country was firmly based on
successful government. The outward signs of her rule were those
made familiar by the earlier Tudors. She was authoritarian, secret
and without conscience. She did not like advice and reminded her
ministers of 'our long experience in government' which had 'taught
us to discover what were fit for us to do in matters of our state'.
Any sign of independent action was sharply checked. She
reminded Leicester that she had raised him from the dust. 'I may
not endure', she told Sir Thomas Sherley, 'that any man shall alter
my commission and the authority that I gave him upon his own
fancies and without me.' Her father used to say, 'If I thought that
my cap knew my counsel, I would cast it into the fire.' She had
the same regard for closeness and secrecy. She wrote to her envoy
in the Netherlands : 'We princes be wary enough of our bargains,
think you I will be bound by your speech to make no peace for
mine own matters without their consent.' In Tudor polity, the
nearer a person was to the throne, the higher the birth and the
better the ability, the greater was the danger. Elizabeth advised
Henry IV of France that it was a 'mild severity' to cut off the head
before ambition rose too high. When Leicester was in temporary
disgrace, Lord Warwick wrote to him not to trust the oath of the
Queen, for her friendship was unreliable and her malice was 'great
and unquenchable'. Essex remarked that the Queen was as
crooked in mind as she was in body.

The policy, however, of this peremptory woman was always
cautious and conservative. She moved very slowly and only made
up her mind after long deliberation, much to the disgust of her
own active ministers. Walsingham, the advocate of an aggressive
policy against Spain which the Queen was loathe to follow,
declared that she was 'daily more unapt to embrace any matter of
weight'. In the event he was right when he saw that a contest with
Spain was inevitable; but the Queen was also right, and wiser, to
put off the battle for as long as possible, to gain whatever she could
from diplomatic sorties and double-dealing, and at last to make
Spain take the initiative and bring the war to England where it
would be fought to the English advantage. In all matters where
she had a choice Elizabeth's instinct was to leave things alone, not

to upset the established order of things. The changes in the reign of Edward VI, and the extreme reaction to them by Mary, had made England Protestant. Elizabeth by all accounts had no deep faith. Her only interest was to preserve the absolute power of the crown which rested on her father's legislation. In theology she was content to follow the wish of the people.

She showed no desire to change the shape of the society she discovered on her accession. She had the usual Tudor distrust for the old aristocracy, and like her father and grandfather chose her confidential ministers from among the 'new men'. But she also had to a marked degree the sixteenth-century love for hierarchy and insisted that ranks were observed and places kept. When her government did legislate for changing social conditions, it did so only out of a sense of practicality, a grudging and usually tardy recognition of a breakdown in the old order. For most of her reign the vagrancy laws, which aimed to keep a man tied to his birth-place and thus prevented the mobility of labour, were applied with great strictness. Only when enclosures and capitalism had made the old rules quite unworkable were new provisions made to free labour and ease the misery of the poor. But if the Queen was conservative, she was not reactionary. She made no attempt to stop the profound changes that were already afoot. The gentry, who had begun their rise in the time of her grandfather, continued their spectacular ascent throughout her reign, encouraged by the long years of peace.

Her economic and commercial policies were also dictated by what she found. She was hardly more successful than her predecessors in dealing with inflation, the bane of the sixteenth century. But her well-known parsimony and her dislike for expensive warfare kept the expenses of her government as low as possible; she still could not prevent James I succeeding to an impoverished crown. If the crown was poor, however, the merchants were not. Her government was naturally suspicious of capitalism, as a new-fangled, foreign device, but the conditions of her reign made capitalist commerce thrive. Peace at home was good for trade, and the great expansion of English curiosity beyond the seas was even better. Elizabeth had a double interest in sea voyages, for she expected them to aid her foreign policy and to fill her treasure chests. Where the pirates and the explorer led, the merchant soon followed. A new spirit of commercial enterprise was about and the wealth of the country grew rapidly, from foreign commerce, from speculation, from the traditional business of the wool trade, from new ventures in mining and manufacturing. About 1600 Thomas Wilson, a knowledgeable writer on all aspects of trade, claimed to have known twenty-four aldermen of Norwich who were worth more than £20,000 each. 'But if we should speak of London', he added, 'and some other maritime places, we should find it much exceeding this rate. It is well known that at this time there are in London some merchants worth £100,000; and he is not accounted rich that cannot reach to £50,000 or near it.' In 1498 the Venetian envoy had been struck by the prosperity of England; nearly a hundred years later a German traveller received the same impression. He also spoke of the fertility of the land and the variety of animals; he saw the stately mode of living of many yeomen. He concluded: 'The peasants and citizens are on the average rich people, not to speak of the gentlemen and noblemen.'

But a critical contemporary might well have wondered what to make of England at the end of Elizabeth's reign. At home, the Puritans were already contesting the right of the government to decide forms of worship. Parliament was attempting to limit the royal prerogative. The rebellion of Essex, who was executed in February 1601, had indicated discontent in several parts of society. The trading classes were wealthy enough, but those of modest means suffered from stiff inflation. The last Parliament of the reign, which met in the winter of 1601, complained that the Queen's use of the prerogative to grant objectionable monopolies to her favourites forced up the cost of living, raised prices all over, and threw men out of work. The people cried in the streets: 'God prosper those that further the overthrow of these monopolies; God send the prerogative, touch not our liberty.' Abroad, victories over the Spanish in the Netherlands were balanced by the fearful waste of men and money in Ireland. The expenditure in Ireland in the last four years of the reign was some £300,000 more than the total revenue of England for those same years. More lives were lost in Ireland than in the famous naval war against Spain; and the calculated barbarity of the conquerors began the implacable resistance to English rule which has been the constant feature of Irish affairs ever since.

The Queen was a despot, and acting as such left a poor inheritance to the weak and foolish Stuarts, so that within forty years of her death the country was once more snarled in civil war. But she was an extraordinary despot, one who listened so carefully to her people that she knew, without having to relinquish her absolute rights, when to bend. In 1601, when Parliament in an ugly mood pressed her about monopolies, she knew she must abandon her favourites to save her prerogative, a lesson which the Stuarts never learnt. She cancelled all monopolies and Parliament wept for joy. 'Though God', she told the members, 'hath raised me high, yet this I count the glory of my crown : that I have reigned with your loves.' With her usual acumen, she knew exactly the reason for her success.

Her minister Sir Christopher Hatton used to say that 'the Queen did fish for men's souls, and had so sweet a bait, that no one could escape her network'. Never has a sovereign in England been so caught up in the emotions of the people. It seemed as if there were between Queen and country something in the nature of a mystical union. The Elizabethan poet, with his ear attuned to the inner life of society, perceived this. Sir John Davies saluted her divinity in a *Hymn to Astraea* :

> Blessed Astraea, I in part
> Enjoy the blessing you impart;
> The peace, the milk and honey,
> Humanity, and civil art,
> A richer dower than money.
>
> Right glad am I that now I live,
> Even in these days whereto you give
> Great happiness and glory;
> If after you I had been born,
> No doubt I should my birthday scorn,
> Admiring your sweet story.

When such a strange occurrence happens, a reign cannot be judged merely on political or economic grounds. Elizabeth found a people reborn into a confident and energetic nationalism. She fostered and directed their ideals while these were still pure and generous, and in doing so presided over one of the great ages in the history of the West.

2
Sir Thomas More

SIR THOMAS MORE has a reputation almost unequalled in English history, yet few lives of the great have been so plain and straightforward. By his qualities he rose to the highest position in the land. He was just, honest, kindly, courageous, intelligent and good-humoured; but these are ordinary virtues hopefully within reach of every man. It is difficult to see the real greatness of a man so like our better selves. No wonder that Erasmus, for all his learning and wisdom, declared himself not competent to write the history of his friend More.

Thomas More was a Londoner, born in Cripplegate on 6th February 1478. His father was a lawyer of Lincoln's Inn, a member of a city family that had come up from obscure beginnings. And though the Mores were prosperous enough, austerity and discipline were still the marks of the household. Young Thomas was sent to a city school, 'brought up in the Latin tongue at St Anthony's in London', where the 'Anthony pigs', as the students were derisively called, learnt their studies by rote from the dictation of the master who alone was likely to have that rare luxury, a printed schoolbook. The aim of this schooling was merely to teach a command of Latin which was dunned into the boys by wearisome repetition and frequent floggings. The method was cruel but effective; by the time More left St Anthony's, perhaps at the age of twelve, he knew Latin well and his wit had been tested in the schoolboy disputations in Latin held once a year in the churchyard of St Bartholomew, Smithfield.

After leaving St Anthony's, More was 'by his father's procurement received into the house of the right reverend, wise and learned prelate, Cardinal Morton'. The old-fashioned practice of farming out children of decent families to serve in the households of the great still lingered on in England. This survival from a past age of chivalry was condemned by forward-looking continental visitors to England. 'The want of affection in the English is strongly manifested towards their children', reported the Venetian envoy; 'for after having kept them at home till they arrive at the age of seven or nine years at the utmost, they put them out, both males and females, to hard service in the houses of other people.' And the envoy uncharitably attributed this practice to the meanness and selfishness of the English who 'being great epicures, and very avaricious by nature, indulge in the most delicate fare themselves', which they were loathe to give to servants and children. Whatever the reason for the custom, More did not regret his time in Morton's household. The great man was already Archbishop of Canterbury and Lord Chancellor, though not yet a cardinal, and no-one was more fit to teach good manners and the arts of government. In *Utopia,* written sixteen years after Morton's death, More paid an affectionate tribute to his old master : 'In his speech he was fine, eloquent and pithy. In the law he had profound knowledge, in wit he was incomparable, and in memory wonderful excellent.' And Morton, it seems, had formed as good an opinion of his young servitor. William Roper, More's son-in-law and first biographer, relates that Morton, delighted by the 'wit and forwardness' of the young man 'would often say of him unto the nobles that divers times dined with him, "This child here waiting at the table, whosoever shall live to see it, will prove a marvellous man".'

Morton was a clear-sighted statesman and a very sound administrator; the success of the early Tudor policies was in a large part due to him. He was also a blunt, homely man whose forthright style pleased Thomas More; serving in the household he learnt wisdom and discretion from the prelate's great experience. Taking note of his good progress, Morton decided to send More to Oxford 'for his better furtherance in learning'. This favour of a great man was invaluable, but John More, Thomas's father, was not entirely pleased that his fifteen-year-old son should go to university. Perhaps he thought it time squandered before the boy buckled down to the law, for which Thomas was destined by family tradition : in this period before the Reformation the universities were for the training of churchmen while young gentlemen got their worldly experience at the Inns of Court. Life at Oxford also drew on the family budget. Students were notoriously poor, and John More kept his son as poor as most of them. In later life More praised his father for this austerity, saying that 'in his youth he did not know

3 MARY I

4 ELIZABETH I

the meaning of extravagance or luxury, could not put money to
evil uses, seeing that he had no money to put to any uses at all,
and, in short, had nothing to think about except his studies'.

Thus Oxford helped to form his moral character; it also started
to widen his mind. His early biographers say that he was 'both in
the Greek and Latin tongue sufficiently instructed'. Good Latin
he knew from his earliest youth, but it is doubtful if he knew much
Greek after his two years at Oxford. English Greek studies were in
their infancy. William Grocyn, the father of English classical
scholarship, had recently returned to Oxford, and More may have
heard his lectures or those of Thomas Linacre. He knew enough
to see that there were extraordinary riches in Greek, but he only
felt this wealth about seven years after leaving Oxford when he
began a serious study of the language. 'You will ask me how I am
getting on with my studies', he wrote in 1501. 'Excellently, nothing
could be better. I am giving up Latin, and taking to Greek. Grocyn
is my teacher.'

After less than two years at Oxford, More came to London for
what were considered his real studies. Like most young gentlemen
whose parents intended them to get on in life, he went to the Inns
of Court, for as Erasmus noted, the English held it 'an honour to
be born and educated' in London. More went first to New Inn,
one of the Inns of Chancery, and then to Lincoln's Inn. From
Oxford to Lincoln's Inn was a great advance in ease and comfort.
At New Inn, More related, one lived well enough, 'wherewith
many an honest man is well contented'; at Lincoln's Inn there was
almost luxury, 'where many right worshipful and of good years do
live full well'. In the pleasant surroundings of Lincoln's Inn he
was called to the bar and began the practice of law under the eye
of his father.

The law, then as now, was the most worldly of professions, leading hopefully to riches and fame. And in the brawling, litigious
Tudor times the lawyers were happy, not only busy in the courts
and in business, but also needed by the sovereign for the places in
the new central administration which all the Tudors built up so
resolutely. Thomas Wilson and other economic writers mentioned
the vast incomes of the successful lawyers, money not always
earned by scrupulous means. Francis Bacon was a type of the
Tudor lawyer, having the keenest mind and the shrewdest judgment in England, but a weak sycophant, the deserter of his

friends and the taker of bribes in his lust for power and place. At first Thomas More was uncertain whether or not to follow the law. It was not that he lacked aptitude; within a short time he was Reader in Law at Furnivall's Inn, a position he held for more than three years. But the religious life tempted him, resulting perhaps not only from his own piety but also from what he had observed in the house of Cardinal Morton and at Oxford. Roper relates that even while practising the law More 'gave himself to devotion and prayer in the Charterhouse of London, religiously living there, without vow, about four years'. Also, his mind was inquisitive, moved by the glimpses of the new learning that he had seen at Oxford, and he was not sure that the business of the law would give him the time he wanted for study and reflection.

In the summer of 1499 a young Dutch scholar called Erasmus arrived in England in the train of Lord Mountjoy. Erasmus was about thirty and was trying to throw off the shackles of his unfortunate life, which had begun with illegitimate birth, passed into the orphanage, and thence into an Augustinian Priory, though he had no vocation for the religious life. His next years were spent trying to escape from this bondage. His talents got him to the University of Paris, and England was the next resting place in his flight. Here at last he found patrons to support his poverty and friends to encourage him in his life's work of scholarship; the first of these English friends were John Colet and Thomas More. Colet, wealthy, widely travelled and learned, was the man who encouraged and influenced Erasmus's studies, but More was the friend of his heart. Thirty-six years later in Basel, when the sick and weary Erasmus heard of the execution of his friend, he wrote : 'In More's death I seem to have died myself; we had but one soul between us.'

The friendship with Erasmus drew young More, not yet twenty-two, into the circle of Englishmen labouring to rediscover the riches of the ancient world. Such were the pleasures and the value of this company, Erasmus wrote, that he no longer wished to go to Italy. 'When I hear my Colet, I seem to be listening to Plato himself. In Grocyn, who does not wonder at that perfect compass of all knowledge? What is more acute, more profound, more keen than the judgment of Linacre? What did nature ever create milder, sweeter or happier than the genius of Thomas More? But why should I run through the whole list? It is marvellous how widespread and how abundant is the harvest of ancient learning which is flourishing in this country.' Erasmus no doubt flattered his hosts, but his account does show that the desire for knowledge was great, and that keen intellects were striving after it.

These men were the 'humanists' and their passion was classical language. To them, and to their fellows on the continent, we owe the recovery and elucidation of many ancient works in Latin, Greek and Hebrew. Though they were scholars first and foremost, their influence went far beyond the lecture halls of universities. They were the standard-bearers of an exact and careful criticism which had hardly ever been applied in the Middle Ages, but was now seized upon with the amazement of discovery and used to examine all contemporary life and society. The mark of their efforts was seen everywhere. The critical examination of biblical sources, especially the attempt to go behind the Latin Vulgate and seek out the Greek and Hebrew texts, brought many humanists into conflict with the Catholic Church and encouraged the reliance on Scripture alone which was one of the distinguishing notes of the Reformation. Reading of the ancients impressed clearly on the humanist mind the Roman civic virtues of gravity and prudence, and they strongly advocated the study of Latin (for humanist culture was predominantly Latin) as an antidote to the barbarous chaos of late medieval times. The humanists attacked medieval philosophy, chiefly on account of its grotesque Latin, and made the 'scholasticism' of Aquinas and his fellows a term of abuse. They had a decisive say on matters as wide apart as the duties of the monarch and the education of women.

The humanists were great civilizers, but their influence was not always for the good. Like most enthusiasts they tended to be fanatical and pedantic; they were keen to set up an orthodoxy, a body of laws, as strict, if not stricter, than the one they had overthrown. This was especially the case in the realm of literature. In the main the humanists were scholars, not artists, and they applied rules, not sympathy. The writers of the Middle Ages, for all their muddle and incoherence, often understood the spirit of a great work far better than the humanists, so concerned with propriety and 'good taste'. Medieval Latin was still a living language, full of strange words and constructions but pithy and forceful, whereas the chaste humanist Latin was careful, artificial and dead. Perhaps the

greatest fault of the humanists was their violent contempt for anything medieval or 'gothic'. Their minds were closed not only to a
large part of history, but also to some of the most impressive works
of the European imagination.

After the meeting with Erasmus, More plunged cheerfully into
the world of humanism and his enthusiasm continued unabated
when Erasmus returned to Paris in 1500. 'Do come back', he writes
to Colet in the country. 'In your absence Grocyn is the sole direc-
tor of my life, Linacre is my tutor in study, and my concerns, all
of them, I share with dear Lily.' He set himself a pattern in Pico
della Mirandola, the young star of the Italian Renaissance who
died in 1494, at the age of thirty-one, while trying to reconcile all
branches of knowledge. Around 1505 More wrote a small *Life of
Picus* which he dedicated to a nun of Aldgate. And such was
More's application to his new studies that he was soon following
the universal genius of Pico in his own small way as a lawyer invited
by Grocyn to lecture on Augustine's *City of God* in St Lawrence
Jewry.

Ardent humanist that he was, More no doubt echoed the pre-
judices of his friends and rejected the work of the Middle Ages,
which Colet termed 'that filthiness and all such abusion, which the
later blind world brought in, which more rather may be called
blotterature than literature'. But what the head judges, the heart
does not always feel. At this time, More, for his own amusement,
was writing some verses in English, and these were wholly medieval
in form and feeling, owing nothing to humanism. One poem in particular, a lamentation on the death of Queen Elizabeth in 1503,
has a simplicity and a real sense of loss, without the artful classical
allusions that a humanist might have added, which make it com-
pare well with the best medieval work.

All the while, More was still living at the Charterhouse and
trying to decide between law and the Church. 'The study of
English law is as far removed from true learning as can be', wrote
Erasmus; and he commented that, while More 'naturally dreaded
these studies', he was very skilled and much in demand. More was
also in some trouble with his lawyer father who was offended by
the humanist studies and nearly disowned his son. But neither
success nor opposition could sway More's mind. Only the desire
to marry finally decided him; he quietly and prudently turned
away from the cloister and into the world.

The whimsical story of the courtship and marriage has been told by Roper. More was attracted to the second daughter of John Colt, of Netherhall in Essex. But seeing that the elder daughter might be shamed to have the younger preferred, 'he then of a certain pity framed his fancy towards her, and soon after married her'. In 1505, when More brought his bride to his new house in Bucklersbury, she was only seventeen. Jane was a country girl, simple and poorly educated, and she found her new life in London, among the most brilliant minds in the kingdom, difficult. Her husband's attempts to teach her ways of the world were sometimes too much for her. After a while she came to terms with her new life and was happy in her marriage until her early death in 1511. More, too, was content with family life. Four children—three girls and a boy—came in quick succession, and he carefully supervised their upbringing, as Erasmus tells us. Erasmus was back in England, translating Euripides, starting the preparation for the Greek New Testament, and together with More translating Lucian. The community of scholars was happily at work.

Now that he had decided on a career in the world, More never allowed the joys of learning to overwhelm the cares of his profession. Erasmus shrewdly noted that in England 'there is no better way to eminence' than the law, and a man of More's ability soon attracted attention. In 1504 he was elected to Parliament where almost his first act, as a 'beardless boy' of twenty-six, was in defiance of the King. Henry VII had demanded a large parliamentary grant on the occasion of the marriage of his daughter Margaret to the King of the Scots. Henry was always greedy for money and the demand was excessive. The grant, in reality a tax, was resented particularly by the burgesses of London whom More represented. The opposition of the bold young man enraged the King. And since he could find no way to hurt young More, who was without property, he turned his anger on the father, John More, whom he gaoled and fined. This was Thomas More's first experience of the arbitrary power of the Tudors. He took note but was not afraid. He had been elected to represent the city of London, and it was in the interests of the city to resist the gross extortion of Empson and Dudley about whose actions (the chronicler Hall wrote) 'noble men grudged, mean men kicked, poor men lamented, preachers openly at Paul's Cross and other places exclaimed, rebuked and detested'. This opposition to the King's agents was a brave act for a young fellow with a growing family to support. Roper relates that More 'was determined to have gone over the sea, thinking that being in the King's indignation he could not live in England without great danger'. The death of Henry VII on 22nd April 1509 relieved him of this worry.

Free from danger, More began the new reign with great expectations. Like all England, he was greatly attracted by the brilliance of the young King. In verses for the coronation More celebrated Henry's good looks, bodily grace and intellectual powers; he recalled the King's descent from such good women as his grandmother, the Lady Margaret, and his mother, Elizabeth of York, and he praised the virtue of the new Queen, Catherine of Aragon, to whom he remained devoted all his life. And the new reign began fortunately for More. At Henry's invitation Erasmus was once again in England, staying with More in Bucklersbury and writing the *Praise of Folly*—the *Encomium Moriae*—written as a playful tribute to the genius of his friend. His career was prospering. Londoners, remembering his stalwart service in Parliament, made him one of the Under-Sheriffs of the city in 1510, a post he held for more than seven years. The two Under-Sheriffs, the chief legal officers of the city, were important but not over-worked. More became well known for his integrity. In the Sheriff's Court, Erasmus says, he usually remitted the fees due from the litigants, which made him very popular in the city. He could afford this generosity, for he was making a good income at the bar; 'there was at this time', Roper wrote, 'in none of the Prince's courts of the laws of this realm, any matter of importance in controversy, wherein he was not with the one part of counsel.' He became a Justice of the Peace, a Reader at Lincoln's Inn and a Commissioner of Sewers. Soon his abilities were required outside the confines of London. In 1515 he accompanied Bishop Tunstall on an embassy to Flanders, an occasion made famous by the beginning of *Utopia*; two years later he was on another embassy to Calais. Nor were his literary studies neglected. About 1515 he began, but never finished, a *History of Richard III*, a pioneer work of English history composed in Latin for his European humanist friends and translated into English for his fellow countrymen.

But in these years, outwardly so prosperous, there were pains and signs of future troubles. His first wife died in 1511 and before the end of the year More had married Alice Middleton, a mercer's widow elder than himself who had a reputation for being a harpy, but who made a good home for his four young children and ran his very busy household efficiently. More was worried by the state of Europe. He was shamed to see the fierce old Pope, Julius II, put on armour and lead the papal forces against enemies while Rome itself was sunk in corruption and nepotism. He feared for the policies of Henry VIII and Wolsey which, largely in support of the papacy, threw away the cautious good sense of Henry VII and drew England into one extravagant and inconclusive European war after another. He feared the growing capriciousness and intemperance of the King's character that caused the peaceful, even cowardly, Erasmus to write that he felt uneasy in Engand. He saw the slackness, indolence and ignorance of the English clergy which his friend Colet had denounced in the most passionate terms in a sermon before Convocation in 1511. He saw, especially through his work in the courts and as a London official, the terrible injustices of the State, the dispossession of the peasants, the beggary of the townsfolk, which were soon to distress so many notable men, from the proud Cardinal Wolsey to the honest Protestant Bishop Latimer. The contemplation of all this caused him to write his *Utopia.*

Utopia, the Isle of Nowhere, the 'fruitful, pleasant and witty work, of the best state of a public weal', was written in Latin and published at Louvain in 1516. It was written for the delight of his scholar friends all over Europe and is perhaps the only work of humanist Latin that is remembered today. No reformer had a better knowledge of social conditions than More, no other writer on the evils of society had more experience of administration and government. Thomas More wrote without illusion, and therefore without hope. What might have been a work of denunciation written in English, was instead a witty fantasy, a make-believe, written in Latin. It is one of the saddest commentaries on the brutal self-interest, intransigence and stupidity of human beings. Nowhere among the nations of Christendom does More's traveller find 'any sign or token of equity and justice'. The rich control all things for their own greed, though the wealth of the country comes from the labour of the common man. The law itself is a futile instrument taking no account of social reality : 'we first make thieves and then punish them.' But change is impossible. 'Where possessions be private, where money beareth all the stroke, it is hard and almost impossible that there the weal-public may justly be governed and prosperously flourish.' That is the indictment. The witty answer appears in the picture of *Utopia* where there is communism, uniformity, no war, no revealed religion, and no liberty. The answer of course is no solution, because if men had it they would not want it and for that reason More makes Utopia the never-never land of Nowhere. The sly conclusion of the book is that man's lot on earth is pain and injustice, that politics can never supply any remedy, and that grand schemes of reform are insubstantial dreams. For More the hope of man lay elsewhere, in faith, and the business of the world had nothing but his condemnation. *Utopia,* the portrait of depraved humanity, is closest to *Gulliver's Travels,* another witty flaying of mankind; and it is notable that Swift makes Thomas More the only modern in his pantheon of heroes.

When *Utopia* was published More was in his mid-thirties, a successful lawyer, an experienced and highly popular city official. Erasmus gave a full portrait of his friend in a letter to Ulrich von Hutten. He was of medium height and healthy, with dark auburn hair and a cheerful countenance. His hands were a little coarse. His clothes were simple and he dressed without much care and without ornaments. He ate the plainnest food without complaint, drank small beer and wine from a loving-cup lest he should seem unsociable. His favourite dishes were milk, cheese, fruit and eggs. He was fond of music but did not sing; his voice was strong and deliberate. He was easy and familiar with everyone and avoided great men because he did not like formality. He liked jokes and laughter and composed epigrams for his own amusement. His son-in-law Roper, who lived in his house for sixteen years, wrote that he never saw More 'as much as once in a fume'. He was not ambitious, Erasmus continued, and had no care for money, spending what he got freely. He loved freedom and leisure to think far more than business, yet took such pains over his court work that he often slept only four hours a night. He liked animals and kept a small menagerie of monkeys, beavers, foxes and other unusual beasts. His piety was constant but unobtrusive. He slept with a block of wood as a pillow and often wore a hair-shirt, though only his wife and eldest daughter knew this. His philosophical, kindly and happy life might have continued until his death but for two events. In 1517 Martin Luther nailed his ninety-five theses to the church door and set the Reformation under way. And at the end of the same year More was drawn into the service of Henry VIII.

No man entered the royal service more unwillingly than Thomas More. He knew well the dangers of court life under the Tudors and spoke with feeling of the 'bondage unto kings'. He had no appetite for money, power or high position. More had already taken part in a foreign embassy at the request of the city merchants. In May 1517, with courage and good sense he helped to compose a riot that broke out among the apprentices in London, and then pleaded their forgiveness to the King. Later, he was retained by the Pope in a court case over a forfeited papal ship at Southampton which the King claimed. More argued so well that he won the case and impressed the King so much that Henry was determined to employ him : 'for no entreaty', Roper wrote, 'would the King from thenceforth be induced any longer to forbear his service.' More could do nothing but obey and was made a member of the Privy Council.

More advanced steadily in the King's service. Henry was pleased with his work and delighted with his company, summoning him on holidays to his private chamber to talk endlessly of astronomy, geometry, divinity and politics, or calling him out suddenly at night and taking him on the roof to look at the stars. After the Council had met, the King would insist that More stayed to entertain him and the Queen at supper and kept him so much from his family that 'he could not once in a month get leave to go home to his wife and children (whose company he most desired)'. He began to dissemble, wearing a long look and refraining from witty replies so that the King would release him. And he had more than his own inconvenience to worry about at court. He could not approve of the pride and greed of Wolsey, nor did he like the policies of Wolsey and Henry which imbroiled England in European wars. A desire for peace was his constant preoccupation. He stated his wish most clearly in *Utopia,* and ever after decried the wasteful horror of any war : 'the world once ruffled and fallen in a wilderness,' he wrote, 'how long would it be, and what heaps of heavy mischief would there fall, ere the way was founden to set the world in order and peace again.' Erasmus, having left England for the last time in 1517, wrote fulsome letters to Henry and Wolsey in which he saw 'an Age truly Golden arising' under these two princes of State and Church who were so wise, learned and kind to the arts. The Cardinal was indeed a great patron of learning, founding six new professorships at Oxford. He was also, despite his own corrupt life, an advocate of Church reform and a keen champion of impartial justice. But it was not enough to make a golden age. The sickness of society, diagnosed so clearly in *Utopia,* was well advanced, and king and cardinal had not the medicines to remedy it.

So Thomas More served Henry as best he could, but he was never the King's man. He became Master of the Court of Requests —known generally as the Court of Poor Men's Causes; he attended Henry when the kings of England and France met at the Field of Cloth of Gold in June 1520; he became Under Treasurer of the Exchequer in May 1521 and was knighted; he went on embassies to the continent where his knowledge of London commerce and merchants was very useful. In April 1523 he was chosen Speaker of the House of Commons. Six years later he reached the pinnacle of his worldly career, following Wolsey as Lord Chancellor.

The years were not restful. The execution of the Duke of Buckingham in 1521, for no other reason than that he was of the royal blood, warned More and the kingdom of Henry's desperation over the succession, and showed the brutality of the King's nature which was soon to be a notorious mark of his reign. In the wake of Luther's action, angry religious controversy had risen up. In 1521 Henry had composed his *Assertion of the Seven Sacraments* against Luther for which he received the title 'Defender of the Faith' from a grateful Pope Leo. Luther replied with his usual blunt language, and since the King could not stoop to a slanging match with this lowly German, More took up the quarrel on Henry's behalf trading violence for violence, acrimony for acrimony, in Latin under the pseudonym of 'Gulielmus Rosseus'. Henry's faithful subservience to papal ambition also worried More. He warned the King that the Pope, in his temporal role, was only 'a prince as you are', and that England should not be tangled by the temporal affairs of this Italian ruler. Perhaps he anticipated the King's disappointment if the papacy should alter its alliance, as Leo later did from England to Spain. He could hardly have foreseen Henry's intense anger when the Pope refused to give him an annulment of his marriage after all the years that England had supported the papacy.

More, therefore, was a critical observer rather than a wholehearted participant in Henry's policies. The actions of a king are especially worrying when he is (as the French ambassador said of

Henry) 'a statue for idolatry'. 'From the prince as from a perpetual wellspring', More wrote, 'cometh among the people the flood of all that is good or evil.' Aware of the appalling power of the monarchy, More thought that the royal prerogative should not be exercised without the best advice. In April 1523, on the one occasion when Parliament met during Wolsey's fourteen years in office, More, the Speaker of the Commons, pleaded with Henry to allow freedom of debate and license to speak the mind. Permission was graciously given, but amounted to little; in the King's view the only purpose of Parliament was to vote funds for his war, and Wolsey bullied the Commons with his usual arrogance until they partly complied. The gloominess of the times, with England slipping without sense into expensive war, with the kingdom at home perplexed by social and economic problems, and with the noise of religious argument always growing, was reflected in More's *Four Last Things,* grim thoughts on man's end, full of medieval pessimism and *contemptus mundi.*

The higher More rose, the worse was the view. In 1527 Henry, now contemplating the divorce of Catherine, asked More for his opinion on the matter. He managed to satisfy the King with some careful answers, but knew that delaying tactics would not work forever. In the same year the sack of Rome by the troops of the Emperor Charles altered the alliances of Europe with disastrous consequences for Wolsey's foreign policy. Hoping to salvage something for England, More accompanied two embassies to the continent, the first with Wolsey to Amiens in 1527 to induce the French to make war on Charles; the second hurriedly to Cambrai in 1529 with Bishop Tunstall to keep the peace with Charles when it appeared that France and Spain were about to unite against England. At this time, walking by the river in Chelsea near his new house, More unburdened his mind to his son-in-law Roper, wishing himself put in a sack and thrown in the Thames if only three things could be established in Christendom. 'The first is,' he said, 'that where the most part of Christian princes be at mortal war, they were all at a universal peace. The second, that where the Church of Christ is at this present sore afflicted with many errors and heresies, it were settled in a perfect uniformity of religion. The third, that where the King's matter of his marriage is now come in question, it were to the glory of God and quietness of all parties brought to a good conclusion.' The achievement of these things had been beyond the cunning of Cardinal Wolsey. He was dismissed and disgraced. On 23rd October 1529 Thomas More took his place as Lord Chancellor.

Now it appeared he had it all—the Great Seal of the Chancellor, the good opinion of the King, the admiration of all humanists, the best regards of the people who remembered his justice in the courts, the love of his numerous family and retainers grouped about him in his new house at Chelsea. But the matter of the divorce, which had tripped Wolsey, was still unsettled, and More had already made his opposition known to the King. The Reform Parliament was about to meet and it was common knowledge, wrote the French ambassador, that the lords and the property owners intended to plunder the possessions of the Church. More hated the rapacity of these greedy men. Why was he chosen? Henry was always patient, and thought in time he could bend the new chancellor to his will; and for the present More was the best man in the kingdom for the position. Erasmus wrote that even Wolsey, who did not like More but 'was assuredly no fool', stated that 'in the whole island there was no one who was equal to the duty of Chancellor except More alone'. Why did he accept? His nephew William Rastell says that he wanted to refuse. But it was too late; twelve years before he had entered the King's service and now he was bound to obey. Also, More was never a man to shirk the responsibilities of his conscience. Queen Catherine had been his friend for many years and he would stand by her now; nor would he desert the faith he believed in.

The Parliament which met in 1529 for the re-ordering of the English faith was one on which the King could rely. The members were the burgesses, landlords, property owners of the country, and they were united only in their lust for possessions and wealth. They scented the downfall of the proud and mighty Church, and they rushed to dismember the vast body. The talk in the Commons was nothing but 'Down with the Church', said Bishop Fisher, and added that this attack was 'me seemeth for lack of faith only'. But the attack was licensed and encouraged by the King. The sins of Wolsey, who died in 1530, were visited on the clergy generally. In February 1531 the Convocation of Canterbury was compelled to pay the King £100,000 and recognize him as 'Supreme Lord, and, as far as the Law of Christ allows, even Supreme Head'. The anti-clerical movement overwhelmed More. He had hoped by

44

his presence to temper the royal irritation with Rome, to prevent Henry, who was no supporter of Lutheran theology, from taking a desperate step against the Church. But the forces behind the Reform Parliament were too strong and various—a real desire to put right a corrupt clergy, the gross venal ambition of the wealthy expressed through Parliament, and finally the King's determination to have his divorce and secure the succession. The work of Parliament was done despite the opposition of the chancellor : 'against this one parliament of yours (God knoweth what manner of one)', he said at his trial, 'I have all the councils of Christendom made these thousand years.' His power was gone by February 1531. In May 1532, the day after the final submission of the clergy to Henry's supremacy, he resigned his office.

More was no enemy to reform. The sombre first part of *Utopia* contained as severe a picture of the corrupt clergy as any written. Like his fellow humanists Erasmus and Colet, he called for a new life in the Church. And he vigorously defended Erasmus from conservative criticism by Catholics. Nor was More a blind follower of the papacy. He knew that the Renaissance popes, as men, were more evil than good, and he opposed Henry's support for these wretched men. But he distinguished carefully between the pope as a man, and the pope as a priest and Christ's vicar. It seemed to More—and to Erasmus—that the spiritual supremacy of the pope was demanded first by scripture, and then by the necessities of Christendom. The humanists, having the ideal of a universal Christian brotherhood, hated the biting partiality of nationalism. They saw that the religious controversy of the Reformation ineviably flowed into nationalism, making sects, destroying the body of Christ's Church, and increasing the distance between people. More would never agree that a national parliament or assembly could legislate on matters of faith. He brought this point home with the greatest force when Rich, the King's solicitor, bated him before his trial. 'I put the case further', said Rich, 'that there were an Act of Parliament that all the Realm should take me for the pope; would then not you, Master More, take me for the pope?' 'For answer', quoth Sir Thomas More, 'to your first case, the Parliament may well meddle with the state of temporal princes : but to make answer to your second case, I will put you this case. Suppose the Parliament would make a law that God should not be God, would then you, Master Rich, say God were not God?'

The authority of the Church was required because the State was not competent to speak on matters of faith. And without authority the universal Church would break apart and disappear. To the Reformers' cry of *scriptura sola*—'the Scriptures alone'—More answered, in his *Apology* of 1533, that 'the Church was gathered and the faith believed before ever any part of the new testament was put in writing. And which writing was or is the true scripture, neither Luther nor Tyndale knoweth but by the credence that they give to the Church'. More thought that Protestant doctrine disordered the individual by giving him a false hope of salvation : 'I could for my part', he wrote in his *Confutation* of 1532, 'be very well content that sin and pain all were as shortly gone as Tyndale telleth us.' And it disordered the State by breaking apart the Christian commonwealth. He therefore wrote many vehement pieces against the Protestants. Tyndale's translation of the New Testament,[1] which began to appear in England in 1526, spurred on the controversial authors. Two years later Bishop Tunstall licensed More to read all Lutheran works so that they might be refuted. In the next five years More set to with energy and wrote several works of great length beginning with a *Dialogue Concerning Heresies* (1528) against Tyndale and Luther, and ending with an *Apology* (1533) for the clergy. They are tedious works. Religious controversy then was carried on with violence and rancour, and More was no gentler than the rest. He did his part out of duty but regretted the labour, the heat and the ill-feeling of it all. He hoped there would be a time, he wrote in the *Confutation,* when all these books, including his own, would be burnt up and 'utterly put in oblivion'. And he would have consigned his own *Utopia* and Erasmus's *Praise of Folly* to the flames as well, as too playful and too open to misconstruction in a frantic, fanatic time. In gratitude for his defence of the Church, the bishops offered him the large sum of £4,000, but he refused even though the resignation of the chancellorship had left him poor.

Later writers such as Foxe, the propagandist of the faith More opposed, and the chronicler Hall, the propagandist of the State that put him to death, claimed that Chancellor More was a fierce persecutor of heretics. He took a severe view of what he thought to

[1] More called for a bible in English, but he was opposed to unauthorized translations. He suggested a translation by approved scholars which would be printed and distributed at the bishops' expense.

be heresy, and perhaps his opinions hardened as the religious strife grew. But he never tried to compel the conscience of an individual by persecution. If a person held Protestant views quietly More left him alone; when the distinguished Lutheran Simon Grinaeus came to consult manuscripts at Oxford while More was chancellor, he was entertained and allowed to go about his business. When heretical views, however, led to sedition no government of whatever faith would tolerate it. Religious persecution began in the late twenties and three men were burnt at Smithfield in the last six months of More's office. But heresy was the business of the ecclesiastical, not the chancellor's, court. Neither did More force the hand of the clergy; when the men died, after February 1531, he had lost all influence and was only waiting a fit occasion to resign. The men died in London, which was always the home of Protestant feeling.[2] Londoners, who would not have forgot or forgiven, reverenced More. After forty-odd years of propaganda to the contrary, the popular play *Sir Thomas More,* written in Elizabeth's reign, still spoke of More with affection as London's hero and the friend of all the poor.

The legal side of the chancellor's office was handled by More with notable speed and integrity. After his fall and at his trial he was accused of corruption, but this was only a ritual attempt to blacken a good name. Wolsey had used the chancellor's court to soften the rigour of the common law. More continued this function, but also, by good humour and diplomacy, managed to soothe the angry common law judges. The cases which had built up alarmingly, because of Wolsey's many interests elsewhere, were cleared off in good time by More. And at a time when even the chancellor's doorkeeper 'got great gains', More would not be bribed. When a rich widow sent him gloves and money as a New Year's gift, he kept the gloves out of courtesy and sent the money back. Another petitioner who sent a gilt cup received in return a cup worth more than the one sent. The Elizabethan, Sir John Harington, remembered More as 'that worthy and uncorrupt magistrate', and the common people commemorated his justice :

---

[2] More's brother-in-law, the printer John Rastell, was associated with Lutherans and was for a time, it seems, an agent for Thomas Cromwell. William Roper, his son-in-law, had a bout of Lutheran enthusiasm while living in More's house.

When More some time had Chancellor been,
  No more suits did remain.
The like will never more be seen
  Till More be there again.

The state of More's health—he complained to Cromwell of pains caused by crouching over a writing desk—enabled him to retire gracefully without offending the King. He had not lined his pocket as chancellor and he now lost his official income. He could not go back to the bar; he was too old and weary, and he had been away from his city practice too long. Henry allowed him £100 a year until his arrest, and he had besides about £50 a year of his own. But he had a large household and many dependants. He placed his retainers as best he could with other great men and cheerfully advised his family to accept poverty, saying he had come up the scale of prosperity from Oxford to the King's court and would now slide down again. His wife, Dame Alice, whom he had once called 'neither a pearl nor a girl', was inclined to nag and fret, but More was his usual equable self. For about a year after his resignation More was left alone, to work on his controversial writings against the Protestants. But he would not appear at the coronation of Anne Boleyn, on 1st June 1533, and perhaps from that moment was marked down. Henry, advised by his new confidant Thomas Cromwell, was determined to bring the English Church irrevocably under the monarchy, and his subjects would have to acquiesce or suffer the consequences of disobedience. More's policy was to keep as quiet as possible, never offering an opinion and answering questions as carefully as he knew how. The campaign against him began with an attempt to implicate him with the Maid of Kent, a nun who made wild prophecies against the King. More barely escaped from this danger. The King was outraged at More, and demanded that his name appear on the Bill of Attainder; but the Lords, knowing there was no evidence, begged on their knees for him and Henry relented. The hunt was close now, and Norfolk came to give him a friendly warning. 'I would wish you', he said, 'somewhat to incline to the King's pleasure; for by God's body, Master More, *Indignatio principis mors est.*' More knew the danger and was resolved to meet it. 'Is that all, my lord?' he replied. 'Then in good faith there is no more difference between your grace and me, but that I shall die today and you tomorrow.'

In March 1534 the Act of Succession was passed, and the time arrived that he dreaded, when he must take the oath before the commissioners at Lambeth. On the evening of 12th April he pulled the wicket gate shut at Chelsea and sadly took the river to Lambeth. He could not take the oath in the form in which it was tendered, as it contained a denial of the papal supremacy and an admission of the invalidity of the marriage of Catherine. He was committed to the Tower for misprision of treason. For the rest of the year he remained in prison while his friends and even his favourite daughter, Margaret, tried to make him change his mind. He refused and the example of his intransigence—and that of Bishop Fisher, his fellow prisoner—was an embarrassment to the government. At the end of the year an Act of Supremacy was passed; non-compliance was high treason for which death was the penalty. A commission came to sound out More on the new Act, but he would give no opinion. 'I do nobody no harm, I say none harm, I think none harm', he told Cromwell, 'but wish everybody good. And if this be not enough to keep a man alive, in good faith I long not to live.' In June 1535 Fisher was condemned and executed. On 1st July More was brought to trial in Westminster Hall. The indictment was long, but though More was ill and weak from his time in the Tower he defended himself with all the agility of his long legal experience. He was finally convicted on the perjury of Richard Rich, the King's solicitor; the jury returned the verdict of guilty in under fifteen minutes. The verdict was no surprise. In his youthful *Book of Fortune* More had written :

> The head that late lay easily and full soft,
> Instead of pillows, lieth after on the block.

On 6th July he was led out to die, and he went firmly with a ready answer for those he met on the path. At the foot of the scaffold he had a jest with the lieutenant of the Tower; he spoke pleasant words to the executioner and, as he had promised, made only a short speech to the crowd. He tucked his beard out of the way, laid his head on the block and died, as he protested, 'the King's good servant but God's first'.

History has dressed Thomas More in numerous, different resplendent robes, none of which quite seems to fit. He was so obviously an extraordinary being that all parties are eager to claim

D   49

him as their own, and censure him when he lapses from their ideal. Was he liberal or reactionary? Wise or foolish? Humble or proud? A benefactor or a persecutor? More was not inconsistent. He was always an orthodox Catholic, a robust, humorous Londoner, conventional in the best sense. A plain, honest man, he was caught in a break in history; he might have reconciled the best of the old with the best of the new, but new passions in religion and politics overthrew him. It was the age that was inconsistent. When he was young the ideal of Christendom still had some force, the Christian commonwealth that united all people under God; when he died each country frankly admitted its nationalism, living for itself alone.

He was born in the dying light of the Middle Ages, his education was medieval, and medieval ways stamped his life and work. His writings, especially his English writings, have all the marks of the Middle Ages : the wordiness, the lack of form, the coarseness, and most of all the irrepressible humour. More can never resist a 'merry tale'; even in his noble *Dialogue of Comfort,* written in the Tower under the shadow of the axe, comedy is always at his elbow, waiting to slide boisterously on to the page. And his life was equally bound to the past as he showed in his devotion to the Church, his ascetic self-discipline, and most of all his care for the community. He had none of the ruthless self-interest of the new age; he was implacably against the new reign of money which sought to enrich the individual at the expense of the poor and the unfortunate. The anonymous playwrights of *Sir Thomas More* saluted his memory as 'the best friend that the poor e'er had', and that tribute from his fellow Londoners would have pleased him as well as any.

But More also became, by his own efforts, a humanist. He was a scholar, a critic, a teacher, a supporter of reform. No work illustrates Renaissance wit and intelligence better than *Utopia,* so deftly handled, so imaginative, so penetrating in its critical view of society, so entertaining in the airy fantasy of Nowhere. The humanist More turned his children's schoolroom into a 'Christian academy', defended Erasmus against Catholic criticism, detested the ambitious and warlike actions of the papacy, and spoke out against the corruption of the English clergy. He hoped to make the new critical temper of the Renaissance enliven the old ideals of the Middle Ages; he wished to reform, not change, to renew, not destroy.

When the triumph of new religion and new policy came, he found he could not live in the new secular world. More was a patriot; in the early days of Henry's reign he vigorously defended the honour of the English navy against the attacks of the French scholar Brixius. But everything he believed, and everything he lived for, was a denial of Tudor nationalism. Since he was a resolute man, he chose to fight for faith and principles. He put aside the urbanity of the humanist and battled his opponents in the old uncompromising, abusive manner. He did not expect to win. In the Tower he wrote with a coal :

> Eye-flattering fortune, look you never so fair,
> Nor never so pleasantly begin to smile,
> As though thou wouldst my ruin all repair,
> During my life thou shalt not me beguile.
> Trust I shall God, to enter in a while
> His haven of heaven, sure and uniform;
> Ever after thy calm look I for a storm.

He went to his death as a man whose life had been justified.

3
Robert Kett

THE HARVEST FAILED in 1527. Wheat rose from six to thirteen shillings a quarter, and the price of rye doubled. The next year was also poor, bringing in a bad decade, the weather hard, the crops thin. Fifty years of abundant yields and cheap prices were at an end. Farmworkers, labourers, all the poor but especially those in the countryside where there were few people and no industry, faced bad days. A solitary fine harvest in 1547, the first year of Edward's reign, brought hopes of relief, but very soon prices went upwards once more. By 1549, the year of Kett's rebellion, wheat stood at sixteen shillings a quarter, barley at eleven, and oats at six. In the good year of 1547 an ox cost thirty-nine shillings; two years later it fetched seventy. In the same time the wages for unskilled labour rose from fourpence ha'penny to fivepence a day.

As prices rose, so too did rents. In the country the changes in agriculture, particularly the move towards sheepfarming, made men greedy for land. As the time for renewal came near, the tenant 'must bow to his lord for a new lease and must pinch it out many years before to heap money together'. The tenant, wrote the reforming Robert Crowley, 'must pay welmost as much as would purchase so much ground, or else void in haste, though he, his wife and children, should perish for lack of harbour'. In the towns the poor were no safer. Ninety per cent of the houses in London were owned and let out by speculators who bought up, said Crowley, 'whole rows and alleys of houses; yea, whole streets and lanes, and raising the rents double, triple, or even fourfold what they were twelve years past'. 'You rent-raisers', Bishop Latimer denounced from his pulpit, 'you unnatural lords, you have for your possession yearly too much'; rents worth twenty to forty pounds a year, Latimer complained, were now puffed up to fifty and a hundred pounds. And John Hales, one of the fiercest critics of enclosures, bitterly lamented the cruel greed of his countrymen. 'Is it not a pitiful hearing', he wrote, 'that man which was ordained of God to be a comfort for man . . . is now clean changed and is become a wolf, a devourer and consumer of men?' The speculators drove on over the protests :

> A man that had lands of ten pound by year,
> Surveyed the same, and let it out dear.
> So that of ten pounds he made well a score
> More pounds by the year than other did before.

But the landlords were not entirely to blame for the oppression of the poor, since the landlords themselves were victims of economic forces they could not control. The abrupt rise in prices in the second quarter of the sixteenth century forced landlords either to raise their rents or to accept a lower standard of living; and the general woe caused by high prices was made worse by the debasement of the coinage, a policy begun by Henry VIII and continued by his successors. By 1545 there was as much alloy as silver in the coins; a mere six years later there were three parts of alloy to only one of silver. A ballad of Edward's reign ascribed the troubles of the time to this debasement :

> This coin by alteration
> Hath brought this desolation,
> Which is not yet all known,
> What mischief it hath sown.

And a report of the Privy Council blamed the debased coinage for its failure to raise money to recover Calais : 'The noblemen and gentlemen for the most part receiving no more rent than they were wont to receive, and paying thrice as much for everything they provide, by reason of the baseness of the money, are not able to do as they have done in times past.'

Though excuses can be found for the landlord, it was he who brought about the agrarian revolution in England; anxious to share in the spectacular profits of the wool trade, the landlord began the work of 'enclosure', turning tilled fields into pasturage, and thereby being the chief cause of rural poverty and discontent in the sixteenth century. As the homely poet Thomas Tusser put it :

Good landlord, who findeth, is blessed of God,
A cumbersome landlord is husbandman's rod.

The growing of corn had never been very profitable; it had served
the needs of the population and little more. The methods of cultivation, using common fields and small tenements, were inefficient,
and many labourers were needed to work the fields. When crops
were good, prices were low; and when prices rose the farmer or
landlord was forbidden to export in order to insure a sufficient
supply at home. But for wool there was always a demand, at first
from the famous looms of the Low Countries, at Bruges, Ghent
and Ypres, and then, after the mid-fourteenth century, from the
native looms of the English clothiers. And English wool retained
its reputation abroad; Flanders and Italy in particular were still
keen to buy, and there was no restriction on export. The profits of
the grazier were very tempting to farmers and landlords, especially when they noted that sheep farming could be done with 'small
charge and small labour', that one shepherd could take the place
of twenty tillers, and that the shepherd was the lowest paid of all
rural workers. 'The foot of the sheep', men truly said, 'turns sand
into gold.'

Enclosures were of various types, and not all of them were made
for sheep raising; some enclosures, for example, brought together
and extended the smallholdings of the arable farmers and thus
made the growing of corn a more efficient business. Moreover, enclosing for the sake of sheep farming had been going on for a long
time. John Hales, the most knowledgeable of contemporary witnesses, claimed that the worst damage was done 'before the beginning of the reign of Henry VII'. From lack of evidence it be-
comes almost impossible to decide just how much of England
was given over to sheep farming. There was perhaps a pardonable
exaggeration in what Bishop Scory wrote to Edward VI in 1551,
that 'there are not at this day ten ploughs whereas were wont
to be forty or fifty', and as a result the country people had 'become
more like the slavery and peasantry of France than the ancient
and godly yeomanry of England'. East Anglia—the birthplace of
Kett—Kent and Sussex, and parts in the West, in particular Shrop-
shire, seemed to suffer worst from enclosures. But most counties
were affected to some extent, for the men of Tudor times were
enthusiastic enclosers; a Venetian traveller was amazed at the

'enormous number of sheep', and another foreign observer, Polydore Vergil, the King's Italian historian, asserted that 'of Englishmen more are graziers and masters of cattle than husbandmen or
labourers in tilling of the fields'.

The observation of foreigners is confirmed by the protests of the
English. 'Sheep have become so great devourers and so wild', Sir
Thomas More wrote in a famous passage of his *Utopia*, 'that they
eat up and swallow down the very men themselves. They consume,
destroy and devour whole fields, houses and cities'. In a sermon
preached before Edward VI, Latimer complained that where there
were before houses and people, 'there is now but a shepherd and
his dogs'. These enclosures, said a satiric ballad, 'be the causes why
rich men eat up poor men, as beasts do eat grass'. By the end of the
sixteenth century the grievances of the countrymen were summed
up in this sad verse :

> Sheep have eaten up our meadows and our downs,
> Our corn, our wood, whole villages and towns.

The policy of the Tudors attempted to stop the enclosing of
the land for sheep farming. The government feared that rural
poverty and depopulation would seriously weaken the defences of
the land, since those liable for military service would be reduced
and enfeebled. The first statute to restrain sheep farming was
passed in 1489. Further Acts followed in 1515, 1534 and 1536.
But as Hales remarked in 1549, the landlords did not mind what
provisions were made against enclosures, so long as none of these
Acts were put into effect. Only two Tudor statesmen, Wolsey and
Protector Somerset, made serious efforts to counter the baleful
effects of sheep farming. In 1517 Wolsey appointed a commission
to enquire into all enclosures since 1488. And in 1548 the fear of
insurrection led to another commission which Somerset supported
with his full authority. It would go forward, he declared, 'maugre
the devil, private profit, self-love, money and such-like the devil's
instruments'. Despite this fervour, Kett's rebellion broke out within a year.

When Somerset spoke of 'private profit' he gave the clue to the
lack of success in regulating enclosures. The motives for enclosures
were many. The increase in the population, the great rise in prices,
the wish for more efficient agriculture all forced on enclosures. But
there had also slowly come about in England a change in thought

as to the use and advantages of land. At one time land was worked not for profit, but for necessity, to support the labourers and to feed the population. Then, as a moneyed class grew up in the towns, made wealthy by the wool trade, merchants became anxious to find outlets for their wealth, and began to speculate in land, regarding it only as a profitable commodity not as a support for life. This was the workings of the new capitalism, already established in the great trading cities of Italy and southern Germany and now creeping into England. Capitalism demanded the best return for the least work, and sheep farming alone gave this return; speculators, therefore, were keen advocates of enclosures.

The drift towards land speculation, and the accompanying evil of enclosures, was hastened by the dissolution of the monasteries in 1536. The monastic estates had been severely criticized by such men as Thomas More in the days before the English Reformation. But whether from conservatism or from a remnant of religious, humanitarian feeling, the old monastic landlords seemed to many good Protestants after the Reformation to have been kinder to their tenants and better to the land than the freebooting Protestant speculators who acquired the monastic estates from Henry's hand in 1536. 'The cloisters', wrote Thomas Becon, 'kept hospitality, let out their farms at a reasonable price, nourished schools, brought up youth in good letters', whereas their successors 'did none of these things'. And Henry Brinklow, writing in 1542, asserted that monasteries 'never enhanced their rents nor took so cruel fines as do our temporal tyrants'. Not for the first or last time the people found economic development to be a crueller oppression than religious dogma.

The government tried to prevent the enclosing of the monastic lands, and as usual the measures were ineffective. The ballad, recognizing better than the government the powerful force of capitalism, scornfully commented:

> We have shut away all cloisters,
> But still we keep extortioners;
> We have taken their lands for their abuse,
> But we have converted them to a worse use.

The old ideal that men had a duty to the land was swept away by the new idea that men had rights over land which they could use to the best profit. The monasteries, though often incompetent

and corrupt, had tried to realize their duty. Now, said the Protestant churchman Thomas Lever, 'those goods which did serve
to the relief of the poor, the maintenance of learning, and to comfortable, necessary hospitality in the commonwealth, be now turned to maintain worldly, wicked, covetous ambition'. The new
despoilers of the monastic lands were at one with their wealthy
brethren in the towns. In 1550 Lever wrote that the London merchants were not 'content with the prosperous wealth of that vocation to satisfy themselves and to help others, but their riches must
abroad in the country to buy farms out of the hands of worshipful gentlemen, honest yeoman, and poor labouring husbandmen'.
Crowley complained that the purchase of land was the only care
of the rich merchant, and Thomas Cromwell even contemplated,
in 1535, a law to stop merchants from owning more than a certain
amount of land.

With the changes in farming, a blight settled on parts of the
land. The tiller of the field, no longer needed by sheep-farming
landlords, was without employment; poverty drove him from his
native village. The villages themselves were destroyed or in decay.
Landlords were so eager to extend their pastures, they did not
hesitate to pull down buildings that stood in their way; 'they throw
down houses,' wrote More in *Utopia,* 'they pluck down towns, and
leave nothing standing but only the church to be made a sheep-
house.' Even more melancholy than the razed buildings were the
abandoned homes decaying in villages unnaturally silent. 'Now
nothing is but pastures and plains', Thomas Starkey wrote around
1538, 'by the reason thereof many villages and towns are in a few
days ruined and decayed.' And Becon spoke of 'utter ruin and
decay; so that by this means whole townships are become desolate
and like unto a wilderness, no man dwelling there except it be the
shepherd and his dog'. 'The towns go down, the land decays',
lamented a ballad from the reign of Henry VIII :

> Poor folk for bread cry and weep;
> Towns pulled down to pasture sheep;
> This is the new guise !

The cultivated land itself soon showed signs of neglect. The monasteries went in 1536, and with them went the monks' large store
of agricultural knowledge gained in so many centuries of estate
management all over Europe. The small arable farmer, struggling

on against sheep farming, ignorant and no longer supervised by the demesne lord, let the standard of cultivation drop. Crops were no longer properly rotated so that the land was over-used and became exhausted. Poor quality seed was sown and it was badly broadcast so that the corn grew thinly and weeds pushed up among it. The fields were poorly fertilized, the poor preferring to dry and burn the dung for want of other fuel. The agricultural author Fitzherbert, writing around 1525, noted that marling and other careful practices of former times were no longer done. Fifty years later Tusser was still complaining of the poor standard of English farming. The picture which Shakespeare drew in *Henry V* of the war-wasted French countryside was most likely taken from his observation of certain English fields :

> her fallow leas
> The darnel, hemlock and rank fumitory
> Doth root upon, while that the coulter rusts
> That should deracinate such savagery;
> The even mead, that erst brought sweetly forth
> The freckled cowslip, burnet, and green clover,
> Wanting the scythe, all uncorrected, rank,
> Conceives by idleness, and nothing teems
> But hateful docks, rough thistles, kecksies, burs,
> Losing both beauty and utility.

In the lanes between the ruined fields, leaving the homes from which they had been evicted or driven out of by poverty, trudged the beggars and the vagabonds, the victims of the agrarian revolution. They tread their woeful paths in More's *Utopia* : 'All their household stuff . . . they be constrained to sell it for a thing of nought. And when they have wandered abroad till that be spent, what can they then else but steal, and then justly, pardy, be hanged, or else go about a-begging? And yet then also they be cast in prison as vagabonds, because they go about and work not; whom no man will set to work, though they never so willingly proffer themselves thereto.' That was written in 1516, and as the century progressed the ranks of the beggars did not diminish. Roger Ascham told Protector Somerset that the existence of the poor was not life but misery. Bernard Gilpin, preaching before Edward VI, declared that 'thousands in England beg now from door to door who have kept honest houses'. The vagabond was so

familiar to the age, he became a common character in the literature, his thieving and conniving ways anatomized in such books
as Harman's *A Caveat for Common Cursetors* (1567). From these
treatises Shakespeare took them, and put them into his plays—
Autolycus the sharp-eyed 'pedlar', Christopher Sly the drunken
'tinker', the 'wild rogue' who shares the straw with King Lear and
the swine, and Edgar disguised as 'poor Tom', who 'walketh bare
armed and bare legged and faineth himself mad'. Most of this
riff-raff, the diseased and the cunning, the mad and the despairing, made for London where they poisoned the arteries of the city
and displayed their pain to the callousness of the wealthy. 'London,' wrote Brinklow in 1545, 'being one of the flowers of the
world as touching worldly riches, hath so many, yea innumerable
of poor people forced to go from door to door and to sit openly in
the streets a begging, and many not able to do for other but lie in
their houses in most grievous pains and die for lack of aid of the
rich, to the great shame of thee, O London!' 'O Merciful Lord,'
Lever declaimed from the pulpit, casting his eye over Edward's
England, 'what a number of poor, feeble, halt, blind, lame, sickly,
yea with idle vagabonds and dissembling caitiffs mixt among them,
lie and creep begging in the miry streets.'

In the country, the labourers left in the crumbling villages were
hardly better off than the town beggars. Rye was the staple crop
for bread, and what with bad farming, bad harvests and high
prices, there was little enough of it for the poor man's table. Vege-
tables, other than beans or peas, were little known; milk and
cheese from a lean cow and a few eggs made the balance of the
diet. Salted meat was sometimes available, fresh meat hardly ever;
fish, as in Caholic times, was still ordained for twice a week, and
in Elizabeth's reign, for reasons of 'civil policy' a third fish day
was added. Oxen were expensive and prized for strength, not fat-
ness; sheep were kept chiefly for their wool. On the poor, ill-
drained land of the common, the miserable livestock of the labourers grazed, half-starved in winter and pestered by gadflies in
the summer so that the scant flesh hung on the bones of the animal.
And the sheepmasters, in their avaricious enthusiasm, even tried to
enclose the common land of the poor villagers. Nor was the shepherd, the one favoured worker of the country, well rewarded by
his master; the shepherd was traditionally the worst paid of the
rural workers, and he benefited little from the prosperity of the

sheep farmers, as Shakespeare's shepherd commented in *As You Like It* :

> But I am shepherd to another man,
> And do not shear the fleeces that I graze.

Robert Kett was born and raised in this time of rural sorrow. His first years were passed in decent obscurity; it is not known where he was born or what age he was at the time of his rebellion. But he came from a Norman family of petty landowners well established in Norfolk for generations. Robert was a tanner and his brother, William, a butcher, and both had prospered. Robert owned land at Wymondham and small properties in other parts of Norfolk; a contemporary chronicler remarked with disgust that he could set out £50 a year for the purchase of land. Kett was, in fact, a minor representative of the new moneyed class who bought and enclosed land by way of an investment.

The counties of East Anglia were much enclosed. And the bitterness of the country folk was the greater since they knew that the rich soil of these counties was particularly good for arable farming. The social discontent of the first half of the sixteenth century broke out into several risings and rebellions. The first one, which followed immediately after the dissolution of the monasteries in 1536, seemed to have religious differences as the chief cause. Uprisings of this kind were the Lincolnshire rebellion and the Pilgrimage of Grace in 1536, and the later West Country rising of 1549 in Devon and Cornwall. Yet even in the earliest revolts the economic troubles caused by enclosures were made part of the grievance. The rebels of the Pilgrimage of Grace demanded the 'casting down of enclosers of commons'; later, the Bristol chronicler of the West Country rising stated that the aim of the rebels was 'to have their old religion restored again as well as the enclosures'. 'Hunger is a bitter thing to bear', wrote the shrewd and sensible John Hales in his *A Discourse of the Common Weal*, explaining why enclosures were 'the most occasion of these wild and unhappy uproars amongst us'; when the people lack, he went on, 'they must murmur against them that have plenty, and so stir up these tumults'.

For many years the murmurs had been heard in Norfolk. In 1537 a canon of Walsingham tried to raise an insurrection to remedy the 'much penury and scarceness' that prevailed. In the same year attempts were made to incite the people against the landowners at Old Buckenham and at Fincham. Three years later John Walker of Griston denounced the gentlemen of the county in the most violent language; he was all for killing the oppressors, 'yea, even their children in the cradle : for it were a good thing if there were so many gentlemen in Norfolk as there be white bulls.' The country people noted that the townsmen of London, Bristol and other cities had from time to time turned on the landlords. Desperation was driving the slow countrymen to copy the quick, turbulent action of the towns.

In the late 'forties, as the noise of discontent grew louder, the government was disposed to listen. The new 'commonwealth party' in Parliament, which stressed the duties rather than the rights of property, under John Hales the member for Preston, carried on an energetic campaign against enclosures in the Commons. This parliamentary action failed against the solid ranks of property holders in Parliament, but it warned the King's ministers that something should be done. In 1548 the powerful preaching of Cranmer and Latimer denounced enclosures, and petitions from countrymen worried Protector Somerset. In June, Somerset issued a proclamation 'against enclosures, letting of houses to decay, and unlawful converting of arable ground into pastures'. A commission led by Hales was sent to make a survey of enclosures; but it met such determined opposition from the gentry, such packing of juries, such fraud and intimidation that its results were useless. Offenders were given a pardon and then returned, said Hales, 'to their old vomit, began immediately to enclose, to take away the poor men's commons, and were more greedy than ever they were before'. Up and down England the poor now resolved to make a fight for their rights and livelihood. In the spring of 1549 the men of Somerset rose and outbursts of rebellion spread from there through the South to Kent. In the North the Yorkshiremen also rose, forgetting the ferocious defeat they had suffered in the Pilgrimage of Grace thirteen years before. These spontaneous outbursts, which were easily put down, were soon elbowed from the government's mind by Kett's rebellion in Norfolk.

The uprising began as a country brawl. On 20th June 1549 the people of Attleborough pulled down the fences of a certain Green who had enclosed part of their common. The country labourers were emboldened by this success. On 7th July, when

the feast of St Thomas Becket was being celebrated at Wymondham, the peasants broke away from the festivities and tore down
the fences of the neighbouring gentry, including those of Serjeant
Flowerdew.[1] Flowerdew was certain that the Ketts were the cause
of this outrage, for he had an ancient quarrel with the family going
back some ten years to the time when Flowerdew despoiled and
ruined the beautiful monastic church of Wymondham, much to
the distress of the Ketts who were the chief citizens of the village.
Flowerdew therefore approached the rebels and gave them 3s. 4d.
to destroy the hedges and fences of Robert Kett. The mob flowed
out towards Kett's lands, and here met a very surprising recep-
tion. Kett himself greeted them and sympathized with their cause
against the landowners, saying that 'power so excessive, avarice so
great, and cruelty of every kind so unheard of, cannot but be hateful and accursed in the sight of both God and man'. He then
willingly joined in the destruction of his own enclosures, proposed
himself to the crowd as 'your general, your standard-bearer, and
your chief', and sent them off to do joyful wreckage against other
enclosures, especially those of Flowerdew. Flowerdew's ditches
were filled and his hedges levelled, and then the crowd surrounded
Kett, acclaiming him as their leader and his brother William as
second-in-command. Kett received this popular mandate with dignity. 'The office', he declared, 'I will never lay down until you have
obtained your rights. Your deliverance and safety are with me
objects of the greatest interest, and to obtain these I refuse not to
sacrifice my substance, yea, my very life itself, so highly do I
esteem the cause in which we are engaged.' The country turmoil
had found its leader and become a rebellion.

Within a few days the band of insurgents, swelling all the time
with new arrivals, had marched to Norwich. On the way, they
had pulled down hedges and destroyed a certain amount of property, but for a band of country rebels their behaviour was re-
strained and their discipline good. Kett brought them to a halt
across the river from Norwich, occupied a hill on the edge of
Mousehold Heath, and there set up his Great Camp. Beacons and
pealing bells let the whole of East Anglia know that at last a stand
was being made against the tyranny of the landowners; the poor,
the desolate and the oppressed hurried to the camp, so too did the

---

[1] 'Serjeant' was a legal title, not a military one.

vagabonds and the outlaws. Soon there were 16,000 rebels on Mousehold Heath. Kett invited the people of Norwich, who were unmolested by the rebels, to come and trade with the camp, an offer which the merchants quickly took up. A regular and fairly orderly commerce developed which spoke well for the peaceful intentions of the insurgents and for Kett's ability to control and administrate.

When the camp was established, the first business was to draw up a list of grievances. These were made out in the name of the delegates from twenty-two hundreds in Norfolk and one in Suffolk, and sent in the form of a petition to the King. The first and greatest complaint concerned the enclosing of the people's common land, and added to this were several other complaints about the conduct of the landowners: the high rents and fees they demanded, their bad way of buying up freeholds and turning them into copyholds, and, in general, the injustice of most of their dealings with the tenant. Unaware of the workings of inflation, the rebels innocently asked that rents, fees and certain prices should be put back to what they had been in the first year of the reign of Henry VII, sixty-four years before.

The petition, however, was not merely the complaint of the tenants against the landlords. Most of the peasant risings throughout Europe from the thirteenth to the sixteenth century were fostered by a vague religious, communistic ideal which demanded, in God's name, freedom and justice for the people. The ideal was most clearly expressed in the twelve articles of the German uprising in 1525, a revolt that was put down with the utmost brutality by the army of the nobles at Frankenhausen in 1526. Kett's rebellion was also moved by this wistful idealism. 'We pray that all bond men', says one of the articles of the petition, 'may be made free, for God made all free with his precious blood shedding.' And the petition demanded that the people should be free to take the fish from the rivers and the fowl from the air, seeing that the gifts of nature were for the well-being of the community not just for the pleasure of the landowners. Indeed, a care for the community was at the heart of the rebels' petition; it asked that ignorant or slothful priests should be dismissed, that each parish church should establish a school, that the evil practices of wardship, whereby the guardian had all the profit from the ward's estate, should be abolished, and even that a parliament of the people—the 'poor commons'—should be set up to assist in the general reform of the laws.

The early historians of Kett's rebellion, members of the property-owning middle classes, picture Kett and his men as dangerous savages out to destroy the laws, customs, property and religion of the land. The mild, temperate nature of the petition suggests otherwise, and this impression is confirmed by the conduct of the rebels on Mousehold Heath. Few people were harmed and none were killed. Hostile landlords were held as prisoners, but they were treated reasonably unless they tried to escape. Kett established himself on a platform beneath a large oak, and from this 'oak of reformation' he administered rough, summary justice to his followers to prevent them rioting and pillaging; Kett also pressed the reluctant mayor of Norwich to sit with him in this rustic court. Anglican services were conducted by a Norwich priest, and Matthew Parker, a Norwich man and a future Archbishop of Canterbury, was allowed to preach to the rebels from Kett's oak. The orderly restraint of the rebel leaders only enraged the gentry. Kett's attempts to keep the peace in the camp were contemptuously described by Sir John Hayward as 'actions covered and disguised with mantles, very usual in a time of disorder'.

When the first news of the rising reached London, the Council feared that the revolt had been set afoot by the Lady Mary, the King's Catholic half-sister. The arrival of the petition stilled this fear; then apprehension gave way to outrage, that country clowns should dare to set their terms for the King himself. Protector Somerset was sympathetic to the peasants' cause. But he had support from none save Latimer, and he knew also, distracted as he was by further outbursts of revolt up and down the country, that the government could not afford to tolerate insurrection. On 21st July he sent a herald to Norwich with a temporizing reply in the King's name, promising certain reforms and a pardon to all rebels who would disperse. Kett was not satisfied with this, perhaps recognizing that there could be no pardon for him as the leader. 'Kings are wont to pardon wicked persons,' he replied, 'not innocent and just men : they for their part have deserved nothing.' The herald called Kett a traitor, and rallying to him some of the moderates, including the mayor of Norwich, retired into the city and shut the gates.

As time went by, the conduct of the rebels in the Great Camp

grew worse. Boredom with the present was added to anxiety for
the future so that Kett could hardly govern them. 'They were content with a licentious and idle life', wrote Hayward, 'wherein they
might fill their bellies with spoil, rather than with labour.' They
certainly filled their bellies. Of sheep, which they naturally considered to be the devil's animal and the cause of their troubles, they
slaughtered and ate twenty thousand in a few days. Three thous-
and bullocks were consumed, and numberless hens, ducks, geese
and swans. Private deer parks were raided, the fences thrown
down and the deer carried off to the cooking pots. Whole woods
were destroyed to provide both shelter and fuel. The citizens of
Norwich were now intimidated by the great, hungry band of
rebels across the river. 'The women resorted twice a day to prayer',
wrote a young inhabitant of the city, 'that God would deal merci-
fully with them, that they might live to talk of it, thinking it
impossible at that time, they were so devoid of hope.'

With the departure of the herald, Kett knew that the rebels
would have to fight for their cause. He began to strengthen the
defences on Mousehold Heath, and moved his artillery to cover
Norwich. The Council in London gave the task of suppressing the
rebellion to the Marquis of Northampton, a genial courtier, who
marched north with some 1,500 horsemen and a band of Italian
mercenaries. But Northampton was no soldier. Almost immediately he allowed his force to be surprised by the rebels, and so
outweighed by the press of numbers that not even the cool fighting
of the mercenaries could make any headway against the enthusiastic rustics. After a day and a night of furious confusion, Northampton fled from Norwich with his remaining forces and Kett
took possession of the city. In the fighting Lord Sheffield was killed;
his horse fell into a ditch, 'and as he pulled off his helmet to show
them who he was, a butcher slew him with a stroke of a club'.

After the failure of Northampton, the task of defeating the
rebels, who now appeared to be a serious menace, was entrusted
to the Earl of Warwick. Warwick was a hardened soldier and a
great supporter of enclosures; the rebels could expect no mercy
from him. He brought together Northampton's scattered troops
and appeared before Norwich on 22nd August. He then sent
another herald to Kett at Mousehold Heath offering once again a
pardon to all who would disperse. Kett was inclined to listen, but
in the course of the negotiations a soldier was offended by the rude

gestures of a young rebel and shot him dead. The negotiations broke up angrily and the rebels chased Warwick and his army within the city walls.

For a week Warwick held out in the city with great difficulty; his numbers were small, and his baggage-train and supplies were waylaid and diverted to Mousehold Heath. On the 26th the arrival of 1,000 experienced German *landsknechts,* originally intended for Scotland, eased his danger. Aware that time was on the side of Warwick, Kett decided to attack; but at the very moment when he needed his best judgment, his usual prudence and good sense deserted him. The strain of controlling the mob on the heath, the certainty that failure would lead to his own death, affected him. The knowledge of the rightness of his cause and the unlikelihood of realizing it overcame him. He was afflicted by omens; 'a snake leaping out of a rotten tree, did spring directly into the bosom of Kett's wife; which thing struck not so much the hearts of many with an horrible fear, as it filled Kett himself with doubtful cares.' He was persuaded by an old country saying to abandon his strong position on Mousehold Heath and to go down into the valley of Dussindale overlooked by the city. It was a fatal decision. The rebels were at the mercy of the disciplined fire of the *landsknechts* and soon surrendered. On 1st September Protector Somerset sent an account of the battle to Sir Philip Hoby : 'On Tuesday last, issuing out of their camp into a plain near adjoining, they determined to fight, and like mad and desperate men ran upon the sword, where a mort of them being slain, the rest were content to crave their pardon. One Kett a tanner, being from the beginning the very chief doers among them fled, and the rest of the rebels, casting away their weapons and harness, and asking pardon on their knees with weeping eyes, were by my Lord of Warwick dismissed home without hurt and pardoned.' The victorious soldiers returned to Norwich where they found at the Cross two barrels of beer provided for them by the city fathers at a cost of 12s.

Kett and his brother fled as far as Swannington, eight miles from Norwich, but there they were overtaken and captured in a barn. On the day of the victory, 28th August, the trial of the leaders began in Norwich. Nine ringleaders were hanged from the 'oak of reformation' and many others were put to death with the full barbarity reserved for rebels; they were hanged, drawn and quartered, and their severed heads were fixed to poles on the city towers. Robert and William Kett were sent to the Tower of London to await their trial and inevitable execution. They were tried and found guilty, and returned to Norwich on 1st December. A week later they were hanged, Robert in Norwich Castle and William from the top of Wymondham steeple. Of their rebellious followers, between 1,500 and 3,000 had been killed in the battle and a large but uncounted number were executed.

Kett's rebellion was snuffed out with ease, and so too were all other revolts against the Tudors. Yet Kett seemed to have good chances to improve the hard lot of the peasant. His grievances were real and sad, and recognized to be so by some of the best men in the kingdom. He had the support not only of the austere churchman Latimer, but also of the all-important Protector Somerset. 'I have heard in deep secret', the Emperor's ambassador wrote to his master, 'that the Protector declared to the Council as his opinion, that the peasants' demands were fair and just; for the poor people who had no land to graze their cattle ought to retain the commons and the lands that had always been public property, and the noble and the rich ought not to seize and add them to their parks and possessions.' Moreover, the Tudors, intent on maintaining their despotic rule, were no friends to aristocratic privilege; they allied themselves with the masses against an upstart aristocracy, and were thus inclined to listen to popular complaints.

But stronger reasons made Kett's defeat inevitable. Complaint was one matter, revolt was another. At Bosworth Field the Tudors had put an end to an age of lawlessness, and they could not allow another to begin. All revolts, for whatever motives, were steps towards anarchy and threats to the centralized power of the monarchy; all were swiftly crushed, whether they were religious uprisings such as the Pilgrimage of Grace in 1536 and the revolt of the northern Earls in 1569, or agricultural uprisings such as Kett's rebellion. Also, though the peasants were suffering from real injustice, the demands which the rebellion presented were conservative and backward-looking. There was no advantage in going back. The feudal system had decayed beyond repair, and the changes that came about were on the way to increasing the prosperity and well-being of the country. Unhappily, the poor peasants were the victims of this change. A peasant turned off his land was not comforted to know that he was now one of the free and mobile workers on whom the rise and success of the new industries depended. The wandering labourer with neither roof nor employment was not consoled by the thought that he was now a freeman, no longer tied by the bonds of the feudal relationship. But the agricultural changes and the rise of industry ensured that bondage gradually died out; ironically they were the means to bring about the prayer of the Norfolk rebels that 'all bond men may be made free'.

The main reason, however, for the failure of the rebellion was the opposition of the moneyed and propertied classes. The accumulation of wealth was the chief enthusiasm of the Tudor age, and neither the King, the lords nor the commons could stand against it. Capitalism was the new, magic means to riches, and no device of the capitalists was more effective than enclosure. Those who fought enclosures felt the enmity of the numerous and bold ranks of property. Wolsey and Somerset, the two Tudor statesmen who opposed enclosures, though they were in their days the most powerful men in England, were brought down. And whatever measures the government made, they could not be enforced against the current of the time. 'We have good statutes made for the commonwealth as touching commoners and enclosers', Latimer said, 'but in the end of the matter there cometh nothing forth.' The enforcement of the law lay in the hands of the justices, and they on the whole were keen enclosers. 'No man', Edward VI shrewdly commented, 'that is in fault himself, can punish another for the same offence.' Tudor policy could not work without the support of the middle classes.

In general, the Tudors found no means to right the injustice caused by the agrarian changes. For the first time in England, the government faced the problem of unemployment, and this malady puzzled the Tudors as much as it has puzzled all other administrations. The best the Tudors could do was to make some provision for the relief of the poor. Kett's rebellion, which brought home very clearly the poverty and the desperation of the countryside, helped to encourage this legislation; this one minute success was the only monument to all those peasant corpses in the Norwich field. The ground for the new poor law had been prepared some years before by the Spanish humanist Luis Vives whose *On the Relief of the Poor* was written in 1526 while the author was living at the court of Henry VIII. When the dissolution of the monasteries added the sick and the destitute from the monastic hospitals to those already impoverished by enclosures, and sent them out on the roads, new relief for the poor was urgently needed. In 1536 the principles of Vives, which had already been tried at Ypres in Flanders, were incorporated into English legislation.

Vives had proposed quite simply that begging should be made illegal; that all vagabonds and beggars who could work should be made to work; and that all those who could not work should be placed in hospitals and almshouses. It was a simple matter to prohibit begging, but the other aims of the Act were harder to bring about. 'Valiant beggars'—those who could work—were to be whipped for the first offence, have an ear clipped for the second, and be put to death for the third; but no suggestion was made as to what work the able-bodied should do and how they should find it. The Act of 1536 and subsequent laws were more successful in providing for those who could not work. In 1547 local authorities were ordered to find houses to lodge the sick, old and useless. But as these houses depended on charity, they were not easily found. Finally, in 1572 the justices were allowed to impose a tax for these lodgings, and to appoint overseers who took the relief of the poor out of the hands of the parish priest.

Poor Kett, what unfathomable affairs he meddled in. An old engraving shows a plump, beaming man of about middle height, sitting in rustic state beneath his 'oak of reformation' with sword at his side, dealing simple justice to his country followers. He was himself a small landowner and prosperous enough, but his modest dealings in the new economy did not blind him to the value of his countryside, its past and its people. When that avaricious fellow Serjeant Flowerdew stripped the lead from the church at Wymondham, Kett, though no supporter of the old religion, was distressed for his community to whom the church meant much. When his fellow countrymen rose up against the evil of enclosures, Kett willingly tore down his own hedges and led the good fight against the oppression of the gentry. He was not the first simple soul to be trodden down by the indifferent steps of material progress.

4
Mary Tudor

STRANGE AND CONTRADICTORY was the life of the Renaissance prince. In England the Tudors had advantages over all former kings. They had magnificence, authority, and control of the land as never before. The country was their estate and they the wilful farmers of it, good or bad according to their whim and judgment. So often frank and easy with their subjects, the Tudors seemed to court and win the good wishes of the populace. Monarchs danced at the maypole, strolled arm-in-arm with commoners, hunted, played, entertained in the full sight of the people. Henry VII was by nature cold and aloof, yet men of no importance easily found places at his banquets and dined with the greatest in the kingdom. His affable second son, though the proudest and most imperious of men, delighted to rub neighbourly shoulders with his subjects. Revels, pageants and progresses were for the entertainment of court and people alike; and when the crowd sometimes intervened, as they did on a famous occasion at Richmond when they broke up the pageant and stripped the King and his courtiers, the Sovereign was not offended by their rude liberties.

Powerful, brilliant and self-willed, still the Tudors were anxious rulers, oppressed by insecurity. With an uncurbed license to do as they pleased they feared that the subject would assert the right to a similar individuality, and their fears made them violent and tyrannical. They were suspicious of the people they governed with such a peremptory power. In his troubles, as his popularity declined, Henry VIII told Marillac, the French ambassador, that he had a miserable people whom he would quickly impoverish so that none would dare raise a hand against him. As the century passed and the problems of the realm grew, the royal family lived amid the whispers of plots and in the fear of assassination. 'Marriage with the royal blood', wrote Francis Bacon at the end of the Tudor age, 'was too full of risks to be lightly entered into.' To forestall the terrors of rebellion, the Tudors would strike first, and queens, bishops, dukes fell under the headsman's axe. At the heart of the royal insecurity was the fear for the succession. The Tudors were a new dynasty without the reverence that attaches to an ancient line. If the succession was not clear, who could prevent the return of the factions and the anarchy from which Henry VII had rescued England at Bosworth Field?

In 1516 Henry VIII was twenty-four and his Queen, Catherine of Aragon, six years older. Catherine had come to England in 1501 to marry the ailing Prince Arthur, Henry's elder brother. The marriage had taken place but according to Catherine was never consummated, and since her life proved her a most honest, upright and religious woman there is no reason to doubt her word; within a year Prince Arthur was dead. The young widow remained in her new country, for there were cordial feelings between England and Spain, and the alliance was important for the English crown. In 1509 she was given in marriage to young King Henry, and though she was a homely person whose short, stocky figure thickened with the passing years and he was the most handsome and accomplished of princes, he had no reason to consider himself mismatched. She was sober, capable and devoted, and the daughter of powerful Spain was a prize for any prince. In 1510 her first child, a daughter, was stillborn; in the next six years she gave birth to four sons but none lived longer than a few weeks. The last three babies had been stillborn and this run of misfortune was taken as a fearful omen. On 18th February 1516 the Queen was at last delivered of a child who lived and the rejoicing in the court and country was great indeed. That the child was a female was taken to be of no account. 'We are both young', the King told the Venetian ambassador. 'If it was a daughter this time, by the grace of God the sons will follow.' Four days later, with the ceremonial and splendour that the King loved, the baby was christened at Greenwich Palace and named Mary after the King's sister, the Dowager Queen of France.

The little princess was given an establishment worthy of the daughter of a resplendent monarch. Her household numbered fifty, presided over by Margaret Lady Brian who administered the budget of more than £1,000 a year—a large sum for the time. The princess was the centre of her own small world and in the extraordinary manner of princes from the earliest age lived away from her parents. Solicitude for her health condemned her house-hold to incessant wanderings. The fear of the plague, always liable to break out when many were gathered together with little regard for hygiene, was ever present in the minds of her guardians. At the first sign of low spirits or sickness a change of air was recom-mended; her unwieldy staff with an attendant flock of domestics set out on laborious journeys to Windsor, Richmond, Greenwich, Eltham, Woodstock, or one of the many royal manors that sur-rounded London. In the course of these flights occasionally father and daughter would rest together at one of the larger palaces, and at the great festivals of the year the royal family was briefly re-united. Despite their long times apart, the parents were affectionate and careful for their daughter. Henry, in his boisterous, jovial way, would himself carry Mary into the presence chamber and invite the admiration of the courtiers and the foreign envoys. And the prudent Catherine ensured that her only child had the best atten-dants and the best attention.

Mary was small, thin and delicate, with a pale, almost trans-lucent skin and a mass of fair hair. The discipline of her life made her seem grave quite beyond her years. 'By immortal God,' her delighted father exclaimed to the French ambassador of his two-year-old child, 'this girl never cries.' Her self-control was a for-tunate accomplishment, for at a very early age, whether she liked it or not, she was drawn into the affairs of state. At the age of two, in a long and wearying ceremony, she was formally betrothed to the French Dauphin. Four years later this solemn and holy pledge was easily set aside in the cause of policy and the child was re-engaged to her cousin Charles V, the Holy Roman Emperor; in 1527 this betrothal, too, was cancelled and the young girl was promised to Francis I of France. From a very early age Mary was used to entertaining the great in her parents' absence. At five she welcomed French gentlemen to her court, feeding them 'straw-berries, wafers, wine and hippocras in plenty', delighting them with her self-possession and her playing on the virginal so that they 'greatly marvelled and rejoiced at the same, her young and tender age considered'.

Despite the heavy labours given to so young a child, Mary's youth appeared to be happy. Between daughter and parents there was a close bond, her father in particular, that tempestuous man, making a rowdy fuss over her which she repaid with the devotion that the delicate often give to the hearty. And growing up she was a credit to her parents. Though small and weak she was a spirited girl; a member of the royal household called her, at the age of nine, '*jocundius*' and '*decentius*'. She burst easily into laughter until the tears obscured her near-sighted hazel eyes. She liked to dance and took to hunting almost as ardently as her father. She was an open, affectionate young girl.

The education of the princess was something which the King and Queen took seriously. The flush of the Renaissance was on England and it was no longer respectable for the royal blood to be rough and ignorant. Henry was a cultivated man of brilliant parts and his court, in the early days before the religious troubles, was a pleasant place where the scholars of England—Colet, More, Linacre and others less famous—were welcomed. Queen Catherine brought with her some of the Spanish learning, then at its height, and also the artistic traditions of the famous Burgundian court, recently incorporated in the Spanish empire. In 1521 Wolsey had met Luis Vives at Bruges and invited the learned Spanish humanist to fill one of the six lectureships that the Cardinal had founded at Oxford. Vives, whose name is connected with so much valuable social reform and whose thought underlay the English poor laws, had given some attention to the neglected subject of women's education. His *De Institutione Feminae Christianae* was published the year he came to England and dedicated to Queen Catherine. She immediately asked him to draw up a plan of studies for her daughter, which he did, and soon afterwards took on the personal supervision of Mary's schooling.

Vives was a stern master; his strictness led his friend Erasmus to remark pleasantly that he hoped Vives would not treat his wife according to the rules of the *Institutione*. For Mary he devised a course solidly based on the Church Fathers and on the more worthy Latin writers, especially the historians, moralists and philosophers. Ambrose, Cyprian and Jerome were well represented; Augustine's *City of God* was read, but not his *Confessions*. Plato, Plutarch, Seneca and Cicero were to be studied, especially for their political views. Of the moderns, the only writers to receive particular notice were Erasmus and Thomas More, whose *Utopia* was published in the year of Mary's birth. It seems that Mary had little instruction in Greek. Greek studies were new to England; even More did not take up the language until his manhood. Nor did Vives recommend the poets and the romancers, all of whom he considered dangerous for women. Mary learnt French from an early age and spoke it well and fluently; her Italian was rather hesitant. She naturally learnt Spanish from her mother and her Spanish ladies, but allowed it to grow rusty so that when she met her husband Philip II for the first time she could understand what he said but would not trust herself to reply in Spanish.

Grave studies were the natural diet of an heir to the throne, and Mary learnt her lessons well. In later years her idiomatic command of Latin surprised and pleased the scholars. And to the serious subjects that Vives appointed for her, she added for her own amusement needlework and music. Like her father, she had a real gift for music which she loved and practised all her life, so that good judges thought her the most accomplished royal performer in Europe on lute, virginal or regal.

For Vives, the aim of Mary's education was not just the acquisition of knowledge, nor a training in government. He believed that the end of man was to glorify God and an education was nothing unless it taught Christian virtue. All writers and all works were made to bear on that point, and Vives's ideal was the one Erasmus found exemplified in the household of Thomas More : 'You would say that his house was Plato's Academy', he wrote to a friend. 'I should rather call it a school, or a university, of the Christian religion.' With the example of her devout mother, supported by the instruction of Vives, and encouraged by the presence at court of such noble men as Linacre, More and Erasmus, Mary from her earliest years showed a strong devotion to the Catholic faith.

In this she was her mother's daughter. Spain, schooled by the long contest with the Moors, was the sternest of Christian countries, and the great Isabella the Catholic, Mary's maternal grandmother, the most uncompromising of Christian monarchs. Queen Catherine brought with her to England the sober virtue of the Spanish. She provided for the religious instruction of her daughter, sometimes herself taking Mary through the catechism, and shielding her to some extent from the easy-going immorality of the King. Catherine appointed to Mary's household a number of Spanish ladies who were as careful and upright as the Queen, so much so that they were in great demand as brides for English lords who valued their sobriety and competence above the more flighty and slovenly girls of the English court. When the emperor asked that

Mary should be sent to Spain for her education, according to the marriage contract, the English envoys refused on the grounds that Mary already had in her mother the finest tutor in Christian virtue that Spain could provide.

The religious influence of her mother lasted the whole of Mary's life. The princess, though learned enough, had a simple, uncomplicated mind which held tenaciously to a few, clear principles. Her upbringing and education had stressed the prime importance of her faith, and the trials which her innocent mother was soon to endure at the King's hands could only confirm her religion. The shifts of policy in the Reformation that made religion a weapon of the State she could never understand. The profound, unbending religion was already something strange in an English princess; the course of English polity in her lifetime made her conviction seem at first eccentric, then perverse, and at last bloody.

The years passed and Henry's greatly desired son did not appear. When Mary was ten, the Queen was forty and soon beyond childbearing. The King was worried about the succession. Only one queen had succeeded to the throne since the Conquest, and the reign of Matilda was an unhappy precedent. While the King did his best to prepare Mary for the throne, sending her at the early age of nine to represent the crown in the Welsh Marches, he also looked for other ways to secure the Tudor dynasty. He thought that his little bastard son, the Duke of Richmond, three years younger than Mary, might succeed him, and gave the boy a household worthy of a Prince of Wales. But as long as Queen Catherine and Mary lived and had legitimacy on their side, the chances of a bastard were slight. The King felt the safety of his line threatened by Catherine's unfortunate inability to bear a son.

Henry had not been faithful to his wife. He was by nature selfish, wilful and amorous, and easily gave way to his desires. His affairs were notorious and his mistresses had their places at court. But like many self-indulgent men he needed the support of a forgiving and capable wife. Catherine ran his household with a careful economy that offset his own extravagance; it was said that she counted the linen with her own hands. He needed her to come home to, to look after his gross body undermined by excess, to bathe his ulcerated leg, to sit by his bed and listen to his complaints and his fears. They had been married so long, since he was a youth of eighteen, that she had become a comfortable habit; and no one could ever deny that she was the most virtuous and loving of wives. The sentiment that Shakespeare put into the King's mouth in *Henry VIII* was no more than the truth :

> That man i' the world who shall report he has
> A better wife, let him in nought be trusted,
> For speaking false in that : thou art, alone.

Once, in the early negotiations over Mary's betrothal, the French envoy had questioned the validity of a marriage between a man and his brother's widow and therefore wondered if Mary was legitimate. Other whispers were heard from time to time, and slowly a convenient doubt grew in Henry's mind. If Catherine, now beyond childbearing, could be put aside and the King marry again, he might yet provide England with a royal son. The scruple about his marriage was aggravated by his new passion. Recently, the cool, quizzical eyes of Anne Boleyn had cast their spell on Henry, and he was writing her hot pleas. But Anne was calculating and her family exceedingly ambitious; she kept the King at a certain distance, aiming to be something more than a royal play-thing, and thus inflamed Henry's desire. Catherine's age and plainness, Anne's beauty and perversity joined together with the King's fear for the succession; Henry decided to divorce his wife.

In the spring of 1527, soon after Mary had celebrated her betrothal to Francis I with dancing, jousting, plays and music, Henry quietly began his proceedings against Catherine : ordered by the King, Wolsey privately cited Henry before a court on the charge of illegally cohabiting with a woman not his wife. Mary was not told of the scheme afoot, but in a court little can be hidden. Catherine was distraught and went to Vives weeping 'over her fate that the man she loved more than herself should be so alien-ated from her as to think of marrying another'. Vives, the prin-cess's fatherly tutor and adviser, left England in disgust. The court was breathless with surprise and anticipation; within a year the King's 'secret matter' was the scandal of Europe. Mary was only an undersized girl of fourteen, but she was intelligent and bred to responsibility. Though the consequences of her father's brutal act could not be clear, she saw enough to fear the pain and humilia-tion ahead.

In May 1529 the trial of the King's cause began in Blackfriars Hall before Wolsey and Cardinal Campeggio, the papal legate.

The evidence for Henry, in the most callous way possible, did nothing to spare the Queen's feelings. Catherine countered with a noble and tragic speech denying the competence of the court, and demanding that the matter should be referred to Rome. Henry had been married by a dispensation of Pope Julius II; he now wanted Pope Clement VII to declare that dispensation void as being beyond the powers of his predecessor. If the cause were tried in England it seemed that the court might be bullied into pronouncing for the King; if the matter were dealt with in Rome, where the Pope only reigned with the consent of the Emperor, who was Catherine's nephew, Henry had no chance. But the legate had instructions to reach no verdict. The trial went on until July, then the court was adjourned and the cause removed to Rome.

Spoiled, pampered and the darling of all eyes from his earliest years, Henry had no doubts about the righteousness of his cause, and the opposition he now met infuriated him. Behind him, he heard the persuasive, nagging tones of Anne Boleyn and her family, daring him to complete the business he had begun, for they knew that their fates were bound up in this cause. He resolved that he would have his way. If the Emperor could play politics with the Pope, he too could bring pressure to bear on the Pope and gain his point by any means. The obstinacy and outrage of his wife also offended him and the two fell into miserable bickering which only drove Henry to the solace of Anne's arms. The policy of Anne was to keep the royal family divided, and under her influence Mary was only allowed short and infrequent visits to her mother. Mary was going through puberty, and suffering with it; already she was showing those symptoms which later caused the French ambassador to ask anxiously if she were capable of bearing children. She was ill, in low spirits, and the doctor bled her too often. She begged to be with her parents, but Henry refused. In the summer of 1531, greatly angered by a summons to appear in Rome, he cut himself off from his obstinate family. Mary was sent to Richmond and Catherine to an insignificant manor called the More. King and Queen never met again. In the five years left to her Catherine was progressively moved to quieter, gloomier, more constricted lodgings, ending finally in one room at Kimbolton Castle, watched at every moment and allowed out for nothing except the Mass. She had with her one or two elderly, unpaid servants. She did her needlework, prayed, smuggled a few letters to her daughter and her friends. She would not give up her claim to be Queen of England. In January 1536 she died; there was some suspicion of poisoning, but death, to one of her faith, could only be a relief from a wretched and tedious existence.

Though Henry had put Catherine away, the influence of the mother on the daughter could not be so easily set aside. The women were too much alike; both were straightforward and courageous, with simple, clear principles undisturbed by subtleties. In a world of shifting policies they inevitably appeared obstinate and bent on self-destruction. At first, Mary was not harassed. Henry's early concern was to break Catherine and the Pope to his will. From 1529 onwards, with the help of a frightened and subservient Parliament, he began to attack the papal rights and privileges in England. In this fortuitous way he began the Reformation in England, though he himself still failed to get what he wanted from the Pope. In 1533 events forced Henry's hand. Anne was pregnant and if the Pope would not annul the marriage with Catherine he must arrange a divorce by his own hand. In April he was secretly married to Anne; in May the new Archbishop of Canterbury, Cranmer, pronounced the marriage to Catherine invalid; and on 1st June Anne was crowned to no applause from a sullen populace. On 7th September the baby Elizabeth was born and the King now had the embarrassment of two daughters.

The desperate logic of Henry's action now made his elder daughter illegitimate in his own eyes. The privileges that Mary had formerly enjoyed were to be transferred to Elizabeth; the household of the elder daughter was dissolved and Mary sent to stay with her baby half-sister at Hatfield. Mary understood the implication of the move, but could not believe that her father had ordered it and earned 'the King's high displeasure' for questioning it. Henry now had both Catherine and Mary opposed to his will, for neither would renounce the title and position they thought were theirs by right; and Henry with his usual heartlessness began to play the two women against each other, threatening Catherine especially that her daughter would be sent abroad, forced into a nunnery, or into a base marriage unless both did what the King wanted. But Catherine, who was beyond fear herself, knew exactly the way to steady Mary's resolution. 'Daughter,' she wrote in the winter of 1533, 'I have heard such tidings that I do perceive, if it is true, the time is come that God Almighty will prove you; and

I am very glad of it, for I trust He doth handle you with a very good love.' She sent Mary a *Life of Christ* and the *Epistles* of Jerome; advised her to play the virginal for her recreation; and cautioned her to be as quiet and obedient as possible : 'Speak you few words, and meddle nothing.' For mother and daughter the King's acts were against the laws of the Church and therefore should be resisted with all the confidence of a serene faith; oppression and suffering were merely the expectations of a good Christian.

The conflict between Henry and Mary was the more pathetic because they kept their affection for each other. The King was exasperated by Mary and threatened 'to abate her stubbornness and pride', but even Chapuys, the Emperor's ambassador and the chief friend and adviser to both Catherine and Mary, noted that he still spoke of his daughter very fondly. Once Mary was removed to Hatfield, Henry left her in peace. But the new Queen, Anne Boleyn, jealous of the hold Mary had on the King's heart and frightened for the future of herself and her own daughter, persecuted Mary maliciously. Anne boasted, Chapuys reported, 'that she will make of the Princess a maid-of-honour in her royal household, that she may perhaps give her too much dinner on some occasion,[1] or marry her to some varlet'. On Anne's orders Mary was kept in the house, forbidden to exercise in the garden or to attend Mass. She was spied upon and her papers searched; she was separated from her old attendants, some of whom were imprisoned and interrogated; she was told to eat at the common table or starve; and the special diet ordered by Mary's doctor was denied her on the grounds that it cost too much—'at the least to the sum of £26.13.4'. And if Mary was not obedient Anne told her aunt Lady Shelton, the guardian of the household at Hatfield, to administer a few slaps across the face 'considering the bastard that she was'. All this Mary bore with dignity; she wept in the privacy of her room, but in public held her head high and insisted as well as she could on her rights as a princess.

With misguided simplicity Mary thought that if only she could speak with her father all would be well. Anne was careful to keep them apart, but Mary's hopes were illusory. Henry was so far gone in despotism that he could see no good but his own desire,

---

[1] i.e., give her a dose of poison.

and no law but his own will. The only limit on his selfish appetite was a canny instinct for the feelings of the people and what they would stand. State and Church he reformed into his own instruments. In 1534 the Act of Succession declared his elder daughter a bastard; later in the same year the Act of Supremacy made the King Christ's English vicar. Mary, the most pious Catholic, could not be expected to assent to either of these measures. Yet, like all subjects of the crown, assent she must. Those who refused the oath faced death. Within a very short time the headsman's axe was busily at work; John Fisher, as saintly a man as there was in England, fell, and not even Sir Thomas More, friend, loyal servant and good companion of Henry's earlier years, was spared.

The oath was brought to Catherine and Mary, and naturally both refused to take it. But Henry, always the astute politician, knew he could not afford to execute Mary. She had a large following in the country and the King, pressed by foreign enemies, would not provoke a rebellion. The Pope had recently judged the royal matrimonial cause in favour of Catherine and had excommunicated the King when he would not take his wife back. The Emperor Charles, Mary's cousin, was increasing his power and must not be goaded into an attack on England. The civilized in Europe were horrified by Henry's barbaric executions, and England had few friends. Henry saw that Catherine and Mary must be made to take the oath, to acknowledge the King's right and to give their assent to their own indignity. He wanted Mary alive and submissive, and he guarded her carefully so that Chapuys and her friends could not smuggle her out of England.

At the beginning of January 1536, Mary heard of the death of her beloved mother. On 29th January, the day of Catherine's funeral, Anne Boleyn miscarried of a boy, an event which doomed her. Thomas Cromwell drew up her indictment and on the 19th May she was executed. A few days later Henry married Jane Seymour and began once again the attempt to provide a son for the English throne. Catherine's death had relieved him from the immediate threat of war, and also of his most embarrassing opponent. In her moving last letter to the King Catherine had commended 'unto you Mary our daughter, beseeching you to be a good father to her', but for Henry policy came before fatherly solicitude and he continued the attack on his ill and grief-stricken daughter, delegating to the task Cromwell, his most wily and competent minister.

5 SIR THOMAS MORE

6 ROBERT KETT

In June 1536 a second Act of Succession made both Mary and the child Elizabeth illegitimate and demanded Mary's submission to the Act. By subtle diplomacy, pretending to be the barrier between her and the King's anger, Cromwell worked his way into Mary's confidence. On 13th June he sent a commission headed by the Duke of Norfolk with the paper for her to sign, but he had misjudged her resolution; she sent the delegation back with contemptuous arguments. Mary was taken from her companions, held incommunicado and watched night and day. Alone, sick and only twenty years old, Mary managed to get word to Chapuys asking what he and his master, the Emperor, would have her do. Judging that Henry was now determined to execute her if she refused and thinking her more important to Spain alive than dead, they advised her to sign. That advice from her warmest and most influential friends decided her. She took the document Cromwell had sent her and signed it without reading it, denying the Pope, recognizing her father as the head of the English Church, acknowledging her mother's 'incestuous and unlawful' marriage and her own illegitimacy.

For the first and perhaps the only time in her life Mary acted against her faith and her principles. Her rigid adherence to both in the future may be put down in part to remorse for this one fall. Henry was determined to break her, and who was she to set her puny powers against the full majesty of the King? For four years, in the sensitive time between sixteen and twenty, she was almost a prisoner and treated roughly and spitefully. With her inexperienced mind she had to resist the persuasive arguments of Cromwell. At last, with her mother dead, with her Spanish advisers counselling submission, and with the likelihood of execution if she refused, she gave way. It is a measure of her character that Henry found it harder to tame his daughter than it was to alter the laws and religion of England to his own convenience.

'As soon as the news of her subscription arrived, incredible joy was shown in all the Court.' The Lady Mary—as she was now called—was re-united with her father and his new Queen; for the remaining ten years of Henry's reign she lived peacefully enough on the sidelines of the court. She was no longer a threat to the King's policy; in 1536 he had put down the rebellious Catholics of the Pilgrimage of Grace; in October 1537 the succession was secured by the birth of his long-awaited son. He could now recognize his eldest child and allow his natural generosity to reign. He gave her a household of forty-two people, and a decent allowance to which he added presents of cash from time to time. Her well-kept accounts are the best record of her daily life.

Having leisure, security and an energetic mind, Mary returned to her studies. A French visitor spoke of her new interest in mathematics, physics and astronomy, besides further studies in the classics, history and languages. She wrote a little, both prose and poetry, and did it competently. Three Latin prayers of hers survive, and also a translation from Erasmus; a lighter Ballade mentioned by Cromwell unfortunately has not survived. She practised her music. Like her father in his youth, she was very active, a great walker and a great rider despite her small, frail body. She was a sociable young woman; indeed, observers at court noted that her little sister Elizabeth was the reserved, contained one, while Mary was jolly. She liked dancing and had her father's appetite for gambling; cards, bowls, riding, any sport was fit for a wager, an indulgence that often strained her budget.

She was both generous and affectionate. Her account books record the presents she gave, not only the gifts to the members of the royal family and to the courtiers, but also the kind offerings to the poor and the humble : 20s. to London prisoners, 15s. to an ill child, 8s. 6d. 'to my Lord Marquess's servant for singing', 20d. 'for bringing unto my Lady's Grace bacon and eggs', and a shilling for a poor woman bringing apples. To Elizabeth and little Edward she appeared to be all that an elder sister should be. 'My sister Elizabeth', she assured Henry, 'is in good health and, thanks be to our Lord, such a child toward as I doubt not your Highness shall have cause to rejoice of in time coming.' When Elizabeth suffered from Henry's neglect, following the execution of her mother, Mary helped her as best she could from her allowance. And Mary doted on her little brother Edward, showering him with the affection that she might have given to her own children had she been blessed with any. Edward responded with a devotion of his own, declaring to her in Latin : 'I love you as much as a brother may love his dearest sister.' Even when the serious youth became a strong Protestant he still preferred his gay eldest sister, though he deplored her Catholicism. With Henry's succession of queens, also, Mary was on good terms. She had a short-lived quarrel with Catherine Howard, but Anne of Cleves and Catherine Parr remained her friends whatever the circumstances at court.

Henry died in January 1547. For the last years of his reign Mary had carefully avoided all interference with politics and religious strife. She was silent when her friends were exiled or executed. When her oldest and dearest companion, the aged Countess of Salisbury, was hacked to death by a bungling executioner, Mary was so ill the doctors feared for her life, but she said nothing. Henry had left the doctrine of his English faith Catholic in most essentials, but with the coming of young Edward VI the Protestant party had their moment and seized it. The practice of the Mass was ridiculed; priests were attacked at the altar; a dead cat was tonsured, dressed in robes and nailed to a board with the Host in its paws. The Catholic Lord Chancellor was dismissed and Gardiner and Bonner, the most Catholic of Henry's bishops, were imprisoned. In 1549 an Act of Uniformity forbade the sacrifice of the Mass and based worship on Cranmer's *Book of Common Prayer*. The penalties for non-conformity were mild enough, but the Protector and the Council had the difficult task of persuading Mary, newly restored as heiress to the throne under the terms of Henry's will, to conform to an Act of Parliament.

The new rulers had neither the authority nor the iron will of the old King, and they faced also a rather different woman from the lonely, inexperienced twenty-year-old who had given way before her father's tyranny. In 1549 Mary was thirty-three, with her title and position confirmed and her income secured. The battle of wills with Henry had tempered her resolution which was, in the manner of all Tudors, already very strong. Her mind had never been flexible; she was on the way to becoming something of an old maid, and her principles were firmly set. Moreover, Henry's faith had been Catholic at heart while Edward's was distinctly Protestant. The ordinary Englishman might, as a cynical foreigner observed, become Moslem or Jew at the King's bidding, but Mary had suffered one great defeat on the cause of religion and was not likely to deny her faith a second time.

She told the Protector in peremptory terms that she could have nothing to do with laws 'against the custom of all Christendom, and in my conscience against the law of God and his Church, which passeth all the rest'. And neither Protector Somerset nor his successor Warwick could move her despite blackmail, threats and the intimidation of her retainers. Warwick had her priests and chief officials imprisoned, and caused the young Protestant King to worry Mary with orders to amend her religion. Despite her reverence for monarchy, her sisterly love, and her sorrow for her servants, she replied that 'her faith she would not change, nor dissemble her opinion with contrary doings'. The persecution of Mary only ceased in March 1551 when the Emperor Charles, as Edward's *Journal* recorded, threatened war if his cousin were not left alone. She was then allowed to hear Mass in private.

The licence given to Mary was not extended to other subjects, for in Edward's reign England went steadily Protestant. In 1552 Parliament approved the second Prayer Book and the Forty-two Articles of Cranmer, which he vainly hoped would lead to 'concord and quietness' in religion. This was not so, and in the same year another Act of Uniformity made stiff penalties for attendance at Mass, and also stripped the churches of their idolatrous Catholic riches—jewels, plate, robes, crosses, all gold and silver—for the benefit of the government which was hard pressed by debt. The conjunction between a stern Protestantism and a corrupt administration made all Catholics and many moderate men of no great religious feeling look to Mary as the hope for the future, to introduce civic peace, traditional ways and good government. On 6th July 1553 young King Edward died of tuberculosis; he left a worried land, burdened with debt, anxiously feeling the pulls of France and Spain, and unresolved in religion. And waiting to take the advantage of the times was the corrupt adventurer Warwick, lately made Duke of Northumberland, but with his eye on a greater place. Northumberland's conspiracy to place his daughter-in-law Lady Jane Grey on the throne failed. His callous double-dealing was so well known that none could trust him, and his only hope lay in surprise; even the Protestants, whom he claimed to represent, hated him. In the crisis Mary acted with prudence and courage. She boldly proclaimed herself Queen, and then, with only a few followers, avoided Northumberland's soldiers until the country rose and acclaimed her. On 19th July the danger was over; the bells began to peal and rang until ten at night, and a mighty *Te Deum* thundered out from St Paul's. 'God so turned the hearts of the people to her and against the Council', her greatest enemy John Knox admitted, 'that she overcame them without bloodshed notwithstanding there was made great expedition against her both by sea and land.'

Hardly ever had an English sovereign come to the throne amid so much rejoicing. 'Money was thrown out of the windows for joy. The bonfires were without number.' 'Yet are we comforted again', wrote a balladeer :

> Lift up, and eke erect :
> By cause the Lord hath placed thus
> His chosen and elect.

London was deafened by the cheering, the dancing, the feasting, the crackling of bonfires and the jangle of the bells. And the reign began well. To the members of the conspiracy Mary was lenient to a fault. Northumberland, two or three notorious ringleaders, and eventually Lady Jane, the innocent victim of Northumberland's ambition, were executed; but several members of the Council, equally implicated in the plot, were not only forgiven but also reinstated in office. She was not vengeful or vindictive; political terrorism, as used by all other Tudors, was never one of her weapons. When Elizabeth dabbled in Wyatt's rebellion, Mary refused to execute or banish her; Elizabeth, in her turn, did not make the same mistake with Mary Stuart. But for all that the new Queen was a Tudor. She intended to rule in the autocratic manner of her family.

Though she made it known immediately that her mind was 'stayed in matters of religion', and though it was not in her nature to compromise with what she considered to be heresy, she began with soft words on religion, calling for an end to back-biting and argument. This policy had been the advice of the wily Charles V to whom, as usual, she turned for wisdom. The choice of adviser was ominous, for it showed that Mary, contrary to the most powerful instinct of Tudor England, was prepared to allow a foreigner to have a hand in English affairs. And the fears of the country were confirmed when Parliament tried to oppose the negotiations for her marriage to Philip of Spain; she angrily interrupted the Commons and rebuked them for their audacity.

The product of nationalism is usually a hatred for foreigners, and this was so in Tudor England. The cultivated combined an admiration for foreign achievements with a fervent English enthusiasm. No man welcomed foreigners more eagerly than Henry VIII, and no king relied on the prejudice of his subjects more than he. But the people had no such subtlety; they heartily detested all foreigners, of whatever complexion. Hall's *Chronicle* quite falsely claimed that the huge number of strangers in London prevented the English workmen from earning a living. Henry's attack on the jurisdiction of the Pope and the subsequent rise of the English Church could hardly have taken place without the native prejudice of the people. When Wyatt raised his rebellion against Mary in 1554, he did so, as it was claimed, to prevent England 'from over-running by foreigners'.

Mary, however, did not share this national prejudice. She was half Spanish by birth and, all her life, had received the kindest help from Spain and the worst treatment from England. She had no thought for the developing commercial rivalry between Spain and England caused by the exclusion of England from the riches of the Spanish New World. She hoped to bring her country back to Catholicism, and thought that this could be done best under the tutelage of Spain, the most Catholic of powers. And lastly, she was a Tudor and did not like opposition; in the matter of her marriage she was determined to have her way. In October 1553, on her knees before the altar, she vowed to become the wife of Philip.

Her decision offended most of the country; even Gardiner, the Queen's ally in Catholicism, recommended her to marry Edward Courtenay, a dissolute nonentity descended from the House of York. When the representatives of Spain came to conclude the match in January 1554, they were showered with snowballs by the London mob. And in the course of three months disaffection turned into Wyatt's rebellion. But the rebels learnt to their cost the august majesty of Tudor rule, sustained by nearly seventy years of autocracy. Mary met the attack on London with disdainful courage, exhorting the citizens to stand fast against the rebels, 'and fear them not, for I assure you I fear them nothing at all'. The attack faltered on Ludgate Hill and Wyatt was taken as he wearily sat on a bench outside a tavern.

Within a year Mary had used up most of the goodwill of her accession. The warning given by Wyatt's rebellion would have checked a more politic or a less stubborn person than Mary. But she pressed on both with the plans for her marriage and with the restoration of Catholicism. On 25th July 1554, at Winchester Cathedral, the thirty-eight-year-old Queen was married to Philip, her junior by eleven years. And now that the marriage was done, the way was clear for the restoration of the Catholic faith. Her new father-in-law, the Emperor Charles V, having by the marriage drawn England under the Spanish cloak, advised her to go slowly in matters of religion; for, like most rulers in the new age of the Renaissance, he preferred to put policy before religion and did not want Mary to alienate her subjects. But Gardiner, the imperial ambassador reported, was 'most ardent and hot-headed in the affairs of religion'; the Queen was impatient for the return of the old faith, and she was supported by the austere Cardinal Pole,[2] an unwavering English Catholic all his life and an unsuccessful candidate for the papacy.

Pole set out to undo the Reformation of Henry and Edward. Mary's third Parliament met towards the end of 1554; on 29th November both Houses were summoned to ratify the reunion with Rome, which they did with only two opposing. Parliament then revived the heresy laws of Richard II, Henry IV and Henry V, and, after lengthy discussion, restored the papal supremacy and jurisdiction. But the Church could not recover her property sequestrated in the last two reigns, and the failure to do this, in the wise view of William Cecil, showed the hollowness of the reconversion. And the imperial envoy agreed with Cecil. The point was soon brought home to Mary and her advisers. When the heresy laws were put into effect at the beginning of 1555, the government was surprised by the strength of the resistance from the Protestant clergy and from the humble laity. At the top of English society, where politics and not religion mattered, the great men and women—Elizabeth, Cecil, Arundel, Pembroke, etc.—easily conformed to Mary's wishes. 'They discharged their duty', wrote a Venetian envoy, 'as subjects to their prince by living as he lives, believing what he believes, and in short doing whatever he commands.' But in the humble depths, and among the clergy, there appeared a Reformed fervour which hardly anyone had suspected. The execution of John Rogers, biblical scholar and the first Protestant to die, inflamed opinion against Mary. And the resolute deaths of Hooper, Saunders, Ferrar, Ridley, Latimer and Cranmer in the same year only strengthened the Protestants and discom-

---

[2] Reginald Pole, son of Mary's old governess the Countess of Salisbury, was of royal descent, and had himself been put forward as a possible husband for Mary: though he was a cardinal, he was not yet a priest. But Pole was fifty-four, an ascetic churchman and not the marrying kind. His own advice to Mary was to remain single.

forted the Catholics. 'You have lost the hearts', a lady wrote to the Catholic Bishop Bonner, 'of twenty thousand that were rank papists within this twelve months.' Before the end of the reign just short of three hundred Protestants had been executed, and their deaths have a triumphant celebration in Foxe's *Book of Martyrs*. Parliament passed the legislation, the ecclesiastical courts condemned the heretics, and the lay arm carried out the executions; but the responsibility for this persecution was with Mary and her Council.

The country was slipping from the Queen's grasp. It seemed that all she did either destroyed Englishmen or lessened the influence of their country. A virulent hatred grew up against Rome, against Catholics, against Spaniards, against all—it seemed—that was dear to the Queen. Her husband had failed her. He had little interest in the middle-aged, narrow virgin who had become his wife; his aim was to win for himself the direction of English policy and to bring the country under the rule of Spain. When this was denied him he soon left for the more pleasant surroundings of the Spanish Netherlands where he amused himself with a young countess. Mary was desolate, and insisted that the dropsical swelling in her belly was Philip's child. Daily, her ardent letters followed her absent husband, to which he replied with cool words, angry that she could not persuade Parliament to let him share the English crown. The common people detested him, and put about provocative rumours concerning his impotence. In March 1557 Philip, now king of Spain on the abdication of his father, returned briefly to England and drew the country into a war against France which none wanted. For two years the harvests had been bad; the coffers of the treasury were empty, and the foreign debt was increasing. The profit of the war went to Philip, the losses to England. On 8th January 1558 the English at Calais capitulated and England's last continental possession passed into French hands after an interval of over two hundred years. Though Calais was not worth the cost of keeping it, and must have fallen sooner or later, its loss was a humiliation to the English for which they blamed the Queen and her husband.

At the end Mary was without hope. She went through the motions of her stubborn policy like a sleepwalker, burning heretics to the last, a tiny, hysterical, sick woman of forty-two. Nothing had come of her policy; England was further from Catholicism than it had ever been in the days of Henry and Edward; the people were more insular than before, cursing Rome and Spain impartially; and the country was poor, debt-ridden and troubled. After much pain and fortified by the rites of the Church, she died on 17th November 1558.

Mary was out of her time—a fervent religious ruler in an age of policy. She had qualities that no other Tudor possessed; she was more honest, more scrupulous, less callous and vindictive than any of her house. Her administration—as distinct from her policy—tried to banish corruption and was kind to the poor. She was generous-hearted and forgiving in all matters except faith. Rebels, traitors, plotters went free while humble Protestants of unblemished life were inexorably condemned. The cruel logic of her faith, which punished trying to preserve the religious purity of the community, made her pitiless towards those who opposed her religion. She had little knowledge and less understanding of English feelings. She was the only Tudor with a foreign parent, and her education was more Spanish than English. The calculating cruelty which her father practised on her in the name of English policy left her too hurt and puzzled to see the particular problems of her native land. As she could not understand her people, so they could never forgive her terrible persecution. Nationalism was their faith, as Catholicism was hers. She could not worship at their shrine and they would not at hers. The division between ruler and people, as wide as at any time in history, caused her own people to brand her with the worst name ever given to an English sovereign : she became Bloody Mary.

5

Sir Thomas Gresham

WHEN THE BUILDING was finished in November 1567, the scaffolding down and the workmen's debris cleared away, the onlookers saw four grasshoppers carved above the corners of the walls, and a fifth, very large upon a puny spire, high in the dull winter sky crouching gigantically over the city. These were the emblems of Sir Thomas Gresham, the brave emblems of capitalism, dominating his new Exchange. On 23rd January 1571 the Queen came in state to the city and dined with Sir Thomas in Bishopsgate. Then they inspected the building and Elizabeth 'caused the same Bourse by an herald and a trumpet to be proclaimed the *Royal Exchange*', setting the final royal approval on a lifetime given to speculation. The great financier, surfeited with property and weary with the accumulation of wealth, his only son dead and his legs lame and gouty, limped amid the extraordinary treasures of his five houses until an apoplectic fit took him off at the age of sixty.

Thomas Gresham was born in London in 1519, the second son of Sir Richard Gresham and the inheritor of a strong merchant tradition. The Greshams came from Holt in Norfolk and had prospered from the wool trade of their native county helped by advantageous marriages. In the generation before Thomas's birth, the family had come to London in search of wider opportunities and had done very well. Sir Richard and his brothers all began in trade. One, frightened by an apparition at Stromboli, forsook commerce and became a priest; the others, with less tender consciences, were members of the Mercers' Company, and all successful. In their trading ventures they saw Russia, the Baltic, France, the eastern Mediterranean; they were well known in Antwerp, the great clearing house for north European trade. The honours that go with successful business came to them. Richard was a financial agent for the government, and both he and his younger brother John were knighted. Both became Lord Mayor of London, Richard in 1537 and John ten years later. They were worthy citizens, substantial, deferential to authority, useful and acquisitive. Sir Richard, adviser to the King's minister Thomas Cromwell, at the dissolution of the monasteries petitioned for, and received, extensive lands in Norfolk.

Thomas Gresham was inevitably destined for trade. He was sent to Gonville Hall, Cambridge, though it was not usual for the sons of merchants to go to university. But the son of a Lord Mayor deserved the extra polish of a classical education, and the Latin and the languages perfected at Cambridge would do a young merchant credit in foreign lands. The real education, the commercial training which was the foundation of his success, he got within his family. After university he was apprenticed for eight years to his uncle Sir John. 'My father', Thomas wrote, 'being a wise man, knew, although I was free by his copy, it was to no purpose, except I was bound prentice to the same; whereby to come by the experience and knowledge of all kinds of merchandise.' In 1543 he was admitted to the Mercers' Company and began to take a part in family ventures. In 1544, with a rather indecent haste he married Anne Read, the widow of one of his colleagues. He prospered and began to make an independent reputation. At the end of 1551 he became the Royal Agent on the continent at the early age of thirty-two.

Among the greatest of the benefits which Henry VII conferred on England was the re-establishment of her commercial well-being. With good reason, John Wheeler, the Elizabethan writer on trade, praised him as the 'peaceful, politic and rich prince'. In former times England's power in Europe had been enforced by arms. Henry VII turned away from military glory and worked instead for the indirect power of trade. While he encouraged the nationalism of the people he secretly soothed the fears of his continental rivals, so that it has been said of him that 'his subjects paid him to levy war and his enemies bribed him to refrain'. The constant care of his reign was to foster trade and to find outlets for English commodities, especially English wool and cloth. To this end he concluded commercial treaties with Spain, with France, with the Empire, with Friesland and the Netherlands. In the North he was anxious to avoid a contest with the powerful Hanseatic League, but he tried to break the monopoly of the Hansards by entering into compacts with Denmark and Riga. In the South, in the rich Mediterranean, Henry faced the jealous competition of Venice.

A war of tariffs ensued, which England eventually won; by the beginning of the sixteenth century 'divers tall ships of London', Hakluyt wrote, 'with certain other ships of Southampton and Bristol had an ordinary and usual trade to Sicily, Candia, Chios and somewhile to Cyprus', taking out cloth and returning with silks, wines, oils, rhubarb and spices.

But the best stroke of his commercial policy was the understanding with Antwerp and the Netherlands. The chief market for English cloth was in the Netherlands, and Antwerp was the trading centre of northern Europe. Political difficulties had interfered with the Netherlands trade and for some years the Merchant Adventurers had removed the mart for English cloth from Antwerp to Calais. In 1496 the *Magnus Intercursus* restored the good relations between countries and the English merchants returned to 'their mansion in Antwerp', Bacon wrote, 'where they were received with procession and great joy'. The vast importance of Antwerp to the English wool and cloth trade was pointed out by an acid Flemish proverb : 'If Englishmen's fathers were hanged at the gates of Antwerp, their children, to enter the town, would creep between their legs.' For the export of wool through the Wool Staplers, and of manufactured cloth through the Merchant Adventurers, most of which trade went by way of Antwerp, was the source of England's riches. And most of the wealthiest merchants in the Tudor age were connected in some way with textiles. Thomas Gresham, his father and his uncles were all members of the Mercers' Company; of the ninety-seven Lord Mayors between 1509 and 1603, seventy-two had made their money from cloth. Exports of cloth rose rapidly; by the middle of Elizabeth's reign Camden put the value of exported cloth at £1,500,000, an increase of more than £500,000 from the start of the reign.

The parsimony and good management of Henry VII left his son a full exchequer which that desperate and extravagant young prince immediately began to squander. Although English trade was still expanding and the King also had to hand the profits from the dissolution of the monasteries, in the last years of his reign Henry sank into debt. The ill-advised expedient of debasing the coinage did nothing to help; money had to be borrowed from abroad to such an extent that the charges for interest and redemption came to £40,000 a year. As a result of lamentable policies, in particular the debasement of the coinage, there was a general and catastrophic rise in prices. 'I think', John Hales, the wisest of economic commentators, wrote in his *Discouse of the Common Weal* in 1549, 'this alteration of coin to be the first original cause that strangers first sell their wares dearer to us : and that makes all farmers and tenants, that reareth any commodity, again to sell the same dearer : the dearth thereof makes the gentlemen to raise their rents and to take farms into their hands for the better provision, and consequently to enclose more ground.' The fluctuations in the exchange rate caused by the poor coinage upset foreign trade and weakened England's international credit, as Gresham later pointed out to Elizabeth. 'It may please your Majesty to understand', he wrote in 1558, 'that the first occasion of the fall of the exchange did grow by the King's Majesty, your late father, in abasing his coin from 6 oz. fine to 3 oz. fine. Whereupon the exchange fell from 26s. 8d. to 13s. 4d. which was the occasion that all your fine gold was conveyed out of this your realm.' The mismanagement of Henry VIII seemed likely to ruin the prosperity that his father had worked so hard to secure. Prices were high and rising, trade was hindered, unrest was stirring and the king's debts were becoming alarming. The state of the royal finances was an embarrassment to Edward and a puzzle to his ministers; having nothing to suggest, the Council fell with displeasure on Sir William Dansell, the Royal Agent, accusing him of 'marvellous ill service' and dismissing him 'by reason of his slackness'.

'I was sent for unto the Council', Gresham recalled, 'and brought by them afore the King's Majesty to know my opinion (as they had many other merchants) what way with least charges his Majesty might grow out of debt. And after my device was declared, the King's Highness and the Council required me to take the room in hand, without any suit or labour for the same.' The government was looking for unusual remedies, and no doubt Gresham's was the boldest plan put forward. Perhaps the King, old-fashioned economic moralist that he was, did not understand Gresham's proposals, his juggling with exchange rates and other capitalist sleight-of-hand; but in the desperate circumstances young Gresham's ideas were spirited and different enough to be given a chance.

And going to Antwerp to try his hand in the international money market, Gresham needed a boldness and an expert knowledge that was hardly to be found in England at this date. Rising out of the stiff, suspicious economy of the late Middle Ages, a world of tariffs, protective legislation, trade restrictions and monopolies, Antwerp waved the banner of free trade and demonstrated to the North the workings of capitalism. The exchange at Antwerp was dedicated *'ad usum mercatorum cujusque gentis ac linguae'* —'to the use of merchants of whatever race and tongue'—and round the exchange were concentrated the men who controlled the money market : the royal agents, the representatives of the great banking houses of South Germany, France, Spain and Italy, the most important of whom were the famous Fuggers of Augsburg, and the rich merchants of all nationalities who found the lending and borrowing of money more profitable than trade. Into the port of Antwerp on the Scheldt came the shipping of the West; in a good season two thousand boats could be seen in the river at a time. Capital from trading ventures flowed into the Bourse, from the mines of Germany and Hungary, from the profits of the English trade—wool brought by the Staplers, and cloth brought by the Merchant Adventurers, the imports of which amounted to some £1,200,00 a year. And from this capital large sums were taken to finance the insatiable demands of governments contemplating, fighting, or recovering from war, or the requirements of merchants expanding their trade across the world, from the East Indies to the West Indies. In Antwerp, in Lyon, Seville, Venice and certain other cities, the techniques of international finance were well developed; bills were discounted, drafts on other cities drawn up, and merchants' papers of all nationalities exchanged. 'No one can deny', the citizens of Antwerp boasted, 'that the cause of the prosperity of this city is the freedom granted to those who trade here.' For fifteen years after 1552 Thomas Gresham was as much at home in Antwerp as he was in London.

The mysteries of the money market were hidden to most Englishmen. Plain men protested against the dubious morality of this traffic, but the government, oppressed by debts, were anxious to have the benefit of the market; Gresham was the English initiate of the subtle arts of finance, taking a place among the 'great bankers or money merchants that use the exchange only for gain by merchandising of money, who lie watching to take advantage of the time and occasion to fall or raise the exchanges to their most profit'. His simple instructions were to use his art for England's benefit. The speculative dealings of Gresham went against the economic morality of the time, and Gresham was as unscrupulous as most financiers, but the government was pleased to allow the Royal Agent a looser conscience while English citizens at home were sternly held by legislation against the practices of capitalism.

It is not known what 'device' Gresham had revealed to the King and Council at his first interview, but a letter to Northumberland on 21st August 1552 showed that he soon had plans to meet the King's pressing debts. First, he suggested that £1,300 should be set aside each week and sent secretly to Antwerp for Gresham to use in paying off the debts. These funds would be used for dealings on the exchange, quietly buying small amounts of sterling each day so that the value of sterling would rise in the market. Next he suggested that the Merchant Adventurers should be compelled to pay the royal debts in Flanders, the money to be repaid to them in London, whereby the government, benefiting from the difference in exchange rates, would save £4,500 on a debt of £30,000, all at the expense of the merchants. Finally Gresham suggested that the royal prerogative should be used to create a monopoly in lead; the King would then export lead to the continent at greatly increased prices.

These proposals were typical of Gresham's approach to business, his devotion to certain ends, and not fastidious how he gained them. The first part of the proposal, the setting aside of funds, was sound practice which had to be abandoned as too expensive. The second part, 'pegging' of the exchanges in Antwerp, was the new capitalism at work. The third part, the mulcting of the Merchant Adventurers, was considered by Gresham to be one of his most brilliant innovations, the deceit being justified by the profit. And the fourth part, the creation of a lead monopoly, was an example of expediency, showing Gresham the merchant forgetting his principles for the sake of Gresham the royal financier. As a successful merchant, he was a great advocate of free trade, yet in the interests of his royal master he was prepared to accept an old-fashioned and objectionable monopoly.

Gresham's operations at Antwerp worked no wonders. Some of his advice was not taken, and other schemes, though profitable, could not satisfy the royal money-hunger. Twice in the next ten years forced loans were raised from the Wool Staplers and the Merchant Adventurers, but the royal debt still crept up. But he had slowed the rate of increase and he had re-established the royal credit. He was able to borrow for Edward at 14 per cent whereas the Emperor Charles V had to pay 16 per cent; and he managed to raise the exchange at Antwerp from 16 Flemish shillings to the pound sterling up to 22 Flemish shillings. The King was well pleased and just before he died presented Gresham with property worth £100 a year.

When Mary came to the throne Gresham was in some trouble. His patrons under Edward did not have the favour of the new government; Gresham was at first dismissed and the former Agent, Dansell, reinstated. Gresham counter-attacked promptly. He pointed out the incapacity of Dansell who 'brought the King in debt and took wares and jewels up, to the King's great loss', asserted his own good services to Edward, and pleaded his own deserving case. 'And now', he wrote to the Council, 'God help poor Gresham.' His pleas, backed by certain influential men and supported by Dansell's unfailing ability to bungle, brought Gresham triumphantly once again to Antwerp, where he continued the royal business as before. He undertook exacting and varied duties with his usual enterprise and cunning. He went on troublesome journeys across Europe in search of capital; he ran discreet errands for important men, and made for them advantageous purchases of silks and jewels and little luxuries; he arranged for the smuggling of currency into England (all countries had stringent regulations against the export of gold and silver) in diplomatic bags, in sacks of pepper and in suits of armour, all of which he advised the Queen to keep secret, 'for if it should be known or perceived in Flanders it were as much as my life and goods were worth'. He kept judiciously silent about the religious and political troubles of Mary's reign, and on the death of the Queen, being in England at the time, he was one of the first to hurry to Elizabeth at Hatfield. He reminded her how much he had done in the two previous reigns, and was well received. Elizabeth would, Gresham proudly reported, 'not only keep one ear shut to hear me, but also, if I did her none other service than I had done to King Edward, her late brother, and Queen Mary, her late sister, she would give me as much land as ever both they did'.

And Elizabeth certainly had need of the very best advice, as the unhappy reign of Mary, despite her reasonably sound administration, had left the royal finances in poor condition. The royal debt was £226,910 of which over £100,000 was owed to foreign financiers. The country was in a restless, impoverished state and

7 SIR THOMAS GRESHAM

8 SIR FRANCIS WALSINGHAM

immediate funds were required for making fortifications, building ships, buying gunpowder and stores. The Queen instituted exceptional economies and Parliament voted heavy new taxes, but these measures could only meet part of the expenses for defence and Elizabeth was forced, as her predecessors had been, to look to Gresham to raise loans from abroad. Gresham set about the problem in his usual way. He put forward once again his old plans. He advocated raising the value of sterling, the reduction of the foreign debt by paying off loans as they became due rather than renewing them. He wanted the Queen to limit the special privileges of the Hanse merchants in London, and thereby put a profitable trade in the way of Englishmen. He was especially keen once more to raise a forced loan from the Merchant Adventurers, and by playing upon the exchanges to make the Adventurers' loss become the royal profit. 'The exchange', he said with a rapt admiration for his own dexterity, 'is the chiefest and richest thing only above all others. This thing is only kept up by art and God's providence.' And last of all he called for the reform of the English currency which had been in a bad state ever since Henry VIII started to debase it.

The reform of the coinage was the first step taken by Burghley and the Council to overcome the prodigious inflation which had so weakened the economic strength of England in the middle years of the century. Gresham had recommended the recoinage, and when the event took place in 1560 it was he who engaged and sent over the chief refiner, Daniel Wolstat of Antwerp, who charged for his labours 5 per cent on the amount of new currency put into circulation. The change went very well. When the old coins had been melted down and the new coins struck the Queen found that she had made a small profit. This was valuable, but much more valuable was the effect of the recoinage on trade. The exchange rates fluctuated less wildly; foreign merchants accepted English currency with renewed confidence; and domestic prices, though they did not fall as the government had hoped, at least rose less steeply.

The reform of the coinage in 1560 was the beginning of a better age for England's economy. The improvement was partly due to the character of the new government. The Queen was notoriously thrifty and managed to execute many of her policies, in particular the Irish campaigns, on the money of her subjects. Burghley, though not the most enthusiastic of mercantilists, at least saw the necessity to reform the conditions of labour in England and to encourage foreign trade. The Statute of Apprentices in 1563 very comprehensively tried to increase the supply of agricultural labour, arrest the decay of 'corporate towns', and improve declining standards of workmanship. Also, in an attempt to defeat inflation, it made the assessment of wages proportionate to prices. Relief of the poor was provided by a number of measures which culminated in the Act of 1572. Having reorganized English labour, Burghley then tried to lessen the country's dependence on foreign finance. Money was needed first of all for *nervi bellorum*—the sinews of war—and it was well recognized that a poor country was a weak one. Gunpowder and ordnance, Gresham wrote to Burghley, were 'better than any treasure'. But the gunpowder and the minerals for the ordnance were mainly purchased from abroad; Gresham indeed had the double function of raising the money to buy the gunpowder in his role as a financier, and of making the actual purchases in his capacity as merchant. Burghley decided to provide for these expensive commodities at home. In 1561 a company was formed to work the mines in Northumberland and to search for copper in Cumberland. German miners trained in the enterprises of the Fuggers were brought over and Gresham gave the Fuggers a bond for their expenses. In 1568 the Company of Royal Mines was incorporated, with Burghley as the Governor, providing iron and copper for ordnance. Patents were issued for the production of sulphur and saltpetre for gunpowder; further mining operations were encouraged in Somerset and Cornwall, looking for calamine, tin, iron and lead.

Thrift, legislation and planning eased the burden of England's debts. Further relief was given by the rapid growth of wealth in the late sixteenth century, a wealth which allowed capital to accumulate at home rather than be expensively bought in the European money markets. 'The realm', it was said in 1579, 'aboundeth in riches, as may be seen by the general excess of the people in purchasing, in buildings, in meat, drink and feasting, and most notably in apparel.' Five years later Sir John Hawkins, treasurer of the navy, thought the native wealth had increased threefold since the accession of Elizabeth. The new wealth came largely from trade, not only from the traditional European trade now greatly extended by such enterprises as those undertaken by the Muscovy Company, formed after the exploratory voyages of Willoughby and

Chancellor in 1553 and 1556, but also from the new trade opened up by the discoveries of the navigators, the wide-flung trade that embraced both the East and the West Indies. And to add to these riches there was the plundered treasure which Elizabeth's privateers brought back to England with her secret encouragement. The bullion which Sir Francis Drake stole on his circumnavigation provided a large part of the capital for the founding of the Levant Company. 'Who doth not understand', wrote the editor of the *Discourse of the Common Weal* in 1581, 'of the infinite sums of gold and silver which are gathered from the Indies and other countries, and so yearly transported unto these coasts?' In 1621 a Member of Parliament calculated that £12 million of plunder came to England in Elizabeth's reign; it was, he said, 'the spring that furnished the kingdom'. The country, because it was prospering, looked formidable to enemies, and the Queen's credit was high. 'The Duke of Alva', Gresham wrote to Burghley about the powerful Spanish governor in the Netherlands, 'is more troubled with the Queen's Majesty's credit and with the vent of her highness' commodities at Hamburg, than he is with anything else, and quakes for fear.'

The new prosperity of England made the work of the Royal Agent less difficult and also less vital. Elizabeth continued to borrow—at her death her debt was said to be £400,000—but England's credit was good and the delicate, sly art of Gresham no longer needed. He had seen three sovereigns through rough waters and his advice had helped to guide them to safety. He had the rewards of his service; trade and speculation, using his advantageous position, made him immensely rich, and Elizabeth knighted him in 1559. His hard tasks in Europe had wearied him. For many years he had been much more than a mere financial agent. He was a roving envoy sent on many a diplomatic mission. He was also the master of an intelligence service, suborning the servants of Spain, bribing and corrupting officials in Antwerp, receiving bribes in return, and all the while sending back to Burghley a precise account of the Spanish strength and intention in the Netherlands; details of private conversations with the Duchess of Parma, William of Orange, and the Duke of Alva; and descriptions of religious troubles, with comments on their possible effect on politics and business. A fall from a horse in 1560, on one of his incessant journeys, left him lame. His family life was disrupted by travel, business, worry. His wife was mostly in England and he was mostly abroad. His son Richard died in 1564 and he was left with an illegitimate daughter only. In 1568, after more than fifteen years in Antwerp, Sir Thomas left that city, now declining in commercial importance, and came home to his many business ventures in England.

In 1537 Gresham's father, Sir Richard, had proposed the building of an Exchange in London. No doubt Sir Thomas remembered his father's plan. Thoughts of an Exchange in his native city came to him again in 1564, after the death of his son left him with great riches and no heir. The decline of Antwerp, harried by the political and religious troubles in the Netherlands, increased the chances for success in London, and Gresham set out to persuade the aldermen.

That London had existed for so long without an Exchange showed the conservative spirit of the English merchants whose economic thought lagged some way behind continental developments. The great banking houses of Italy and South Germany did not find it necessary to keep agents in London, and the English government, as Gresham knew only too well, was forced to raise loans abroad. Such financial business as there was in London still went largely to the resident Italians, men like Palavicino, Spinola and Vellutelli, men so omnipresent and dexterous that they raised suspicions in Burghley's cautious mind. In 1553, in an effort to control the exchanges, he wanted to limit the powers of these Italians; they 'go to and fro and serve all princes at once,' he complained, 'work what they list and lick the fat from our beards'. Nonetheless, Elizabeth made use of them, as her predecessors had done, and knighted Palavicino for services to finance and diplomacy. And English merchants, coming haltingly after where the Italians had led, soon saw the value of a money market. Successful merchants, accumulating capital from foreign trade and learning something of markets, found that the financing of foreign ventures was more profitable and less of a risk than trade itself. Such a merchant was able 'to get a part and sometimes all his gains that employeth money taken up by exchange on wares, and so make others travel for his gains'. The persevering merchant was transforming himself into the radiant capitalist financier (though confusingly he kept the name of 'merchant'), and such men appreciated the value of an Exchange in London with the organization and international connections to aid their financial dealings. The government, too, looked favourably on an Exchange, for then it could raise loans within the realm.

Formerly, the London merchants had met in St Paul's, or walking in Lombard Street where they were constrained, wrote Stow, 'either to endure all extremities of weather, viz. : heat and cold, snow and rain, or else to shelter themselves in shops'. Gresham's plan was accepted and money was raised by subscription for the purchase of a site. In 1566 some houses were cleared off Cornhill and the ground prepared; then possession (as Stow related) was 'given to Sir Thomas Gresham, Knight, Agent of the Queen's Highness, thereupon to build a Bourse, or place for merchants to assemble in, at his own proper charges'. The design of the building was modelled on Antwerp's Exchange, having a piazza in the middle surrounded by cloisters. It was a handsome building, and hopefully a profitable one for Gresham; for besides the exchange rooms, there were more than a hundred shops round the exterior on two floors, and from the rent of these Gresham hoped to recoup the cost of building. Into these shops came milliners and haberdashers, sellers of mousetraps, bird-cages, shoe-horns, lanterns and jew's harps. In short time the Exchange also became the meeting place of idlers and rogues. A complaint of 1574 mentioned noise, rowdy behaviour, molestation of honest citizens and interruption of church services. But these annoyances were a small price to pay for the joys of enhanced profits. In December 1568 the Exchange was open for business. Just over two years later the Queen stamped the Exchange with her royal approval. Capitalism had at last come of age in England.

The money-lender, the financier, the provider of capital was in practice no stranger in the Middle Ages. But in the ideal Christian theory he was a pest and a thief from the community. In an agricultural land, such as England was, an economy may be more or less self-sufficient. But when men move into cities, as they did in Italy, turning from farmers into merchants and drawing the wealth of the society not from the land but from the great trade routes to the Orient, then the large volume of trade must be carried either on credit or on other people's capital. As the wealth of a nation rises and trade expands, the capitalist comes into his own. The rise of England's fortunes came first from the success of the wool growers; from being merely an exporter of wool England became an exporter of manufactured cloth which was sought all over Europe to the great profit of the wool masters. They in their turn grew rich, had capital to share and wanted to use it. In the fifteenth century families enriched by wool, such as the Celys, made their capital available for all the various processes of the cloth industry—the purchase of sheep, the providing of pasturage, the shearing and weaving. They also bought and enclosed the land to the despair of Kett and his poor countrymen.

Money invested in the woollen industry made further profits, and more capital accumulated. This was available for trade in general, supporting ventures of a size and over a distance beyond the resources of the ship-owner. Rich clothiers like Spring of Lavenham, Byrom of Manchester and Winchcombe of Newbury could do much as they liked; they were independent of the Merchant Adventurers, lived well, married well, and thought themselves equal to the landed aristocracy. And the capital of the great wool-masters and landowners was also available for industry and mining. Bacon wrote of a certain nobleman who was 'a great sheep-master, a great timber-man, a great collier, a great corn-master, a great lead-man, and so of iron'. The Willoughby family of Nottingham throughout the sixteenth century supplemented their income from land by the manufacture of iron and glass and the mining of coal. Towards the end of the century they were spending £20,000 a year on the iron mills at Codnor. Tin and lead were mined in Cornwall, lead in Somerset, coal in Durham; all these industries required large amounts of capital to keep them going. Tin from the Cornish mines was paid for only twice a year. In the meantime the miners wanted their wages and the tin masters needed money for the day to day costs of production. Capital was essential and the speculators like Bulmer, Maynard, Palavicino, Gresham himself, and Stoddard the former grocer's apprentice, were pleased to supply it.

The capitalists, who now found themselves indispensable to the commercial well-being of the country, were irked by the regulation of trade and the restrictions on enterprise which were part of the economic legacy from the Middle Ages. They were against monopolies and privileges, whether those privileges were enjoyed by the English cloth exporters banded together in the Merchant Adventurers, or by the foreign merchants of the Hanse who controlled most of the trade to the North and had been resident at the Steelyard in London since at least 1350. They were against the exclusive rights of the gilds and of municipal organizations, and they resented the restrictions on apprentices which prevented the growth of business. They demanded the right to trade where, when and with whom they could. They felt that the only restriction on trade should be the limits of finance, and they were in business to extend that. So they set out to break down the medieval barriers to free trade; they infiltrated the gilds and captured their organization; they evaded municipal regulations by taking business outside the towns; they became Merchant Adventurers themselves; they harried the privileged foreign merchants and finally drove the Hansards from the Steelyard in 1578; and they pressed unceasingly for legislative changes.

As the old exclusive trading corporations died away, business ventures were now undertaken through a new device called the joint stock company. This kind of company, which grew out of certain medieval partnerships, became prominent in the second half of the sixteenth century. The Muscovy Company, founded in 1553, was an early and famous example which was followed by the Africa Company and the Levant Company; even the plundering expeditions of Elizabeth's privateers were organized as joint stock ventures. The old regulated company such as the Merchant Adventurers was an exclusive club of fortunate merchants; entrance was difficult, admission fees were high, rules were strict. But the joint stock company was a much more democratic affair and, drawing its stock from all sections of the public, a much better source of capital. 'Divers noblemen, gentlemen and persons of quality, no ways bred up to trade or merchandise' purchased their shares and left the running of the company to the few powerful merchants who directed the trade. Undisturbed by the competition and jealousies of merchants within the company, and blessed with adequate capital from the shareholders, the joint stock companies were both efficient and profitable. Men who had before never thought of trade could now buy their shares, taking a profit without any knowledge of sails, tides and harbours, or bills, exchanges and dockets. The wider the rewards spread, the less was the criticism. By the accession of Elizabeth in 1558 the secret victory of capitalism was accomplished. Only the poor, the dispossessed, the moralists, and the government would not see it.

In the new economic age after the mid-century, with so many opportunities for speculation and trade, the capitalist merchant wove around him a complex web of business. Besides being the Royal Agent, Gresham was a Mercer and a Merchant Adventurer; he was the constructor and owner of a paper mill and engaged in the production of iron. As part of his financial dealings he loaned money to the aristocracy. He advanced £4,000 to Viscount Bindon, held a mortgage on the manors of Lord Thomas Howard and of Sir Henry Woodhouse who was foolish enough to take an action against Gresham for usury. In this expansive and inflationary time the aristocracy were committed to luxury and show. 'We that be courtiers', says an Elizabethan play, 'have more places to send gold to than the devil had spirits.' But the revenue from ancestral lands was no longer sufficient for such conspicuous expense, and the aristocrat was an eager client of Gresham and his kind. The aristocrats were not the only large spenders. Throughout society affluence was at work, and the financier was the gainer. In the house of the merchant or gentleman, William Harrison wrote in the *Description of England* he compiled early in Elizabeth's reign, one could see 'great provision of tapestry, Turkey work, pewter, brass, fine linen, and thereto costly cupboards of plate, worth five or six hundred or a thousand pounds'. Within his lifetime, Harrison wrote, he had seen chimneys added to the meanest houses; flock beds taking the place of straw pallets; pillows used instead of logs or sacks of chaff; and wooden platters and spoons giving way to pewter vessels and tin or silver spoons. And few citizens lived as well as the financier. The description of luxury in Shakespeare's *Taming of the Shrew* would have been a fitting tribute to Gresham House in Bishopsgate, the home of the wealthiest commoner in England :

> My house within the city
> Is richly furnished with plate and gold :
> Basins and ewers to lave her dainty hands;
> My hangings all of Tyrian tapestry;
> In ivory coffers I have stuff'd my crowns;
> In cypress chests my arras counterpoints,
> Costly apparel, tents, and canopies,
> Fine linen, Turkey cushions boss'd with pearl,
> Valance of Venice gold in needle-work,
> Pewter and brass, and all things that belong
> To house or housekeeping.

The riches piled up. Gresham had his house in London; he also had houses at Osterley in Middlesex, Mayfield in Sussex, and at Westacre, Kingshall and Intwood Hall in Suffolk. The furniture at Mayfield alone was valued at £7,500. When he died he was able to leave his widow an income of over £2,000 a year. Was Gresham content in the midst of his magnificence? After the final return from Antwerp he was a lonely man perhaps. His money made more money without him looking at it; though still not old, he retired from business entirely in 1574. Also, whatever his wealth, he was still a commoner and subject to the peremptory whims of the Queen. In 1569 Lady Mary Grey, the youngest sister of Lady Jane, who had unwisely married a 'sergeant-porter' of the Queen's household, was sent to lodge with Gresham. Why Sir Thomas should have been made her gaoler is not known, but for more than three years her unhappy presence poisoned the life of his home. He drank Rhenish, cursed his gout and was dissatisfied. Was it conscience or philanthropy that caused him to endow Gresham College in his will?

'Was it not for prodigality', wrote Bernard Mandeville, the unconventional mocker of the next century, 'nothing could make us amends for the rapine and extortion of avarice in power.' In 1575 Gresham made his will. He left his house in Bishopsgate to his wife for her lifetime, and then it was to become Gresham College. Seven professors were to teach seven subjects. The lectures were to be free and the professors paid £50 a year (a generous salary for the time) from the rents of the shops in the Royal Exchange. The government of the College was vested in the Corporation of London and in the Mercers' Company. When Lady Gresham died in 1596 the College began; for a hundred years and more it was London's university, attracting some of the greatest scholars in the land. Then the income that supported it fell off, the building was in disrepair, and covetous eyes wanted the valuable city site. The professors were turned out of their pleasant lodgings, their wages left unpaid, and the building razed. Occasional lectures in a gloomy room at the Royal Exchange were all that were left of Gresham's grand design of a university. It was founded on commerce and commercial values killed it. On 21st November 1579 Sir Thomas himself died. 'Coming from the Exchange to his house', wrote the chronicler, 'he fell down in his kitchen; and being taken up, was found speechless, and presently dead.'

'In the world of commerce and finance', the Greek orator Demosthenes had said, 'it is thought remarkable if a man is both clever and honest.' The arrival of capitalism brought in a new age of deceit and notable greed. In England men were, John Lyly wrote in *Euphues,* 'as in every place all for money'. And in pursuit of it men preyed on each other remorselessly. The terms of the ubiquitous money-lenders were extremely hard, interest of 20 per cent and above being the rule rather than the exception. A country gentlemen seeking £100 to help a needy friend approached a scrivener. The scrivener demanded 20 per cent interest, a £2 fee, £20 for legal expenses, the repayment of an old debt owed by another friend of the gentleman, and when all these charges were met 'there was no bond delivered'. A grocer who had loaned money to another gentleman discounted the bills at 25 per cent, renewed them at compound interest and, having sold up the debtor, became lord of the manor. Needy gentlemen were an easy mark, but the great were equally put upon. For a loan of £3,000, the powerful financier Sir Horatio Palavicino suggested that Lord Shrewsbury should convey to him land worth £7,000, pay all legal and other fees, and forfeit an interest in the land unless the mortgage was paid off within three months. The great financier was an even more rapacious hawk than the small money-lender. The little group of London capitalists who supported the tin mines of the West Country diverted between 40 and 60 per cent of the profits of the industry into their own pockets.

In this world of sharp practice Sir Thomas Gresham, the richest financier of them all, was no sluggard. His rates of interest for his loans were as high, and higher, than those of his fellows; the unfortunate Sir Henry Woodhouse was driven to try to bring Gresham before the courts for usury. And Gresham had no scruples about his dealings. His dishonest plan to help the royal debts by cheating the Merchant Adventurers was a matter of great pride to him, even though he was himself a Merchant Adventurer! Nor can it be said that he made an honest profit from the government for his official work, though perhaps his conduct here was retaliation for the notorious meanness of Elizabeth to her servants. He was allowed a brokerage of $\frac{1}{2}$ per cent, and he calculated this at an arbitrary rate of exchange well in advance of the actual market rate and naturally in his favour. When his books were audited at the end of his time as Royal Agent it was discovered that he owed the crown £10,000. Gresham was not dismayed. He immediately produced a fictitious counter-claim for £11,500, and when the auditor spurned this went behind the man's back to the Queen's favourite, Leicester, who persuaded the Commissioners of the Treasury to discharge him from the debt.

'Treasure doth then advance greatness', wrote Bacon, when 'the wealth of the subject be rather in many hands than few.' The fear of Tudor government was not only that the individual enterprise of capitalists concentrated wealth into very few hands, but also that the greedy self-interest of the capitalists hurt the life of the community. The dreadful social havoc caused by certain types of enclosures was a warning of the danger of speculation and profiteering too sad to be ignored. And the grip of the capitalists on emerging industry often had unhappy consequences for the poor workers. In the tin mines the capitalists squeezed the mine owners and they in their turn imposed upon the miners, to whom they had made advances in money or in truck at usurious rates of interest. The Tudors, who always relied on the support of the many against the ambition of the few, were not naturally advocates of capitalism. The young, inexperienced and religious Edward VI, in his *Discourse about the Reformation of Many Abuses,* put the social idealism of the Tudors in its most simple, naïve form : 'I think this country', he wrote, 'can bear no merchant to have more land than £100; no husbandman nor farmer worth above £100 or £200; no artificer above 100 marks,[1] no labourer much more than he spendeth. . . . This Commonwealth may not bear one man to have more than two farms, than one benefice, than 2,000 sheep, and one mind of art to live by. Wherefore as in the body no part hath too much or too little, so in a commonwealth ought every part to have *ad victum et non ad saturitatem.'*

It was a sentence of St Jerome that 'the merchant can never please God', and much of the economic thinking of the Middle Ages seemed to have been governed by this text. The medievals did not object to a reasonable profit from trade, but they considered money itself to be barren and financial dealings to be a sin against the community. The money-lenders were, as a later writer put it, 'the true drones of the commonwealth, living upon the

[1] The value of the mark was 13s. 4d.

honey without any labour'. These views on finance were perhaps endearingly simple, arising out of an agricultural economy that had no experience of problems of widespread trading. But because they had in mind the well-being and moral cleanliness of the community, they were actively promoted by the Church. The Renaissance, which changed so many things, brought to England a new view on finance, a new sense of individual enterprise (often at the expense of the community), and a new Reformed religion. All these combined to make the government slowly and reluctantly alter its economic ideas. And, as usual, the new capitalist practice was well entrenched before the regulations of the old theory were swept away.

In the sixteenth century the argument between the government and the capitalists was largely over 'the damnable sin of usury'. Conservative opinion, holding that money was barren, was against all interest on loans. English churchmen, even Protestants, and especially those who cared about social reform, regretted that Calvin had made interest respectable. In 1543 Cranmer wrote to Osiander protesting against the economic immorality of the Reformation. Tudor government, from conservative suspicion, and from a desire to stop the oppression of the poor, agreed with Cranmer. In the cause of trade, interest was grudgingly allowed. A maximum rate of 10 per cent was set in 1545, withdrawn in 1552 and imposed once again in 1571 in an Act which nonetheless denounced usury as 'forbidden by the laws of God'.

The regulations were not effective. The growth of trade led to an increase in financial dealings. Gresham, the realist, insisted that Englishmen who subscribed to government funds should be exempt from the Usury Acts; otherwise, as he well knew, no money would have been forthcoming. The government itself was forced to pay 14 per cent and more at Antwerp. The instinct of Tudor government was to regulate all aspects of national life, but the new money market was international in its scope and provisions and did not respond to the Tudors' bluff attempts to intervene. Nonetheless the Tudors still tried. 'How little', wrote an official, giving the typical government opinion of merchants, 'they regard the commonweal for advancement of their private lucre.' Seeing the obvious excesses of the system, Tudor government continued to lay crude hands on the delicate mechanism of the capitalists. Private exchange business was suspended more than once.

An official Royal Exchanger was appointed whose hopeless task it was to try to steady and control the market. In 1576 some attempt was even made to nationalize exchange business.

Complete freedom from government control was the ideal of the capitalists, and while Parliament was stumbling over ineffective laws the merchants were loudly calling for the repeal of these laws entirely. And the capitalists had the most persuasive argument. 'If we were not,' they said, 'the State could hardly stand. Where is money to be had in time of need if the city should fail?' In particular, they objected that interest should be called usury and themselves made into criminals for demanding interest. When, in the late sixties, the political troubles of the Netherlands destroyed the Antwerp money market and the English government was forced to look for money at home, it at last saw the necessity to come to an agreement with merchants and speculators. Recognizing that capitalists were not saints and that they lived in an imperfect world, the Act of 1571 at last made the distinction between moderate interest, which the law would allow, and excessive interest which constituted usury. 'It is', said the Act, 'biting and over sharp dealing which is disliked, and nothing else.'

This reluctant compromise was in fact the legal recognition of the capitalist practice which Gresham and his kind had already made quite usual in England. The Act of 1571 and the building of the Royal Exchange were equally part of Gresham's triumph. To him, credit, interest and the like were problems of business, not of morals. None knew better than he the greed of speculators, but he thought that the market would control business where legislation could not. Instead of puzzling itself with moral considerations, the government was invited by Gresham to join the financiers for the common benefit of country and capitalist. With a rather bad grace, the government at last agreed.

6
Sir Francis Walsingham

OBSCURE STEPS LED from the feudal state to an autocratic monarchy. The final and successful acts in this progression were taken by Henry VII when he united a fractious land after the Wars of the Roses, and the particular colour that Henry gave to the English state lasted throughout the Tudor age. The Tudors are rightly called despots, and each reign bore the personal mark of the sovereign. But Henry VII was no political philosopher; he was a cautious, practical administrator who learnt his lessons from experience. During the English civil wars he had spent some time in France and the advantages of Louis's centralized power had impressed him. The powerful French state was founded on nationalism and on the strong control that the king maintained over all parts of the national life, and when Henry came to the throne of England in 1485 he determined to govern his new land in the French manner. Ayala, the Spanish ambassador, noted Henry's intention to rule 'in the French fashion', but added that he was not able to do so. What was possible in France was naturally not always practical in England; and perhaps this was to the good of the country. The actions of Henry VII were tyrannical enough, but Louis XI of France was a sterner scourge of his people. The lawyer Sir John Fortescue observed that Louis oppressed his subjects, levied arbitrary taxes, imprisoned without trial and executed secretly—all by virtue of the *jus regale*.

Even though English law and custom tried to check the arbitrary power of the sovereign, the Tudor monarchy began, in the French manner, to establish its absolute authority and to introduce some of the features of government that had worked so well in France. The first task of the Tudors was to subjugate the arrogant nobility and to diminish their feudal power which had caused such destruction in the civil wars. They went about this business with their usual blend of good sense, cunning and cruelty; within a century they had completely destroyed the power of the old aristocratic families. Sir Walter Raleigh commented that an earl who might once have put a thousand horses into the field could now hardly raise twenty-five. Very astutely, the Tudors left the peers their privileges. The Garter was reserved for them; they retained their ceremonial functions at court; and certain prizes, such as lord lieutenancies, were for them alone. But political power was carefully kept from them and they were no longer the sovereign's advisers. The Duke of Buckingham complained with some truth that the King would rather give offices and rewards to boys than to noblemen.

Ambitious lords were quickly cut down. Henry VIII executed Buckingham merely for having royal blood : the Tudors ferociously established their family dynasty and woe betide him or her who stood too close to the throne. Aristocrats who transgressed the law were severely dealt with, for the Tudors wisely used the law as the leveller of the people. In 1498 the Earl of Sheffield was outraged that he should be indicted for manslaughter before a common court, even though he was later pardoned by the King. Henry VIII insisted that Lord Dacres be tried for poaching; he was condemned and executed. Raleigh claimed that if the greatest lord should lift a finger, he would be locked up by the nearest constable. And Surrey at his trial accused the King of wishing to be rid of all the old nobility.

Having lost the favour of the monarchy, the aristocracy seemed to abandon the fight for political power. Depending on fixed incomes from land and subject to the gross inflation of the time, the lords could no longer support their old extravagance; and political ambition is usually expensive. The young Earl of Essex, one noble who dared to set himself against Elizabeth's policy, right at the start of his career, in 1589, admitted to debts of about £23,000. The more their influence waned, the more conservative the nobles became. They refused to compete in the rude Tudor marketplace for preferment, but chose to retire with their pride and idiosyncrasy to their dogs and hawks. Dudley, the hated minister of Henry VII, accused the aristocrats of neglecting the education of their sons so that 'the children of poor men and mean folk are promoted to the promotion and authority that the children of noble blood should have'. Latimer deplored the ignorance of the upper ranks of society, and Ascham, Elizabeth's tutor, roundly blamed the nobles for their own eclipse. 'The fault is in yourselves, ye noblemen's sons,' he wrote in his *Scholemaster,* 'and therefore ye deserve the greater blame that commonly the meaner men's children come to be the wisest counsellors and greatest doers in the weighty affairs of this realm.' These commentators were deceived by the conventional ideals of Tudor society, and by its love of order. They expected the lord to have an influence commensurate with his exalted rank. But the Tudors, deliberately and subtly, had cut away the power and left the prestige of the lord. In their sulky way, the nobility recognized this and retired from the contests of the public stage.

'The wanton bringing up and ignorance of the nobility', wrote a Tudor official, 'force the prince to advance new men that can serve.' The instinct of the French monarchy had been to employ men of low birth who repaid the king's favour with an unquestioning loyalty. A visitor to the court of Louis XI had the impression that the King's closest advisers were his barber and his doctor. Henry VII, copying France in this as in much else, also had humble men as his great officers. Even Perkin Warbeck denounced the 'caitiffs and villains of simple birth' in Henry's administration. And Henry VIII followed the example of his father. One of the pleas of the Pilgrimage of Grace in 1536 was that Thomas Cromwell should be removed from the Privy Council because of his villain blood. Wolsey was the son of an Ipswich butcher, and his enemies never let him forget it. Dukes and barons, however great they were, wrote William Roy:

> But they are entertained to crouch
> Before this butcherly flouch.

And another poet, the impetuous John Skelton, spoke contemptuously of Wolsey's 'greasy genealogy':

> He came to the sang royal
> That was cast out of a butcher's stall.

But the poor and the humble were generally uneducated, and though the exceptional man might rise by the royal favour, the monarchy could not rely on the lower classes to provide the large number of officials and administrators that the new centralized organization of the State required. The gentry now came enthusiastically forward to fill the gap in the royal service, and began the startling rise that was to make them the dominant group in

English society. The members of this class were hard to define but easy to recognize. Despite the Tudor love for order and strict social hierarchy, the middle ranks of society were in a constant state of flux, and there was plenty of movement both up and down. In general the gentry occupied the middle ground between the yeomen and the aristocracy, 'neither in the lowest grounds . . . nor in the highest mountains', as Raleigh put it, 'but in the valleys between both'. The members of this class were mainly small landowners, but rich yeomen, farmers and merchants belonged as well, and the class also included the professional men, lawyers, doctors and divines. The distinguishing mark of the class was prosperity, for the common opinion was that 'gentility is nothing but ancient riches'; speaking on behalf of the class to which he belonged Sir Thomas Smith claimed, with a cynical realism, that a gentleman is he who spends his money like a gentleman.

These men were confident, ambitious and ready for public service. Very many of them were enriched by the expansion of trade in the sixteenth century and sought the places and honours that the crown could grant to go with their new wealth. Others were the restless younger sons of landed families, forced to make their own way in the world by the English system of inheritance which refused to split up estates between the children, gave all to the eldest son and no land to the younger. Others benefited from the increase of civic business. The lawyers especially did very well; the economic writer Thomas Wilson stated that the leading Elizabethan lawyers were making over £20,000 a year. All the spoils of society seemed to come the way of the rising gentry. They benefited from trade and from enclosures; they bought or mortgaged the lands of the old nobles, reduced by extravagance and conservatism to live like 'rich beggars, always in want'; they bought the crown lands sold off by the monarchy to cover its debts. By the end of the sixteenth century the aggregate income of the gentry was three times that of the peers, clergy and yeomen added together. In their new success it is no surprise that they began to look for political advancement.

And in this, too, circumstances were right for them. The Tudors would not employ the aristocracy, yet needed men of education. The educated gentry were no threat to the throne, for rebellion was hardly likely to form around men whose names were unknown beyond their village or county. In the past many officials had been churchmen; with the Reformation, the dissolution of the monasteries and the formation of the secular State, churchmen were no longer available, and their places were taken by the gentry. For the young man of good, but not high, birth, reasonable ambition and some talent, political service was the best career open to him.

Francis Walsingham was a member of this bold class. He was born about 1536 into a family, descendants of a London shoemaker, which had slowly progressed up the ranks of the gild hierarchy and had come finally to a country house in Kent. His father was a London barrister, his mother a member of the very Protestant Denny family; his step-father, the man who brought him up, was the brother-in-law of Anne Boleyn's sister. His inheritance was Protestant and prosperous; members of his family had attended at court and knew something of the perils and rewards of the King's service. Francis was given the education suitable to a gentleman, and went in time to King's College, Cambridge, where his Protestantism was greatly strengthened by the enthusiastic Reformers of that university. At an early age Walsingham was a Puritan, even something of a fanatic, and he retained his strong religion until his death. In the way then customary for the wealthy student, he travelled abroad after his degree. Soon after his return to England the Catholic Mary came to the throne and Walsingham, the Puritan, found it wise quickly to bend his steps to the continent once more.

From his earliest years Walsingham seemed by disposition to be grave and industrious. Other young students, such as the notorious Robert Greene, had filled their time abroad with sport and debauchery. But Walsingham was a model student and a model traveller, using his laborious days for the pursuit of knowledge. He read law at Padua, the foremost European university for legal studies. He perfected his command of foreign languages, and he travelled to Switzerland and Germany to talk with other Protestant refugees from England. Italy, that subtle, intellectual land, seed-bed of the Renaissance, had the greatest effect on him, as it did on all European men of culture. Men of the North usually had a great suspicion for Italian ways. Roger Ascham condemned the Italianate Englishman who brought home 'the religion, the learning, the policy, the experience, the manners of Italy'. In his *Schole-master* he defined these as follows : 'for religion papistry or worse :

for learning less commonly than they carried out with them : for policy a factious heart, a discoursing head, a mind to meddle in all men's matters : for experience plenty of new mischiefs never known in England before : for manners variety of vanities, and changes of filthy living.' But the effects of Italy were too profound to be anatomized so easily. The sober Walsingham certainly did not give way to papistry or atheism, nor was he notable for 'filthy living'; the only marks of Italian vanity on him were the shape of his doublet, the cut of his beard, and the elegant polish of his manners. But he did learn from Italian policy and experience. In the land of Machiavelli he studied the statecraft of the Italian princes, and prepared himself for public service according to their cold, unscrupulous principles. Old-fashioned scholars like Ascham decried the new Italian policy, but the forward-looking Tudors knew that mercy and conscience had been banished from international affairs and were determined to take advantage of the new secular morality. 'There is a Fate, that flies with towering spirits Home to the mark, and never checks it conscience', wrote Ben Jonson in *Mortimer,* expressing the cruel faithlessness of Renaissance polity :

> But we
> That draw the subtle, and more piercing air,
> In that sublimed region of Court,
> Know all is good, we make so, and go on,
> Secured by the prosperity of our Crimes.

Some time in the early years of Elizabeth's reign Walsingham returned to England. For the next decade or so little is seen of him. He married a prosperous widow, and when she died within a short time, he married another; he had one daughter. He entered Parliament and sat whenever the Commons met (which was not often for the Queen did not like the restraint of Parliament) for the rest of his life. And all the while his ambition was aiming at the court. His path to that promised land is not recorded, but the journey was well known in Tudor times to be a weary pilgrimage requiring patience, influence, skill, boldness and bribery. 'My lord', said a contemporary, 'advancement in all worlds be obtained by mediation and remembrance of noble friends.' But even with that help the course was difficult, as Spenser, who had suffered the pains of the attempt, wrote in *Mother Hubberd's Tale* :

To have thy asking, yet wait many years;
To fret thy soul with crosses and with cares;
To eat thy heart through comfortless despairs;
To fawn, to crouch, to wait, to rise, to run,
To spend, to give, to want, to be undone.

Through his family Walsingham had certain influential friends; he is known to have helped the government secret service on occasion, and this perhaps brought his name to the attention of Elizabeth's ministers. But his best credentials for service were his own qualities. He was serious and hard working; he was well educated, cultured and a very proficient linguist; he had studied the art of statecraft; and his years on the continent had given him many useful connections abroad, especially among Protestants. In 1570 Elizabeth sent him to be her ambassador in France. It may be that the careful hand of Lord Burghley was behind the Queen's choice, for it was said that Elizabeth never resolved 'any private suit (or grant) from herself, that was not first referred to his consideration; and had his approbation before it passed'. In any case, the new ambassador was just the man that the Queen and her great minister required.

In former times the ambassador was often an insignificant figure. Much of the diplomacy between countries had been undertaken through the international organization of the Catholic Church, and the lay envoy, when he existed, had a rather low place. Merchants were sometimes delegated to represent their countries abroad; otherwise the envoy was a simple clerk. John Stile, the English ambassador to Spain at the beginning of the sixteenth century, had neither rank nor education. And Puebla, Stile's counterpart at the court of Henry VII, lodged with a mason who kept a bawdy house and took his meals daily with the prostitutes. But the religious Reformation also brought in a new, complicated age of international relations, and the lay ambassador advanced in ability and prestige. Henry VIII, who needed to count the pulse of Europe for the good of his own plans, appointed such eminent men as Sir Thomas Elyot and the poet Sir Thomas Wyatt and had in return elegant reports and swift, reliable information. The French ambassador, Marillac, reported that the English were the first to hear any rumour from any quarter.

Walsingham's embassy, which lasted three years, was up to

the standard set by his notable predecessors. He was sent to negotiate the marriage between Elizabeth and the Duke of Anjou, the brother of the French King. But the Queen's hand in marriage was, as always, merely a ploy in the diplomatic game : she made it clear to the French envoy La Mothe that she never intended to marry. 'Her real aim', a French observer reported, 'is to bring the French gradually into the offensive and defensive league which many of the German princes and the Duke of Florence are said to have joined.' Differences of religion, colonial and commercial rivalry had severely strained the alliance between Spain and England that had lasted since the reign of Henry VII. England's prosperity was based very much on trade with the Netherlands, and the Protestant revolt in the Spanish Netherlands, which was disastrous for commerce, worried England. This issue divided England and Spain; England was driven to help the revolt in the Netherlands, and Spain encouraged rebellion in Ireland and plots in Scotland. By 1570 the alliance with Catholic Spain was at an end, and Walsingham's task was to make a new Protestant coalition into which France might be drawn. He arrived at the end of the third French religious war when the Protestant Huguenots were gaining influence at the French court. His Puritan sympathies were naturally with the Huguenots and the negotiations with Catholic Anjou, a man who had successfully fought against the Huguenots at Jarnac, were no doubt a sore trial. But he subordinated his feelings to the wishes of his government and with great skill forged the new alliance.

The marriage negotiations with Anjou were, as Philip of Spain commented, 'nothing but a trick'; they were soon decently forgotten and Walsingham, to his relief, was left to form the defensive alliance against Catholic Spain. He succeeded so well that the Huguenot leaders now began to dominate the French court, much to the distress of the Catholic party. In April 1572 the defensive treaty between England and France was concluded at Blois. On 24th August the fear and hatred for the Huguenots burst out in the Massacre of St Bartholomew. For eight days the Protestants were put to the sword. 'While I write', the Spanish ambassador reported on the 26th, 'they are casting them out naked and dragging them through the streets, pillaging their houses and sparing not a babe.' And he commended this as holy work : 'Blessed be God who has converted the princes of France to his purpose !

May he inspire their hearts to go on as they have begun !' At a low estimate some 10,000 Huguenots were killed in France. It is said that on hearing the news Philip of Spain laughed for the only time in his life.

To Walsingham the massacre was a terrible blow, first because his co-religionists were suffering, and then because his own diplomacy had helped to make the massacre certain. He became convinced that a Protestant country should fly from Catholics—that Christ, as he put it, should not lie down with Belial—and after St Bartholomew he longed to return to England. He thought that religion was still the main-spring of international policy, and his own Puritan faith was too strict to allow him to be at ease in the faithless realm of national intrigue. Elizabeth and Burghley knew better. They saw that national interest, not religion, was at the heart of European affairs and they patiently set about the reconstruction of the French alliance which the massacre had threatened to destroy. Catholic France had kept quiet when Elizabeth executed the two Catholic leaders, Norfolk and Northumberland, in 1572. Elizabeth had her testing moment after St Bartholomew. Since her people were outraged by the slaughter in France, Elizabeth had her court wear black to receive the ambassador, La Mothe. But she treated him kindly and pretended to believe his stammering explanations; to the Queen, national security overrode all religious arguments.

The callousness of Elizabeth's policy may have puzzled Walsingham, and his conscience disqualified him for the immoralities of international intrigue, but while he was ambassador he followed his instructions exactly and was as successful as any man could have been. His reports were models of clarity; he was loyal, hard-working and efficient. The Queen was pleased with him and for the rest of his life used him for the most delicate diplomatic negotiations. In December 1573 she recalled him from Paris and appointed him to be one of her principal secretaries, a position he retained until his death in 1590.

'I wish first God's glory', Walsingham once wrote, 'and next the Queen's safety.' By these bright lights he advanced surely. The duties of his position were never exactly defined; his powers and his responsibilities were too large to be covered simply. 'Among all particular offices and places of charge in this State', one of his officials wrote about his master's post, 'there is none of more necessary use, nor subject to more cumber and variableness than is the office of principal secretary, by reason of the variety and uncertainty of his employment, and therefore with more difficulty to be prescribed by special method and order.' He was in fact responsible for the efficient working of the centralized Tudor government, and such was the nature of Tudor despotism that he was liable to be held to blame for any failure in government policy. 'Only a secretary', said his successor, 'hath no warrant or commission in matters of his own greatest peril but the virtue and word of his sovereign.' How frail that virtue was, Wolsey and Cromwell had found to their cost, though they had most assiduously done the King's bidding. It is a measure of Walsingham's careful and successful attention to 'the Queen's safety' that he was never called to account for any act of his time in power.

By 1573, after fifteen years of trouble and worry, Elizabeth was in firm control of the country, and the nature of her rule had become clear. The old lords whose power, religion or ambition had threatened the early days of her reign were all gone, executed, imprisoned or dead. There were no political parties. She was England's policy-maker and she ruled with the help of a Privy Council composed of new men recently ennobled by the Tudors, dependent on the monarchy for patronage and in general devoted to her interests. 'All these Lords', Burghley said in 1565, 'are bent towards her Majesty's service, and do not so much vary amongst themselves as lewd men do report.' And for himself he declared that he had 'no affection to be of a party, but for the Queen's Majesty'. Among these supporters of the Queen there were naturally different factions who advocated different policies, and it was Elizabeth's wise habit to play one faction off against the other. Leicester and Walsingham were usually bold spirits, clamouring for aggressive acts against Spain and Catholics, while Burghley and his son were the advocates of peace and restraint. The Queen valued men of both factions, yet insisted on deciding her own mind; she was careful not to allow either group to become dominant, and when she disposed of her patronage, shared official positions between the factions. 'The principal note of her reign', Sir Robert Naunton commented in his *Fragmenta Regalia*, 'will be, that she ruled much by faction and parties, which herself both made, upheld, and weakened, as her own judgment advised.'

This policy maintained a balance in the government which

pleased Elizabeth's cautious nature. From time to time a leader of a faction would have a deluded sense of his own power—Essex was the most notable example; but by a skilful use of opposites, the Queen soon curbed such ambition. The partisan *Leicester's Commonwealth,* in a virulent attack on Leicester, claimed that the earl was paramount at court : 'nothing can pass but by his admission, nothing can be said, done, or signified, whereof he is not particularly advised.' But the reality of Leicester's position came home to him while he was away in the Netherlands. Advised by Burghley (or so the French ambassador claimed), Elizabeth appointed Whitgift, Buckhurst and Cobham to the Privy Council, all men who worked against Leicester's interests. 'I pray you', the worried earl wrote to Walsingham, 'to stand fast for your poor absent friends against calumniators.' This stroke showed where the true influence lay; for the one man who always had the ear of the Queen was William Cecil, Lord Burghley. He was the greatest statesman of the age; his advice was the most disinterested and the closest to the Queen's own mind, and he himself was less corrupt than most others at court. Unlike Essex, he was not a man of brilliant parts, but the Queen trusted him the more for that; as he told his friends, 'he had gotten more by his patience than ever he did by his wit'.

Walsingham had a lesser place than Burghley and he was too coldly fanatical for the witty, calculating Elizabeth to like him. But he shared some of Burghley's virtues and the Queen trusted him for them. He was as efficient and hard-working as the great minister, and he was also as honest. He was not ambitious for more power, and he was devoted to the Queen. Even his excessive Puritan enthusiasm was tempered by the wish to preserve the Tudor authority at all costs. 'I would have all reformation', he wrote in a clear statement of Tudor doctrine, 'done by public authority. It were very dangerous that every private man's zeal should carry sufficient authority of reforming things amiss.' He was just the man to supervise the work of the central administration.

The formal structure of Elizabethan government was not complicated. The Queen ruled and had for her assistance and advice the Privy Council, further councils in the North and in the Welsh Marches, and Parliament. The administration of the realm was divided between several departments, the most important of which were the exchequer and the judiciary; this central administration was in the hands of the principal secretaries. In Walsingham's time financial affairs were largely attended to by Burghley and justice was naturally in the hands of the lawyers under the Lord Chancellor and the Chief Justices. Beyond these men, Walsingham seemed to be the co-ordinator of all departments. As his functions were never defined, so his operations were multitudinous, varied and often obscure. Foreign affairs were part of his business, so too was the defence of the kingdom from enemies both within and without. He hunted down priests, prepared the case against Mary Stuart, mustered the forces in time of trouble, and organized military expeditions to France, Ireland and the Netherlands. His faith helped him in his many tasks, for he always had at the back of his mind the ultimate victory of the Protestant cause over Catholics, and in particular over Spain. 'The proud Spaniard', he wrote at the beginning of his official career, 'whom God hath long used for the rod of His wrath I see great hope that He will now cast him into the fire.' This hope, which was never quite realized, influenced all his actions. It made him the chief advocate of war with Spain, and the natural ally of Protestants everywhere; it also made him the great patron of Drake, Hawkins and all English voyagers who opposed the Spanish empire in the New World; and lastly it made him the scourge of Catholics at home and the implacable enemy of Mary, Queen of Scots.

The English sea voyages interested Walsingham on two counts : first, like most Elizabethans from the Queen downwards, he was attracted by the speculative profit which these voyages offered; and secondly, he came to see that England's expansion must be at the cost of Spain and Portugal; English privateers and adventurers became useful instruments for his attack on Spanish power. His patronage of the voyagers began in 1576 when he contributed £25 to Frobisher's first expedition. For the second expedition in 1577, in search of the worthless stuff which Frobisher foolishly thought to be gold, Walsingham gave £200 even though he had commissioned the analysis from the London goldsmiths which declared that Frobisher's ores were pyrites not gold. For the third expedition Walsingham contributed yet again, adventuring in total some £800 on Frobisher's success, all of which was wasted.

This loss did not blunt his enthusiasm. When Drake came to court with his dream of a plundering circumnavigation, he found in Walsingham his best advocate, for here appeared most clearly

the chance to serve mammon and the Protestant cause. Walsingham took on himself the weary task of winning cautious Elizabeth's assent. Drake was allowed to sail in 1577 and set off backed
by the Queen, Leicester, Hatton and Walsingham among others.
When Drake returned three years later his profits were said to
have repaid his promoters 4,700 per cent on their investment. The
success of Drake swept away all memories of Frobisher's failure,
and for the rest of his life Walsingham was an eager supporter of
maritime enterprise. He was interested in all projects, warlike, trading, exploration and colonial. He was for sending Drake to the
Azores to harry Spain; Edward Fenton to the East in search of
trade; and John Davis to the North-West to find that elusive passage. Most unusual and far-reaching of his plans was the support
he gave to Humphrey Gilbert's colonizing ventures on the understanding that Gilbert would take with him certain prominent English Catholics thus ridding the country of their religious influence.
As he guided the voyagers through the labyrinth of court intrigue
and persuasively put their case to the Queen, so he contributed
his own money to the joint-stock companies which launched the
expeditions. When Richard Hakluyt came to dedicate his *Principal Navigations* he could offer it to no fitter person than Sir Francis
Walsingham. If, as Hakluyt immodestly claimed, 'in this most
famous and peerless government of her most excellent Majesty,
her subjects through the special assistance and blessing of God, in
searching the most opposite corners and quarters of the world, and
to speak plainly, in compassing the vast globe of the earth more
than once, have excelled all the nations and people of the earth',
it was in a large part due to Walsingham.

The encouragement of the English voyages was a great work
which Walsingham undertook for the Protestant cause. His ruthless and efficient persecution of English Catholics was the darker
side of his Puritan nature. But in this unpleasant task he was only
carrying out the wishes of the government; that he used spies, informers and deceit of all kinds, that he countenanced torture and
murder of good men, cannot be held against him alone. His
methods were the universal methods of his age. He believed in the
central Tudor doctrine, that the authority of the State must be
preserved at all costs. 'Our unity', he wrote, 'might be a strength
to ourselves and an aid to our neighbours, but if we shall like to
fall to division among ourselves, we must needs lie open to the

common enemy and by our own fault hasten, or rather call upon ourselves, our own ruin.' It was his duty and his interest to prevent this happening.

Until the excommunication of Elizabeth by Pius V in 1570, Catholics in England were not treated severely. There were fines for recusants who would not accept the state religion, but the Queen only required lip service to legal forms. After 1570 the complication of international affairs sadly condemned the Catholics to persecution. The reconversion of England was the aim of the papacy. The political attack was undertaken by Philip of Spain, and organized by his wily ambassador Mendoza who helped to ensnare Mary Stuart in a tangle of plots. The spiritual onslaught was directed by the expatriate Englishman, Cardinal Allen, and carried out by missioner priests chiefly from the newly formed Society of Jesus. The English defence against this double threat was in the hands of Walsingham. The simple aim of most Jesuits may have been to speak only of religion, but political events made their task impossible. England, after the way of the Reformation, had made religion part of state policy, and acts of faith now constituted acts of treason. After the Massacre of St Bartholomew in 1572, the English people had a horror of aggressive Catholicism, and the unfortunate connection between Mary Stuart and the bigoted Guise family, the villains of St Bartholomew, made England fearful of Catholic intrigue. Moreover, several priests, influenced by the forthright revolutionary propaganda of Cardinal Allen and Father Parsons, were implicated in the plots of Philip and his agents; the saintly Edmund Campion, the first Jesuit to be caught and executed, in 1581, was innocent of any intrigue, but his companion Parsons, who escaped, was a notorious meddler and plotter.

The plotting of Spain and the advent of the Jesuits caused something of a panic. Parliament met in 1581 and began to draft penal legislation against Catholics. Very large fines were imposed for recusancy and for attendance at Mass; to be converted to Catholicism carried the death penalty; priests of all kinds were to leave the country within forty days under pain of death for high treason. The spying out of Catholics was left to Walsingham and his secret service. By the end of Elizabeth's reign 187 Catholics had been executed. But the operation of penal laws was only part of the problem. Walsingham was convinced that there could be no security in England so long as Mary Stuart lived. While she was alive, he wrote to Leicester in 1572, 'neither her Majesty must make account to continue in quiet possession of her crown, nor her faithful servants assure themselves of safety of their lives'. With his usual efficiency Walsingham set out to find the evidence to convict her, for Elizabeth was very reluctant to execute a fellow sovereign. At last, after the foolish Babington conspiracy of 1586, Walsingham had his evidence. Mary was condemned, the Queen signed the warrant, and Mary was executed on 8th February 1587. Walsingham was careful that his colleague William Davison should hand the death warrant, for he knew the Queen. With the hypocrisy of which she was always capable, Elizabeth wanted a scapegoat for Mary's execution, and visited her guilt on poor Davison whom she dismissed, fined and imprisoned.

Camden spoke of Walsingham as 'a most sharp maintainer of the purer religion', and his record against Catholics, both English and foreign, bears this out. But his relations with his fellow Puritans are less easy to follow. Since the Puritans slowly became as grave a threat to Elizabeth's religious authority as the Catholics had been, Walsingham must have had some difficulty in reconciling his faith with his royal service. That he put the State first can hardly be doubted, otherwise the Queen would never have tolerated him. Perhaps she even deferred the persecution of Puritans until after her faithful servant's death in 1590. He may also have been useful in her dealings with Parliament. Throughout Elizabeth's reign Parliament was Puritan in tone and critical of her use of the royal prerogative, so that she had little time for the Commons. She summoned Parliament as infrequently as possible and in typical Tudor style blatantly packed it with her supporters. Walsingham first entered Parliament as a member for Lyme Regis in 1563; at the start of his official career, in 1573, he became one of the members for Surrey and retained this seat for the rest of his life. He was at the same time a member of the Privy Council, and Elizabeth used her councillors who also sat in Parliament, men such as Walsingham and Sir Christopher Hatton, to guide and influence parliamentary decisions in the way she wanted. Walsingham perhaps had an extra use. His brother-in-law was Peter Wentworth, the most outspoken of the Puritan parliamentarians. Walsingham was thus excellently placed to be the middleman, testing and reporting on the Puritan temper for the Queen's benefit, warning his co-religionists of the limits to the Queen's patience, and if they overstepped that limit perhaps shielding them from her displeasure.

Elizabeth's contemptuous handling of Parliament was but an example of the personal rule of the Tudors, yet this despotism was a danger to Elizabethan government. Since all the power was at the court, men were desperate to get there, rightly counting their future, their fame and their wealth to be dependent on the Queen's patronage. She had about 1,200 places to dispose of in the central administration and she husbanded this resource carefully. Henry VIII, in his last years, had scattered political rewards profusely and unwisely, and Elizabeth's successor, James I, was to do so again. But Elizabeth was economical and wary. Competition for places under Elizabeth was ferocious, and the more so because there were so few of them. Driven by their new-found ambition, and by gross inflation, the gentry besieged the gates of the court, clamouring for admission. And the best way to gain entry was to have the ear of the ministers and faction leaders at court. The edifice of Elizabethan administration was built on the shifting ground of bribery and corruption.

This state of affairs was openly recognized, and was no doubt allowed because the crown was poor and could not afford to pay much in salaries. Officials were expected to make up their income through various fees and gifts. The Lord Keeper officially received £919 a year, the Lord High Admiral £200, and the Principal Secretary only £100. Yet in 1601 John Manningham noted that the Lord Keeper's office was 'better worth than £3,000 per annum', the High Admiral's worth a little more and the Secretary's a little less. The same practice operated from highest to lowest. 'There liveth not so grave nor so severe a judge in England', wrote Samuel Cox, the slippery secretary of Hatton, 'but he alloweth his poor clerk under him, even in the expedition of matters of greatest justice, to take any reasonable consideration that should be offered him by any man for his pains and travail.' The Queen herself was not averse to bribes; when Leicester was in disgrace he was advised by friends at court to send her a valuable gift.

The system had its practical advantages for an impecunious monarchy, but it encouraged that crude strain of avarice and venality which everywhere went hand-in-hand with the expansion of trade and the accumulation of wealth in the sixteenth century. And the system was very hard to control. Burghley was certainly a reasonably honest man by the lights of his time; as the Queen's first minister he was the chief disposer of places, and his watchfulness helped to limit the greed at court. Yet he persistently accepted bribes and payments for the places in his gift and died an extremely rich man. An incorruptible official, like Sir Henry Sidney, the father of Philip Sidney, was almost as rare as the unicorn. As Elizabeth grew old and lost some of her vigilance and Burghley declined into the 'old Saturnus' of English government, the venal men flourished: clergymen bought bishoprics, judges sold justice, and great men hired underlings for their factions. The Earl of Essex spent and spent; when he was disgraced at court in 1599 his income was cut off and he grew mad with hurt pride, frustrated ambition and debt. His rebellion in 1601 was the last act of desperation.

Speaking of the court in *Mother Hubberd's Tale*, Spenser wrote :

> For nothing there is done without a fee :
> The courtier needs must recompensed be.

The corrupted morals of government were all too plain in Elizabeth's last years. 'I will forbear to mention', said one of Burghley's panegyrists, 'the great and unusual fees exacted lately by reason of buying and selling offices, both judicial and ministerial, as also the privileges granted unto private persons to the great prejudice and grievance of the common people.' The old Queen herself found her grip slipping as the tide of materialism swept over the kingdom. In 1601 she voiced her resentment to her antiquary, William Lambarde : 'Now the wit of the fox is everywhere on foot, so as hardly a faithful or virtuous man may be found.'

Walsingham, in an official career of seventeen years, naturally received a good share of the spoils. He received few honours, for Elizabeth gave these out with a mean hand. He was knighted in 1577, became chancellor of the Garter in the next year, and chancellor of the Duchy of Lancaster in 1587. These posts increased his dignity but not his income. His wealth was based on the many perquisites of his office. He was allowed a farm of the customs, and was given on occasion licences for the export of cloth and wool. The Queen granted him several parcels of land, some of which he retained for his own use and some of which he used for specula-tion. In the patent rolls of the reign are very many sums of money put down to the name of Walsingham without any explanation. And his influential position made him one of the chief brokers at court, the happy receiver of innumerable gifts and fees for favours done. It was said by Camden that he died in debt having spent his wealth on the secret service he had built up. Certainly he was put to great expense by this and by the complicated debts left to him at the death of his brilliant son-in-law Sir Philip Sidney in 1586. But he always lived in great style and had numerous houses. In London he lived at first in London Wall, near Sir Thomas Gresham, in a house that almost rivalled the financier's fabulous mansion. Later he moved to Seething Lane where he was a neigh-bour of the Earl of Essex. But in the manner of great gentlemen his favourite house was in the country just outside London. At Barn Elms, a few miles up the river from Westminster, he kept a large establishment; the stables were said to house sixty-eight horses.

To the observer, Walsingham was composed, calculating and silent. King James of Scotland called him 'a very Machiavel'. He was in ill health for much of his life, and often had to rest from his strenuous duties. 'My disease groweth so dangerously upon me', he wrote to Burghley from France in 1571, 'as I most humbly desire her Majesty to take some speedy order for some to supply my place.' The French ambassador in London reported that he had some kind of recurring bladder or kidney trouble, and he be-came something of a hypochondriac, dosing himself excessively with medicines. Neither his affliction nor his unpalatable medicines was likely to sweeten his temper. Hawking, hunting and sports of all kinds, which the Elizabethans loved, were not for one of such delicate health. He caught some of the contemporary enthusiasm for gardens, and was content to saunter there gently. His powers and his interests were intellectual, not physical.

But at home he was an affectionate man and the pleasant har-mony of his private life was at variance with the austere front and unremitting labour of his public appearance. He married twice, both times perhaps more for money than love. Of his second wife Ursula, who bore him two daughters, he seems to have been very fond, and this capable, homely woman supported her husband well all his life. The younger daughter died at an early age; the elder, Frances, grew to be something of a beauty and made two of the most brilliant marriages of the time. In 1583, when she was only sixteen, she married Sir Philip Sidney. This was more a political arrangement than a love match, intended to bind fast the alliance between Walsingham and Leicester, who was Sidney's uncle. But Walsingham soon came under the spell of his most attractive son-in-law. The young couple stayed in his house, and the grave secretary delighted in the notice which came to Sidney from all sides. When Sir Philip was killed in 1586 Walsingham conscientiously looked after the tangled finances though it cost him dearly. Frances then married the Earl of Essex, a man almost as brilliant as Sidney, but the most wayward, proud and troublesome man in the kingdom.

Walsingham's Puritan faith did not override his natural generosity; nor did his severe views on religion prevent him from being a man of cultivated refinement. Puritans too often became known for a carping, censorious criticism of art and society, but Walsingham was not one of these. From the early day of his Italian travels he had been something of a dandy. His keen mind and wide reading kept up with art and thought. He took upon himself the duties of patron, and hardly anyone encouraged arts and sciences as faithfully as he did. Much of what he did was for the good of the country. He was a great friend of both Oxford and Cambridge, doing more for Oxford though he himself had been to Cambridge. He pressed forward the English sea voyages and encouraged the writers on discovery and the arts of navigation; Nicholas, Peckham and Horsey dedicated to him the accounts of their travels; and Dr John Dee, inventive scientist and great charlatan, was indebted to him. Hakluyt, in his dedication, commended Walsingham's 'wisdom to have a special care of the honour of her Majesty, the good reputation of our country and the advancing of navigation'.

All that can be seen as part of his duty to his Protestant island, but he did not forget his pleasure and his curiosity. Edmund Spenser in an introductory sonnet to the *Faerie Queen* called Walsingham 'the great Maecenas of this age' :

> As well to all that civil arts profess,
> As those that are inspired with martial rage.

Though the compliment, as usual with Spenser, was overdone, Walsingham was well known for his wide interests. He knew poets and wits such as Sidney, Spenser, Thomas Watson and John

Harington. He was kind also to the obscure; he favoured alike John Rider, the laborious compiler of a Latin dictionary, and Richard Tarlton, the Queen's fool. Nor was his interest confined to England. No man in the realm had a wider knowledge of continental affairs. He was called the best linguist of his time; and his knowledge of ancient literature was equal to his command of modern languages. He was able to carry off conversation with the greatest in Europe : 'He could well fit King James his humour with sayings out of Xenophon, Thucydides, Plutarch or Tacitus, as he could King Henry's with Rabelais's conceits and the Hollander with mechanic discourses.'

For all his remarkable talents, the sum of his life was service. 'You have fought more with your pen', Drake wrote to him, 'than many here in our English navy fought with their enemies.' The bulk of his official correspondence was incredible; there was hardly any business of government that did not come under his eye. He came to public service not only driven by ambition and the hope of gaining wealth, but also fired by a great devotion to the Queen and to the country. The success of Elizabeth's government depended on the learned, ambitious, patriotic new men like Walsingham, and for the greater part of the reign the compelling character of the Queen and the manifest destiny of England attracted them in sufficient numbers. Walsingham died on 6th April 1590 and his old colleague Burghley recognized that 'the Queen's Majesty and her realm and I' had suffered a great loss, the more so because his kind of service was now hard to find. He died just at the point when Elizabeth's system began to break down. Greed, fraud and ambition displaced the idealism of former years. The strength of Tudor government rested on the strength of the Tudor despots. Elizabeth was old and weary; the country was no longer in danger; the firm grip of the monarchy relaxed, discipline slipped, corruption thrived and a problematic inheritance gathered to dismay her weak successor.

7

Sir Humphrey Gilbert

ON MONDAY, 9th September 1583, undone by idealism, Sir Humphrey Gilbert and his little ship the *Squirrel,* a mere cockleshell of ten tons burthen on the black sea, vanished beneath the Atlantic waves.

Gilbert's short and vigorous life was a continuous preparation for this calamity. Uncertain in his inheritance, schooled by pedants, trained in the courtly modes of a departed heroic age, he sought a new England overseas which he imagined as the grand Platonic form of the old England he knew, through whose perplexed ways he wandered dragging his abstract ideas and leaving incidentally a trail of blood. He was born to the sound of water, about the year 1539 at Greenway on the River Dart. The Gilberts had grown wealthy from maritime business pursued with energy and ruthlessness. They had been, and were, warriors, merchants, smugglers and privateers. Among his relatives were many West Country adventurers—Carews, Champernowns, Grenvilles—turbulent men full of seamanship and egotism, who knew the atrocious loneliness of small ships far from land. Humphrey's father died in 1547, and soon after his mother married Walter Raleigh, another Devon sailor; from this union came, in 1552, the famous Sir Walter Raleigh, destined, like his half-brother Humphrey, to laborious journeys, to obscure triumphs and ultimate defeat.

At the early age then usual, young Humphrey was sent to Eton, which until 1541 had been under the rod of Nicholas Udall, scholar, playwright, thief of the college plate, and the 'greatest beater' of his time. At Eton, the too familiar acquaintance with Lily's *Latin Syntax,* the text book of the age mentioned in no less than eight of Shakespeare's plays, the mere repetition of Latin grammar which Roger Ascham's *The Scholemaster* (1570) called 'tedious for the master, hard for the scholar, cold and uncomfortable for both', failed to prevent Gilbert from becoming modestly learned in the manner of the gentlemen of the time, sound in the classics and proficient in French and Spanish. But the method was rough and deficient, as Gilbert saw; twenty years after his school-days he wrote a work on education called *Queen Elizabethes Achademy* in which he tried to reform the schooling of rich youths who were, he said, 'obscurely drowned in education'. Leaving Eton, Gilbert took the lean fruits and sore bruises of Udall's method and went on to Oxford; for no doubt he had suffered the kind of barbarity that caused his cousin, Peter Carew, to be chain-ed like a mad dog in the school-yard until he broke his fetters and ran away. In Gilbert's short time at Oxford—he entered the service of Princess Elizabeth at sixteen[1]—he remembered the tradi-tions of his family and studied navigation and the arts of war.

The Gilberts were Protestants, and relatives of Humphrey were implicated in Wyatt's unsuccessful rebellion against Mary in 1554. Oxford, where the Protestant churchmen Latimer, Ridley and Cranmer were burnt to death in 1555 and 1556, was Catho-lic and no place for young Gilbert. He left puzzled. The study of Latin, which had taken up the greatest part of his education, was intended by schoolmasters under the influence of the enthusiastic humanists of the Renaissance to teach the pupils the grave Roman ideals of probity and public service; the humanist Vives, praising the advantages of Latin, wrote that it expressed 'the image of a right prudent and valiant man born and nurtured in a well-ordered commonwealth'. But as to the nature of that common-wealth, education was silent. Under the torment of the whip the young came to know Cicero, but the relevance of these republican views to mid-sixteenth-century England was not explained. The young, Gilbert complained in *Queen Elizabethes Achademy*, were 'estranged from all serviceable virtues to their prince and country'. As he was a Protestant, Gilbert followed the great example of Luther and Calvin and made nationalism a large part of his belief. But his serious aspirations to do good for his country were blocked by a neglectful education and by a Catholic queen whose policies would consign England to a minor place in a Christendom dominated by the Spanish power.

---

[1] It was not unusual to go to university at a very young age. John Fisher took the grammar degree at Cambridge when he was fourteen, and Wolsey, the famous 'boy bachelor', received his B.A. from Oxford at fifteen.

From the pain of his inchoate idealism Humphrey Gilbert was rescued by a kinswoman. Katherine Ashley, a close relative of Humphrey's mother, had been appointed companion and womanly guide to Princess Elizabeth before the death of Henry VIII. With her excellent talent for intrigue, Mrs Ashley had kept the affection of Elizabeth until her death in 1565. At the end of 1555, when the Queen finally absolved Elizabeth from complicity in Wyatt's rebellion and allowed her to return to the peace of Hatfield, Katherine Ashley preferred young Gilbert to a place in the princess's household.

The princess was thin, active, sardonic, learned, riding easily among the complexities of her State. Her new page was ardent, handsome, a sturdy young skiff from the Devon slipways. She was twenty-two and he was sixteen; 'such was his countenance, forwardness and good behaviour', said the continuation of Holinshed's *Chronicles* in 1587, giving a likely elaboration to events long past, 'that her Majesty had a special good liking to him, and very oftentimes would familiarly discourse and confer with him in matters of learning.' He now began his proper education, learning that 'serviceable virtue' to prince and country that could not be found at Eton and Oxford, and which Elizabeth was extremely apt to teach. He saw the image of England's future greatness in Elizabeth's Protestant court. 'O noble prince', he wrote to his Sovereign in *Queen Elizabethes Achademy,* 'that god shall bless so far as to be the only mean of bringing this seely, frozen Island into such everlasting honour that all the nations of the World shall know and say, when the face of an English gentleman appeareth, that he is either a soldier, a philosopher, or a gallant courtier.' He saw also his own advantage, his position at court saving him from the desperate place-hunting forced upon the gentry and small landholders by a vertiginous inflation. He saw his own small glitter as part of Elizabeth's royal resplendence; at the end of his life, in 1581, Gilbert wrote truthfully that he had 'served her Majesty in wars and peace, above seven and twenty years . . . from a boy to the age of white hairs'.

By 1563 Gilbert's training was almost complete. Guided by such works as Castiglione's *Il Cortegiano,* the most famous of the courtesy books which Sir Thomas Hoby translated into English in 1561, Gilbert had acquired the graces of peace and was proficient in music, dancing and the composition of lyric verse; it now remained for him to put his courage, his fencing and horsemanship to the test of war. In his twenty-fourth year he left for France in search of honour and reputation.

He endured a small, cautious campaign, pretending to be in aid of the French Protestants, but really an English attempt to take the Channel port of Havre de Grace as compensation for the recent loss of Calais. He saw a few skirmishes and more dishonour. Having driven the trusting citizens from the town, the English settled in Havre de Grace and awaited the boredom of the siege. Soon the greater dread of the plague was upon them; the ominous buboes appeared at the groin and the armpit and soon the English soldiers, whose worst enemy until then had been heat and fatigue, screamed in painful contractions and died covered in pus from ruptured swellings. On 5th June Gilbert was wounded. In July the English capitulated and withdrew.

Though the chronicler John Stow wrote that Gilbert served in France 'with great commendation', no honour comes from a deceitful campaign and courage makes no headway against the plague. The reality of his military apprenticeship had been in grim contrast to the debonair assumptions of the courtier's training. The brutal may show a disinterested lust for blood, but the courtier of gentle breeding, if he is to gain honour from the squalors of war, must endow the terrible business with noble purpose. Despite polishing, the little enterprise in France was without a gloss of nobility. Three years later an outbreak of rebellion in Ireland gave Gilbert the chance to acquire reputation, for this campaign was undertaken in a high national cause, to put down treason. Gilbert's serious love for England promised the greatest severity for the Irish rebels; the aim of the war, as the commander-in-chief Sir Henry Sidney admitted, was to make the name of an Englishman 'more terrible now to them than the sight of a hundred was before', and this purpose, Sidney informed the Council in London, Gilbert achieved. Moreover, the Irish were miserable specimens and cruel rectitude is most easily practised against wretches : 'they came creeping forth upon their hands', Sidney wrote of his enemies in Munster, 'for their legs could not bear them; they looked like anatomies of death; they spoke like ghosts crying out of their graves; they did eat the dead carrions, happy when they could find them; yea they did eat one another soon after.'

For more than three years Gilbert fought the Irish, first against

Shane O'Neill in Ulster and then against James FitzMaurice in Munster. He rose to the rank of colonel though he protested his 'insufficientories to be such, both for want of years, experience, and all other virtues necessary for such an officer'. Several times he left Ireland, trying to escape from this savage assignment which he found expensive, distasteful, barren; but he was ordered back, for his distaste did not prevent him from being horrifically effective. At the end of 1569 Gilbert sent Cecil an account of his methods in Munster. If a town would not yield, he took it by force 'how many lives so ever it cost, putting man, woman, and child of them to the sword'. The poet Thomas Churchyard, who left a description of this campaign in his *General Rehersal of Wars* (1579), wrote of piles of heads from the day's slaughter put before Gilbert's tent which did 'bring greater terror to the people, when they saw the heads of their dead fathers, brothers, children, kinsfolk and friends, lie on the ground before their faces as they came to speak with the said Colonel'. Captain Ward, one of his officers, reported that the Irish accounted Gilbert 'more like a devil than a man, and are so afraid of him that they did leave and give up twenty-six castles'. The commander-in-chief Sidney thought that Gilbert had made the highways safe and the towns free, and for all this, Sidney wrote, 'I had nothing to present him with but the honour of a knighthood, which I gave him.' Gilbert was allowed to leave Dublin for England in January 1570, and although he returned later in the year in an unsuccessful attempt to recover the expenses of his campaign, £3,315 in all, his days of notorious slaughter were over.

In an age of mutability death loses some of its terrors. 'One day one sees a man as a great lord,' a French traveller to England noted in 1558, 'the next he is in the hands of an executioner.' A man who has some contempt for his own eclipse will send others that way the more easily : Gilbert's efficiency in Ireland, not his ferocity, was unusual. John Keats, in a famous passage on Shakespeare, remarked on the playwright's 'negative capability', the power to look on death, despair and uncertainty with detachment. The power which Shakespeare showed in art, many of his contemporary men of action showed in life. 'For conversation of particular greatness and dignity,' wrote Raleigh, Humphrey Gilbert's half-brother, 'there is nothing more noble and glorious than to have felt the force of every fortune.' Terrestrial events were merely accidents that proved the character. To be great was to think greatly, the mind following its abstract star; then the ruthless pursuit of high endeavours, causing perhaps the death of many others and even one's own demise, could be looked on with equanimity. Hawkins the slave-trader, Drake the circumnavigator, Gilbert, and later Raleigh, the scourges of Ireland, men practised in ruthlessness, were all proud and ambitious, and were all in the grip of large ideal notions.

Gilbert fought in Ireland for the cause of England's greatness—to put down treason, to secure English rights and property, and if possible to establish English rule throughout the land. Despite the barbarity of his methods he quickly saw that rapine and destruction were no way to make Ireland an obedient and peaceful province of England. It is to his credit, and supports his own contention that he had no military ambition and no desire to command, that he looked for peaceful ways to subdue Ireland. The policy of 'plantation' was first attempted in Ireland in 1556, in the reign of Queen Mary, when English soldiers were given the land of rebellious chiefs in the counties of Leix and Offaly. Soon after he went to Ireland, Gilbert pressed for an English plantation in Ulster. Elizabeth was sympathetic, seeing that the scheme would cost her nothing, and wrote to Sidney that Englishmen 'were to be allured to plant in Ulster'. The plan failed, but in 1568 Gilbert, being then in Munster, again petitioned for grants of land : 'Sith it seemeth good to the Queen's Majesty to use means to reduce the Realm of Ireland to civility and obedience.' Although this plan went little further than the former one, Gilbert was convinced of the advantages of colonization. In 1572 he wrote a *Discourse on Ireland* setting out the benefits for England; he mentioned the increase in trade, the value of Irish minerals and fishing, the good harbours in Ireland for English shipping, but chiefly he thought of the security and glory of England, to keep 'the Irish empire from the conquest of the Spaniards, Frenchmen and other nations'.

A courtly education and his desire to serve the Queen had turned Sir Humphrey Gilbert into a soldier. For ten years, from the age of twenty-four, he followed this profession in France, in Ireland and in the Netherlands. But his mind—the wistful mind that aspired to a great and singular enterprise for the glory of queen and country—became aware that his destiny would not be realized on the numerous and bloody battlefields of Europe. From the restrictions of the European land, where each field and path had a profound history, he turned his thoughts to the sea whose unfenced immensities allowed the imagination a corresponding freedom. Son of a sailor, born by the sea, friend and colleague of Devon seamen, and living in an age of great discoveries, he could not have forgotten the sea. In the intervals between campaigns he thought of ships and voyages. In 1566, on his return from France, he was eager to try the north-west passage to China and was only stopped by the opposition of Sir John Gilbert, his elder brother; 'thereupon he wrote this treatise unto his said brother, both to excuse and clear himself from the note of rashness and also to set down such authorities, reasons and experiences, as had chiefly encouraged him unto the same.' This treatise was *A Discourse of a Discovery for a New Passage to Cataia,* written in 1566, but not published until 1576 when the poet George Gascoigne brought it to the press and contributed a preface.

This short pamphlet, written with persuasive charm, drew proofs for a north-west passage from the usual erroneous sources of antiquity—from the myths of Plato, from the history of Pliny, from the geography of Strabo, and from others even less reliable —and added to this much puzzling information of tides and currents, of travels and migrations. It set out also the advantages of the passage, the benefits to England's trade, and the possibility of finding new, rich lands beyond the reach of Spain and Portugal. None of this was new. The geographical misinformation and the naïve surmises were common to the age; the wish to outflank Spain and Portugal on the way to the riches of the East had caused the Merchant Adventurers to send Willoughby and Chancellor on their voyages to the North-East in 1553 and 1556. The only novelty in the treatise appeared in this surprising hint: 'Also we might inhabit some part of those countries, and settle there such needy people of our country, which now trouble the commonwealth, and through want here at home are inforced to commit outrageous offences, whereby they are dayly consumed with the gallows.' In these poor criminals may be seen the forerunners of all England's imperial millions. And Gilbert, hell-bent on distinction, made it clear that he was the man to undertake such an enterprise; 'he is not worthy to live at all,' he wrote in the closing passage of his treatise, 'that for fear, or danger of death, shunneth his countries service, and his own honour : seeing death is inevitable, and the fame of virtue immortal. Wherefor in this behalf, *Mutare vel timere sperno.*' Something must come of such a desperate resolution.

In the rush for possessions, wealth and power released by the sea voyages of Portugal and Spain, England had been left behind. While the Portuguese sailors, guided and encouraged by the royal family, moved steadily down the coast of Africa, discovering Madeira in 1419, the Azores in 1448 and rounding the Cape of Good Hope in 1486, England was still convulsed in the last brutalities of the Wars of the Roses. And when that struggle was over none of the early Tudors had the vision of King John of Portugal or of his more famous son, Prince Henry the Navigator. England established no naval college, as Portugal had done; there was no equivalent of the Spanish Casa de Contratacion in Seville, where the lecturer in navigation instructed and examined all captains bound for the Indies. England had no writers on geography and the theory of navigation. Pedro de Medina's important *Arte de Navegar* (1545), the text-book for world voyagers, was not translated into English until 1581. England's rulers were insular, cautious, poor; her sailors, the Spanish Ambassador at the court of Henry VII wrote, 'are generally savages'. The line drawn by Pope Alexander VI in May 1493, dividing the new discoveries between Spain and Portugal, recognized the pre-eminence of these nations in the work of exploration.

It was impossible that Spain and Portugal should enjoy their new worlds in peace. The vast riches brought back inflamed the greed of less fortunate nations, and strange tales moved the imagination of all Europe. The pity of it was, the poet of *A New Interlude* complained in 1517, that England had no foreign possessions :

> what an honourable thing
> Both to the realm and the king,
> To have had his dominion extending
> There into so far a ground.

In 1513, Robert Thorne, a Bristol man who went to live in Seville, had exhorted Henry VIII to encourage exploration. In 1527, at the invitation of the English ambassador, Thorne wrote a long account of Spanish and Portuguese successes, and then set out a way in which England could redress the balance. His advice was to go north, so shortening the passage to the Spice Islands and, on the way, opening 'the navigation of all Tartary, which should be no less profitable to our commodities of cloth, than these spiceries to the Emperor and King of Portingale'. And to the objection that the northern seas were blocked with ice, and the lands too cold to live in, Thorne replied with the confidence of one resident in warm, beguiling Seville that 'there is no land uninhabitable, nor sea innavigable'.

The North slowly became England's particular territory. John Cabot had prepared the way, sailing from Bristol in 1497 to discover Cape Breton. Within a few years the English fishermen were out in force, making the arduous journey to the Newfoundland fishing banks. Henry VIII encouraged shipbuilding and protected English fisheries so that Hakluyt could justly claim that the Newfoundland trade 'was common and frequented in the reign of Edward VI'. And Hakluyt's judgment had the support of the Spaniards. The geography book *El Yslario General*, written in 1536 by Alonzo de Santa Cruz, an experienced navigator from the Casa de Contratacion, affirmed that Labrador was 'frequented by the English, who go there to take fish, which the natives catch in great numbers'.

But the fishing trade with its traditional modest rewards was of no interest to the new English adventurers. Envious of the riches of Spain and Portugal, they wished to use the routes of the North only as a means to the East, to the wealth of Cathay and the Spice Islands. 'The preciousness of these things,' wrote Robert Thorne, 'is measured after the distance that is between us and the things that we have appetite unto'. Serious attempts to lessen this hateful distance were taken by the Merchant Adventurers in mid-century. In 1553 three ships under Willoughby and Chancellor were sent to find Asia by the North-East, and further journeys in that direction were made in 1556 and 1558 by Stephen Burrough and Anthony Jenkinson. Despite the oppression of fog, cold and ice which killed so many, these expeditions established trade with Russia; but the larger aim to win through to the East seemed impossible by this route, and so men's hopes turned once again to the North-West.

By the mid-sixties envy of Spain, private greed, national pride and the cautious hints of Elizabeth's policy had inflamed all England with a desire to claim a place in the new worlds. The partial success of the ventures to the North-East was hopeful. The black enterprise of Hawkins, pirating and slave-running in defiance of Spain, had to prove the weakness of the Spanish giant, a weakness that Elizabeth and her sailors were delighted to exploit. The West Country seamen, many of them friends and neighbours of Hawkins, were rigging vessels, subscribing to ventures to which the Queen as often as not gave a surreptitious encouragement. Too poor to challenge Spain directly, she looked upon her privateers —her state pirates like Drake and Hawkins—to snatch for England a part of the Spanish wealth. She knew that a powerful state was built on money, and instituted the policy which Francis Bacon later set out and commended in his *Considerations touching a War with Spain*. The greatness of Spain, he said, 'consisteth in their treasure, their treasure in the Indies, and their Indies (if it be well weighed) are indeed but an accession to such as are masters by sea. So as this axle-tree, whereupon their greatness turneth, is soon cut in two by any that shall be stronger than they by sea.' Hawkins, Drake, Raleigh and many lesser men made themselves masters by sea. But to steal hardly diminished the wealth of the Spanish, supported as they were by the unbounded riches of the Indies. It would be better for England to find her own source of treasure, either in the North of the Americas or in Cathay and the Far East, and the way to those parts, since the journey around Russia had proved so difficult, lay by the North-West.

Sir Humphrey Gilbert was the man who re-awakened England to the possibilities of the north-west passage. As a young man from a Devon seafaring family he had naturally caught the fever for both the adventure and the profits of exploration. He had joined the Merchant Adventurers and subscribed towards their journeys to the North-East. The Adventurers, finding the way to the East blocked, settled for ordinary commerce with Russia, but Gilbert could not forget Cathay so easily. The way east was tedious and known; the way west was full of imaginative possibilities: who knew what gold, what lands, what clear passages were in the North-West? At Havre, during the French campaign, Gilbert had met Richard Eden whose translation of Peter Martyr's *Decades,* in 1555, had given Englishmen the first full account of the New World. In his own West Country Gilbert talked to 'our yeerly fishers to Labrador and Terra Nova'; he recalled the voyages of

Rut and Hore to Newfoundland in 1527 and 1536. In 1566 he wrote his *Discourse of a Discovery of a New Passage to Cataia* and set English sailors on a quest that was not resolved until the Norwegian Amundsen made the first passage in 1905. Frobisher, Davis, Hudson, Baffin, to name only the most famous, tried to find the passage, failed, and gave their names to some part of the desolation that defeated them.

Discovery in the sixteenth century, set about with so many uncertainties, was a field for the contest between practicality and idealism. Treasure was the spur that drove most of the adventurers; their lust for riches caused them to commit murder, piracy, robbery, perjury, blasphemy, and whatever lesser sins besides which might help them to the money they sought. Proud Protestant merchants willingly compounded with the Catholic Church for the benefit of trade with the Indies. 'The merchant in England', Hakluyt lamented in his *Discourse of Western Planting* (1584), 'cometh here devoutly to the communion, and sendeth his son into Spain to hear Mass. These things are kept secret by the merchants; and such as depend upon the trade of merchandise are loth to utter the same.' Gilbert also was in search of profits; he was an early member of the Merchant Adventurers, and advocated the north-west passage as a route to certain riches. But his thought went beyond greed and sought the ideal put forward by Richard Eden in his preface to the translation of the *Decades*. England, said Eden, should possess the coast lands of North America, from Florida to Newfoundland, as yet unexplored and uninhabited by Christians. Colonization was the ideal tentatively suggested in Gilbert's *Discourse of a New Passage,* and in the petition that Gilbert addressed to the Queen at the same time for 'license and favour to enterprise and give the attempt with all possible speed, for the discovery of a passage to Cathay, and all other rich parts of the world, hitherto not found', he asked the Queen 'to grant me during my life the Captainship unto the government to Your Majesty's use of all such countries and territories as shall by me or my advice discovered'. The Merchant Adventurers opposed this petition, and the Queen had need of Gilbert's service in Ireland. At the end of 1566 he was ordered back to his military command, to complete his brutal work in the bogs, to try out his ideal of English 'plantations' in Ireland, and when those failed to dream of the infinite space and liberty of the North American shores.

For some years after his return from Ireland in 1570 Gilbert was kept from his dreams abroad by the press of affairs at home. In 1570 he married Anne Ager who was to bear him, in the thirteen years of their marriage, six sons and one daughter. In the next year he entered Parliament, he and Sir John Hawkins being the representatives for Plymouth. In Parliament, he was an outrageous supporter of the Queen against the Commons and won the enmity of Peter Wentworth, that independent parliamentarian, who called Gilbert 'a flatterer, a liar, and a naughtie man'. As a reward for his flattery, the Queen appointed him Surveyor of Artillery. He dabbled in alchemy; seeking as usual rare knowledge and profit, he tried to turn iron into copper and thereby lost £400. With unabated curiosity, and still thinking of England's needs, he put his mind to education and composed his *Achademy*. He was, said his friend and poet Gascoigne, 'endowed with great gifts of mind and well given to the advancement of knowledge and virtue'. And between the times of his studies, in 1572, he took up arms again. Accompanied by his young half-brother Walter Raleigh, Gilbert went to the Netherlands on one of Elizabeth's typical double-dealing ventures, designed to get the advantage of Spaniard, French and Dutch alike. This expedition, which culminated with the rout of the English at Tergoes in the winter of 1572, won no praise for either English diplomacy or English arms.

The disappointment, even ignominy, of this campaign can only have increased Gilbert's resolve to serve the Queen in the free airs of the Americas where his nationalism could make some notable mark unconstricted by the perils of European policy. By 1574 he was in his prime, a man of reputation and achievement. He now gave himself wholeheartedly to enterprise beyond the seas. His first attempts, in March 1574, were petitions to the Queen and to the Lord High Admiral, 'Supplicated of certain gents in the West parts for a new navigation'. These petitions, asking permission to discover rich and unknown lands 'fatally, and as it seemeth by God's providence, reserved for England and for the honour of Your Majesty', were refused. It seemed that Elizabeth, though assured of divine providence, hesitated to annoy Spain. In the next year, under pressure from the Privy Council, the Merchant Adventurers took up once again the search for a route to Cathay. Martin Frobisher was chosen for this venture, and at first he intended to go by the North-East. But Frobisher had known

Gilbert in Ireland and met him again in London in 1575, and after talks between the two, talks which incidentally led also to the publication by Gascoigne of Gilbert's *Discourse* written ten years before, Frobisher decided to try the north-west passage.

Although Gilbert did not sail with Frobisher in 1576, his hand may be seen behind the expedition. He turned Frobisher from the North-East to the North-West, and perhaps it was he who suggested that a colony of one hundred men should be left in Meta Incognita—as the wilderness was called—to possess the land and make an English staging-post on the way to Cathay.

Frobisher's voyage was a failure; he found no passage and he planted no colony. But he did bring back a lump of black ore which the assayers wrongly pronounced to be rich in gold, and so this dismal voyage caused a great excitement. Frobisher hurried back to the North-West in search of gold and brought his ships to England laden with stones; 'when neither gold nor silver nor any other metal could be extracted from them,' wrote Camden, 'we have seen cast forth to mend the highways.' The way in which Frobisher's voyages were transformed from scientific exploration to a gold-rush confirmed, if any proof were still needed, that plunder was the chief end of English voyages. The Queen was not interested in colonization; the accepted opinion was that England was under-populated, and the Queen needed all her subjects at home to face her rivals on the continent. Perhaps learning from the example of Frobisher, Gilbert saw that Elizabeth would give way to his plans only if there were advantages in them for the Queen. In November 1577, therefore, he sent her a paper entitled 'How Her Majesty may annoy the King of Spayne', in which he suggested that, under the pretext of forming a colonizing expedition, a large fleet might be sent to St Lawrence Island from where it could attack the fishing boats of Spain, Portugal and France, taking and keeping both the fishing-boats and their catches. Since Gilbert knew the Queen well, he cunningly arranged his scheme so that no blame would attach to her, and so that it would cost her nothing. In June 1578, he received a patent from Elizabeth for the occupation and settlement of Newfoundland.

To win these Letters Patent from the Queen had been a desperate business. For more than four years Gilbert had looked for a way to make his colonizing plans acceptable, and had managed at last only by a piece of notable dishonesty. Was Sir Humphrey

Gilbert really interested in plundering defenceless fishermen? No doubt he was thoroughly confused. In the manner of his time he was quite prepared to accept the profits from robbery, and a persuasive, specious argument could be made that his action would weaken England's enemies. But most of all he showed the ruthlessness of the idealist—that same terrible purpose which had first appeared in Ireland—and had won by this the charter he longed for, 'to inhabit and possess at his choice all remote and heathen lands not in the actual possession of any Christian prince'; this was the first serious attempt among Englishmen to establish a colony overseas.

Perhaps the dubious foundation for this expedition ensured its complete, and almost farcical, failure. Amidst many quarrels, and with the Spanish Ambassador Mendoza keeping watch, the fleet met at Dartmouth. In September 1578, with winter coming on, they put out to sea; in October they were driven back. Finally, on 19th November they left for unknown parts and disappeared from sight and mind. They were gone, wrote Churchyard:

> But whither, no man knows,
> Save that they are in Bark.

On 26th February 1579 Gilbert slipped back into port, and hardly anyone would have known had not the careful spies of Mendoza been keeping watch. The ambassador reported to Spain: 'Not only have they abandoned the navigation to Cathay, but they have been so sickened with the little profit produced from their last voyage that not a man or a sailor has been paid his wages.' The details of this voyage have never come to light; but Spain, convinced that Gilbert's party had been pillaging the coast of Galicia, complained so loudly that the Council temporarily withdrew the patent and sent Gilbert to subdue the rebellious ships of his old enemy James FitzMaurice off the coast of Ireland, a venture that caused him much vexation and expense.

The original terms of Gilbert's patent had allowed him six years to complete his enterprise. The failure of 1578 had cost him dearly; he had mortgaged his family, lands and credit to the limit, and now he saw time running out. In order to mount a final attempt he needed money and hit upon the brilliant idea of selling off some of the rights granted to him by the Letters Patent. The wastes of Labrador were sold to the ingenious alchemist, Dr John

Dee, but the greatest part of the capital was provided by Sir George Peckham and Sir Thomas Gerrard, two moderate Catholics, who wished to purchase land in the Americas to which English Catholics could emigrate away from the persecution they suffered at home. The all-knowing Mendoza reported that this scheme was devised by Walsingham, the Queen's secretary, who promised to spare Peckham and Gerrard if they would take their troublesome Catholics away; if this was so, and Mendoza was always well-informed, Elizabeth had at last found a use for colonization. Gilbert granted the two Catholics the right to explore between Florida and Cape Breton, and contracted to sell them 2 million acres of their choice. A further 3 million acres were granted to Sir Philip Sidney who immediately assigned his rights to Peckham. And yet still more money was required. A joint-stock company was formed with Walsingham at the head, and the funds were raised. Gilbert made his Will, grandly disposing of his future commonwealth; the Queen sent a token and good wishes by her new favourite Walter Raleigh; learned Stephan Parmenius of Buda composed an *Embarkation Ode* in three hundred elegant Latin hexameters; in June 1583 the five ships of the expedition, varying in size from the *Raleigh* of 200 tons to the minute *Squirrel* of 10 tons, sailed from Plymouth on 'the trade way to Newfoundland'.

The voyage, like all journeys of the time, was full of incident, danger and disappointment. The *Raleigh,* the 'Vice-admiral' and the largest of the fleet, turned back for England pleading a strange sickness. Fog and contrary winds delayed the rest, and then the remaining ships were separated only to meet up again with great joy in Conception Bay. On 30th July they sighted Labrador and fled south along this forsaken coast of 'hideous rocks and mountains, bare of trees and void of any green herb'. On 3rd August the small fleet entered the harbour of St John's, Newfoundland, where Gilbert, despite the great number of foreign fishermen about, took possession of the place, promulgated laws, imposed taxes and demanded the revictualling of his fleet. 'And afterwards', wrote Edward Hayes, captain of the *Golden Hind* and historian of the expedition, 'were erected not far from that place the Arms of England ingraven in lead, and infixed upon a pillar of wood.' Gilbert had claimed for England her first colonial possession. Sir Humphrey was cheerful; his plans were developing well and Newfoundland pleased him.

But at St John's his good fortune ended. Several of his crew stole away and took to piracy; 'some were sick of fluxes and many died : and, in brief, by one means or other our company was diminished, and many by the General licensed to return home.' A gold-strike was claimed, but Gilbert, dreaming of the richer prize offered by uncounted acres on the American shore, took sail; Sir Humphrey now travelled in the tiny *Squirrel*, the better to explore the crannies of the coastline. At the Island of Sablon the flagship, the *Delight*, went aground and was lost while the remaining ships were help-lessly driven on by a south-east gale. When the wind dropped, the navigators had lost their bearings. The skies look ominous, the cold increased; the men were in rags and without food; they pleaded to go back to England. Gilbert agreed 'withal protesting himself greatly satisfied with that he had seen and knew already. Reiterat-ing these words : Be content we have seen enough, and take no care of expense past; I will set you forth royally the next Spring, if God send us safe home'. On 31st August they altered course for England and saw immediately the ugly portent of a walrus who 'to bid us farewell he sent forth a horrible voice, roaring or bellowing as doth a lion'. At the start of the return Gilbert was as variable as the weathercock, sometimes bold and swaggering, dar-ing the devil himself to contest the passage home, and sometimes morose, beating the cabin-boy and lamenting the loss of certain unspecified possessions or papers. Hayes thought that these were the plans of secret mines. His men entreated Sir Humphrey to transfer from the *Squirrel* to the much larger *Golden Hind*, but he refused, saying he would not 'forsake my little company going homeward with whom I have passed so many storms and perils'. They reached the Azores and set course for England when a great storm sprang up. On Monday, 9th September, the ships were dashed about; in the little frigate Gilbert, 'sitting abaft with a book in his hand, cried unto us into the *Hind* (so oft as we did approach within hearing) "We are as near to heaven by sea as by land." Reiterating the same speech, well beseeming a soldier resolute in Jesus Christ, as I can testify he was.' At about midnight Hayes saw the lights of the *Squirrel* disappear and the ship and her crew swallowed up by the sea.

So much difficulty and so little achieved. The plans for coloniz-ation came to nothing. Even St John's, Newfoundland, though claimed by Gilbert, had to wait another thirty years for the arrival of the first permanent settlement. The cause for the failure was partly in Sir Humphrey himself. His expedition was built upon ambiguity. As with so many of his contemporaries, his ideals quarrelled with his practice; his heart desired a colony, but his hands were continually pulled towards riches. Moreover, despite his Devon birthplace, he was a poor seaman, perhaps from lack of experience and too many years ashore; even the Queen noted that he had 'no good hap at sea'. If he had wanted wealth only, he might have sailed with a sound navigator and trusted his military training and his intrepid spirit to win him plunder, in the manner of Drake. But he chose to be the leader of a great sea enterprise which he guided and commanded poorly, though the aims of the venture were a mystery to most of his men. They taxed Gilbert, like the disappointed Edward Hayes of the *Golden Hind,* 'with temerity and presumption' in that 'he was too prodigal of his own patrimony and too careless of other men's expenses on a ground imagined good'. He consumed the solid ground he stood on in pursuit of the ideal he could not reach.

If Sir Humphrey Gilbert had too much idealism, England had too little, and this also prevented the success of the early colonists. When Raleigh took up the work of his half-brother and sent two ships to explore the American coast, the land which they found and called Virginia contained gentle and friendly Indians. The expedition that Raleigh sent to possess it, in 1585, under Sir Richard Grenville and Ralph Lane, and manned by the usual criminals and riff-raff, pillaged, tortured and slaughtered to such effect that the Indians revolted and wiped out the colony. 'It is the sinfullest thing in the world', commented Bacon, 'to forsake or destitute a plantation once in forwardness : for besides the dishonour, it is the guiltiness of blood of many commiserable persons.' But the Queen and the Council looked on colonies as places which favourite courtiers could exploit for their profit, using for their purpose rogues and criminals unwanted in England. Again, Bacon pointed out the folly of this : plantations abroad were like plantations of wood; they needed careful tending and only gave their profit after many years. And criminals were not the men to do the tending. 'It is a shameful and unblessed thing', Bacon wrote in his essay on *Plantations,* 'to take the scum of the people and wicked, condemned men, to be the people with whom you plant, for they will ever live like rogues and not fall to work, but be lazy and do mischief, and spend victuals, and be quickly weary, to the discredit of the plantation.'[2]

Sir Humphrey Gilbert takes his proper place among the imaginative men, the artists, of the age. His memorial is not his practical success, but rather the example of his thought and trials. 'We and the French', wrote Richard Hakluyt, 'are most infamous for our outrageous, common, and daily piracies.' Gilbert was the first influential voice in England to assert that colonization was a nobler work than piracy, and one more likely to advance England's wealth and power. And he asserted this against the general opinion of the country: the robbers—Hawkins, Drake, Grenville and the like—were the popular heroes whose thefts were blessed by the Queen's policy. But Gilbert, with the confidence of the visionary, saw before the Queen and her Council that England was strong enough to turn from destruction to building. 'The time approacheth,' wrote Hakluyt in the preface to the first edition of his *Principal Navigations,* written just before Gilbert's last voyage, 'and now is, that we of England may share and part stakes (if we will ourselves) both with the Spaniard and Portingale, in part of America and other reasons yet undiscovered.' Hakluyt, the epic chronicler of England's voyages, was the disciple of Gilbert's thought, and so great a believer in colonization that he wanted to accompany Gilbert in 1583; but his duties as chaplain to the Earl of Stafford stopped him.

It is no surprise that the sea voyages so laboriously collected by Hakluyt and published in his *Principal Navigations* between 1582 and 1600 should have possessed the imagination of his fellow countrymen:

> Thy Voyages attend,
> Industrious Hakluyt;
> Whose reading shall inflame
> Men to seek fame,

wrote Michael Drayton, in his *Ode to the Virginian Voyage.* The new riches, so astoundingly and suddenly revealed, brought forth new riches from the mind. 'Gold', Columbus said, 'is the most precious of all commodities; gold constitutes treasure, and he who possesses it has all he needs in this world, as also the means of

---

[2] Bacon became a shareholder in the Company that planted the first successful English colony at Cupid's Bay, Newfoundland, in 1610.

rescuing souls from purgatory, and restoring them to the enjoy-
ment of paradise.' The mystical properties of gold exercised their
powerful influence on the English mind. Lust for wealth and power
invaded the writing. 'I'll have them fly to India for gold', says
Marlowe's Doctor Faustus of the spirits he controls:

> Ransack the Ocean for orient pearl,
> And search all corners of the new-found world
> For pleasant fruits and princely delicates.

The mariners returned with the raw wealth of their experience
from which the poets cut the jewels of their imagery. For writing
itself showed a splendour not seen before, so that the very language
seemed like George Chapman's *Guiana*:

> whose rich feet are mines of gold,
> Whose forehead knocks against the roof of stars,
> Stands on her tiptoes at fair England looking.
>   (*De Guiana Carmen Epicum*)

The divinity of riches caused strange changes in men and art, a
power that was recognized in the opening to Ben Jonson's *Volpone*:

> Good morning to the day; and, next, my gold:
> Open the shrine, that I may see my saint.
> Hail the world's soul, and mine.

Marlowe, Chapman, Jonson—three men whose ambitions and
unruly, high-flown spirits matched those of the great plunderers
Hawkins and Drake. The former raided the resources of language
as boldly as the latter pirated the treasure ships of the Spaniards.
But the voyages opened up another, quieter vein of the imagination inspired more by Gilbert's geographical inquisitiveness than
by the rapacity of the sea-dogs. The plays of the time, Sir Philip
Sidney complained, were so bespattered with foreign places that
the audience was hard put to know where they were: 'you shall
have Asia of the one side, and Affrick of the other, and so many
other under-kingdoms, that the Player, when he cometh in, must
ever begin with telling where he is; or else the tale will not be con-
ceived.' Gascoigne, in his preface to Gilbert's *Discourse of a Discovery,* pictured the author in 1576, planning the north-west passage at his house in Limehouse with the maps and tables of Ortelius
by his side. And when Marlowe took Tamburlaine on his vast

journeys of conquest, he did so with the same Ortelius in his hand :

> Give me a map; then let me see how much
> Is left for me to conquer all the world.

With the voyages before him, what other material did a poet need for his imagination? 'But read the report of the worthy Western discoveries, by the said Sir Humfry Gilbert', Gabriel Harvey advised a fellow writer. Who in the past, Edmund Spenser inquired in the *Faerie Queene:*

> in venturous vessel measured
> The Amazons huge river now found true?
> Or fruitfullest Virginia who did ever view?

And did not the noble work of exploration increase the fame and power of England? Again, Humphrey Gilbert was the inspiration of the poet; he was the first, said Thomas Churchyard, who :

> all for countreys cause, and to enrich the same,
> Now do they hazard all they have.

Gilbert's bold motto had been *Quid Non*—Why Not?—and the possibilities opened up by his thoughts on colonization intrigued the mind. Even Chapman, for whom exploration was the pursuit of infinite riches, admired the idealism that put riches to the country's service. In *De Guiana* he commended the 'patrician spirits'—the true nationalists—

> That live not for yourselves, but to possess
> Your honour'd country of a general store.

Others, equally possessed by Gilbert's idealism, had a more generous vision of England's work in the new lands. Samuel Daniel, in his *Musophilus* published two years before the death of Elizabeth, saw England as the gentle civiliser :

> And who, in time, knows whither we may vent
> The Treasures of our tongue? To what strange shores
> This gain of our best glory shall be sent
> To enrich unknowing nations with our stores?
> What worlds in the yet unformed Occident
> May come refin'd with the accents that are ours?

In his will, Gilbert had also dimly perceived a golden age where the virtue and knowledge of Europe, released from the historical problems of the homeland, could establish the ideal commonwealth in foreign parts. Others, also seeking a golden age, saw colonization not so much as an extension of European power and influence, but rather as a corrective to the fiery temper and greedy itch of Europe; gentle natives with simple and uncorrupted ways would teach Europe how to live.

And when Amadas and Barlow brought the first news from Virginia in 1585, it seemed that this idyllic place might tempt the English colonists to live a life of quiet and natural justice. No doubt Shakespeare had both Gilbert and the Virginian venture in mind when he borrowed the words of Montaigne to describe the ideal state in the *Tempest:*

> All things in common nature should produce
> Without sweat or endeavour : treason, felony,
> Sword, pike, knife, gun, or need of any engine,
> Would I not have; but nature should bring forth
> Of its own kind, all foison, all abundance,
> To feed my innocent people.

But Shakespeare, so much wiser than Gilbert and so much aware of human frailty, knew that the dream of simple justice could not withstand the energy, greed and ambition of his contemporaries. 'You are gentlemen of brave mettle', says Gonzalo in the *Tempest,* explaining why the ideal would never work : 'you would lift the moon out of her sphere, if she would continue in it five weeks without changing.' It is a fitting epitaph to the impossible hopes of Sir Humphrey Gilbert.

8
Richard Hooker

ENGLISH RELIGION in the sixteenth century was a puzzle to the Christian world. Cardinal Allen, an Englishman banned from his homeland by his Catholicism, wrote at the end of the Tudor age that his country's inconstancy was its shame : 'We have had to our Prince a man who abolished the Pope's authority by his laws, and yet in other points kept the faith of his fathers; we have had a child who by the like laws abolished together with the Papacy the whole ancient religion; we have had a woman who restored both again and sharply punished Protestants; and lastly her Majesty that now is who by the like laws hath long since abolished both again, and now severely punished Catholics as the other did Protestants; and all these strange differences within the compass of thirty years.'

The Middle Ages were a time of high Christian endeavour and the Tudors, inheriting a part of this legacy, could not help but show their religion in their lives; but the manifestations seemed odd, inconsequential. Henry VII, the founder of the dynasty, was a simple, orthodox son of the Church. Three successive popes resisted his attempt to have Henry VI canonized, lest the King's naïvety should bring sainthood into disrepute. Henry VIII wrote on theology and for his work against Luther was proclaimed by the pope 'Defender of the Faith'; within a few years Henry had utterly repudiated the papal claims. Marillac, the French ambassador, was amazed that the King, in the same hour, could condemn three men to death for Protestant heresy and another three for speaking in favour of the Pope. Edward VI was a pious Reformer with an interest in theology; his half-sister Mary was the most rigorous of Catholics. Elizabeth amused herself with religious argument but showed little religious feeling. In the interests of the State she executed Catholic and Puritan impartially.

The true religion of the people was equally puzzling. Only his confessor knew that Wolsey, the proudest and most worldy of prelates, wore a hair shirt beneath his cardinal's silken robes. The noble piety of Sir Thomas More was an example to his time, yet the faith he gave to the inhabitants of his *Utopia* was a kind of deism : 'there is a certain Godly power unknown, everlasting, incomprehensible, inexplicable, far above the capacity and reach of man's work, dispersed throughout all the world, not in bigness but in virtue and power.' In the three years of his chancellorship, the humane, gentle More was no friend to heretics. In 1500 the English people were commended for their religious practice. The Venetian ambassador reported that 'they always hear Mass on Sunday in their parish church and give liberal alms', and he found the churches well furnished : 'there is not a parish church in the kingdom so mean as not to possess crucifixes, candlesticks, censers, patens, and cups of silver.' Yet some notable churches were put to strange use. Fair booths were set up in Exeter Cathedral, and St Paul's in London was the business place for merchants, lawyers, pickpockets and prostitutes. Another commentator feared that the rich decoration of the churches was but for show; 'men do it more for pomp and pride of this world to have a name and worship thereby in the country.' At the dissolution of the monsteries the same men were quick enough to strip the riches from the monastic churches.

The religion of the masses was for the most part a question of habit; and the English Church, even in the days before the Reformation, had acquired English habits. It acknowledged the papal jurisdiction, but England was far from Rome, and to the Pope and the Curia these northern islands were cold, inhospitable, unattractive. Almost free from Roman intervention, the English Church was hiddenly national. In 1351, in the reign of Edward III, the Statute of Provisors prevented the Pope from making appointments to English ecclesiastical positions; two years later the first Statute of Praemunire decreed that there should be no appeals beyond the realm. And the doctrinal arguments of the fourteenth century only encouraged the latent nationalism of the English Church. The reformer Wyclif demanded that local men be appointed to local offices, that the Scriptures be translated into English and the laity instructed in the vernacular tongue. Thomas Fuller, describing the burning of Wyclif's corpse by order of the Council of Constance, saw Wyclif as the inevitable precursor of the Reformation. The ashes were cast into the Swift; this brook led into the Avon, that into the Severn, and so by degrees to the ocean. 'And thus the ashes of Wyclif are the emblem of his doctrine, which is now dispersed all the world over.'

Nationalism lay hidden, but close to the surface, barely covered by old habits, old traditions, old objects of reverence. It was the conscious task of the Tudors to bring nationalism out, to tend it and strengthen it for the safety of the crown. In 1485 Henry VII came to the throne of a lawless country. The feudal barons were puffed up with independent power and ambition, the populace was turbulent. Henry packed his coffers by new taxes and used the money to establish a strong centralized administration; he broke the power of the old nobility, and he gave a new form and authority to Parliament. In all this he was helped by the ardent desire of a tired, impoverished nation for peace. But with the ghost of discord and rebellion so close behind, the monarchy was still uneasy. If the 'very and true commonweal' was to be founded in England, the Tudors needed some doctrine which made it a religious duty to obey their authority. Henry VIII, with an obscure but intuitive understanding of what was required, set about the fashioning of this doctrine. And the lucky tool that came to hand, enabling him to shape the country to his wishes, was the Protestant Reformation.

The Catholic Church was then, as it always had been, ripe for reform. The King could count on the hearty national prejudice of the English who for two hundred years had taken scant notice of the Pope. He had also the enthusiastic support of the landed and wealthy classes who coveted the possessions of the Church. Jean Bodin in France and Sir Thomas More in England, the greatest political thinkers of their time, both concluded that the sixteenth-century reformation in Church and State sprang from greed. 'When I consider and weigh in my mind all these commonwealths, which nowadays everywhere do flourish', More wrote in *Utopia,* 'so God help me, I can conceive nothing, but a certain conspiracy of rich men, procuring their own commodities under the name and title of the commonwealth.'

The time was right, then, for Henry VIII to proclaim himself the head of the native English Church. The dangers of this action came more from Henry's unstable and despotic character than from the opposition of the people. The English, then as now, were not theologians. They had no understanding of the arguments for papal supremacy; and since they did not love the Pope saw no reason why they should not change religious masters, putting their palpable, haughty and powerful King in the place of some obscure foreigner in Rome. When the Reform Parliament met in 1529 it had behind it not only the vague approval of the masses, but also a weight of argument, as tedious as it was long, proving that God had intended national kings to rule national churches. The Scriptures proved, said the *De Vera Differentia,* setting out the characteristic Protestant argument in 1534, that the Pope's claims were unfounded and that authority lay only in the prince. And Tyndale complained that the priest had stolen the power of the prince. 'Kings they are, but shadows; vain names and things idle, having nothing to do in the world but when our holy father needeth their help.' The title that Henry VIII assumed in the Acts of Supremacy was said to be merely the re-assertion of the ancient powers of the English monarchy. The power, said Bishop Gardiner, was there already, and Archbishop Cranmer agreed, saying that 'all Christian Princes have committed unto them immediately of God the whole cure of all their subjects, as well concerning the administration of God's Word for the cure of souls, as concerning the ministration of things political and civil governance'. That was the legal and ecclesiastical argument, and those who were too Catholic to be convinced by it were executed.

The Acts of Supremacy gave Henry what he needed. Obedience to the sovereign now became a religious duty, and the King felt safer from sedition and rebellion. And when that stroke of policy was done, Henry saw no necessity to go any further towards Protestantism. When he dissolved the monasteries in 1536, he was merely after their property; the dissolution implied no doctrinal change, and there were many good Catholics who wished to see the slack monastic orders rigorously shaken. Henry's reformation made so few alterations to the ordinary religious practice of the people that it might have passed almost unremarked but for the exceptional wilfulness and bestiality of the King's own conduct. The squalid affair with Anne Boleyn, which Henry used as the excuse for the break with Rome, was very much resented by the people. 'The king's grace', the mouths of rumour muttered in 1532, 'is ruled by one common stewed whore, Anne Boleyn, who makes all the spiritualty to be beggared and the temporalty too.' They called for the King to take back Queen Catherine, and when that silent, dignified lady, after the crowning of Anne, was reduced to princess-dowager and banished to Buckden, the crowd, in defiance of the royal proclamation, lined the way and saluted her respectfully as still the Queen. When Catherine died at Kimbolton, on 7th January 1536, Henry ordered the court to wear yellow and danced all night. 'God be praised,' he said, 'We are now free from all fear of war.'

The King's fear of opposition, his rage at being denied, his callous and intemperate character brought in a new age of pain and death. Cranmer and the bishops preached the King's supremacy from the pulpit, but the lay minister, Thomas Cromwell, was the King's vicar-general in spiritual matters, and the clergy took their orders from him. With his usual ruthless efficiency he sent spies and informers to sniff out contrary opinions. In April 1535 orders were given for the arrest of those who still recognized the jurisdiction of the Pope. Among the first to be taken in were the monks of Charterhouse in London, and of Sion in Middlesex. At the end of April they were condemned by a special commission under the Duke of Norfolk, and on 4th May six men were led out to execution. An astounded crowd, unused to such barbarity, saw their limbs chopped off, their chests ripped open and the spurting hearts torn out and ground into their faces. Faced with the possibility of such a death, most of the clergy very willingly and meekly followed the royal will. And the execution a month later of John Fisher, the saintly old bishop of Rochester, and of Sir Thomas More, the noblest Englishman of his age, convinced the country that the tyrant would have his way. For the rest of the century, religious argument in England, as on the continent, was carried on against the sombre music of the drum roll on the scaffold.

The reformation of Henry VIII was more an act of polity than an act of religion; it was a triumph of nationalism. The scriptural text from Corinthians, that 'the spiritual man judgeth all things; and he himself is judged by no man', was completely turned about. 'Lo, I have set thee this day over the nations, and over the kingdoms', Pope Pius V proudly quoted from Jeremiah when he attempted to depose Elizabeth in 1570. In England his words were as empty as the air, for the Tudors had made the Crown in Parliament the only governor of English life. The reform of church law which Cranmer drew up in the reign of Edward VI declared that it was for the sovereign to decide, in the last resort, what was heresy. The English position was summed up in 1583 by Sir Thomas Smith : 'Parliament legitimateth bastards, establisheth forms of religion, altereth weights and measures.' The State was supreme.

Religious questions are not solved by political acts. From the death of Henry VIII to the time of the religious settlement made by Elizabeth, the belief of Englishmen was confused and changeable. What Henry himself believed may only be guessed. At the bottom of his profound egotism perhaps there lay only a simple belief in the supremacy of his own will. He certainly had not made England Protestant, but his acts of national self interest and his defiance of the Pope agreed with the thinking of the European Reformation, and so were an invitation to Protestantism. Continental Reformers such as Bucer, Peter Martyr and Ochino were attracted to England; their disputations and their command of the Protestant arguments no doubt helped the English Church to become more Protestant under Edward VI. But in the muddled years after Henry the English episcopacy could include men like Bonner and Gardiner, supporters of the Acts of Supremacy but Catholics for all that, and men like Ridley and Hooper, Calvinists in all but name. Many good men, worried in conscience and harried by prying commissions and coercive Acts of Parliament, hardly knew what they were. And for those whose belief was capriciously individual there was always the possibility of martyrdom. Many good men changed their opinions as the theology of the Church swung to Protestantism under Edward VI and severely back to Catholicism under Mary. Mary, who like her grandfather Henry VII had a strong and simple piety, was forced by her father to sign a paper disavowing the Pope, declaring her mother's marriage incestuous and her own birth illegitimate. Elizabeth, who like her father Henry VIII looked on religion as a mere adjunct of state policy, pretended a devotion to Catholicism as long as her sister reigned.

In 1553, with the coronation of Mary, a true religious fervour intruded itself into the English confusion of religion with politics. The Queen was a Catholic and wished her realm to become Catholic once more. At first she was not intolerant; she asked her subjects to live together 'in quiet sort and Christian charity' avoiding the 'new found devilish terms of papist and heretic'. But her Catholic enthusiasm had appalling consequences. In the name of religion she seemed about to undo the independent national state which her father had so carefully created. Her chief adviser was the Emperor Charles V, and under his influence and from her own desire she made the calamitous decision to marry the detested foreigner, Philip II of Spain, despite the urgent appeal of Parliament that she should marry an Englishman. She had, after all, been treated extremely badly by the English, and supported her injured Spanish mother against her brutal English father, boasting, so the Venetian ambassador said, of her Spanish descent. At the thought of a Spanish king and a hated pope taking away the English liberties, Parliament and the country became thoroughly alarmed. Though she was warned by Wyatt's rebellion in 1554, Mary pressed forward the restoration of Catholicism. With an acquiescent Parliament, packed with her supporters, behind her, and encouraged by the grim orthodoxy of Philip, who firmly believed in the execution of heretics, Mary began the religious policy which sent nearly three hundred Protestants to their deaths in the four years of her reign, a catalogue of executions which Foxe's *Book of Martyrs* has never allowed English people to forget. She was the only Tudor who persecuted for faith and not for treason. It is a mark of her misunderstanding of her country and her people, that she should consider acts against the State hardly important and acts against belief as worthy of death, while her subjects thought differences of religion of no account, but acts against the State to be the ultimate sin. Mary caused one final blow to national pride. At the end of her reign England lost Calais, the last of her continental possessions, and the Queen was powerless to recapture it. When Mary died in November 1558 'all the churches in London did ring, and at night men did make bonfires and set tables in the street, and did eat and drink, and made merry for the new queen'.

In 1554, the year made ominous for Protestants by the marriage of Mary with Philip, Richard Hooker was born at Heavitree, Exeter. His parents were poor, sober citizens whose Reformed faith had been put to trial and strengthened by the old beliefs, as much conservative as Catholic, of the West. In the western rising of 1549 against Edward's Act of Uniformity and his new prayer book, the Catholic rebels of north Devon had besieged Exeter for five weeks. And the start of Mary's reign promised more afflictions for western Protestants. So the household of the Hookers was full of earnest devotion. The Bible was ever at hand, either in Tyndale's translation or in the impressive large folio of the Great Bible, first issued in 1539 to satisfy the need for the Scriptures in English and soon the favourite reading of the people. Its sonorous language was not only incorporated into the Book of Common Prayer for use in every church, but also found its way into the ordinary speech and greatly enriched the prose of the age. Young Richard flourished in this devout air; for though he was a country lad in looks, his gentle biographer Izaak Walton described him as 'sanguine, with a mixture of choler'; he was a natural student and wise beyond his years : 'his motion was slow even in his youth, and so was his speech, never expressing an earnestness in either of them, but an humble gravity suitable to the aged.'

To his masters he was 'a little wonder' and lapped up knowledge like a hungry kitten at a bowl of milk. His parents had no means to continue his education and had intended him to become an apprentice. But when it was seen how well the child did, a prosperous uncle, John Hooker, came to his aid, paid for the continuation of his schooling and then, in the first years of Elizabeth's reign, brought the boy to the attention of John Jewel, the bishop of Salisbury. Jewel was a strong Protestant who had fled from England during Mary's reign. He was impressed by the gravity and the learning of the lad and perhaps saw him as a hopeful recruit to the Anglican ministry. In 1567, through the influence of the bishop, Hooker entered Corpus Christi College, Oxford.

Jewel died in 1571, and with the loss of his patron Hooker feared for the future. But his quality had been noted; the head of his college assured him that his place was secure, and Sandys, the bishop of London, having heard of his excellence from Jewel, appointed young Hooker as tutor to his son Edwin. The peaceful rotation of the academic year at Oxford absorbed Hooker. Younger students gathered round him, in particular Edwin Sandys and George Cranmer, the influential friends of his life. At nineteen be became a scholar of Corpus Christi, and at twenty-three a fellow. Oxford and Cambridge had always been the great breeding ground for churchmen, and Hooker, doubtless as his patrons intended, moved easily from the study of the classics and languages to the study of religion, applying a rational, lucid and temperate mind to the problems of faith : 'the Scripture', he said, 'was not writ to beget disputations and pride, and opposition to government; but charity and humility, moderation, obedience to authority, and peace to mankind.' In 1580 he took orders and became a modest, obedient member of the Anglican priesthood.

Hooker was not a contentious or a proud man. At the age of twenty-six he had done well enough; the obscure rewards of university life, surrounded by books and pupils, would have suited his small ambition. The first sign that he was to be drawn out of the university quietness came in 1581 when he was appointed to preach at St Paul's Cross in London. To preach this sermon, in the open air before a large, critical audience, was a considerable honour for a young man. The Elizabethan public came to the sermon to be entertained as well as instructed and expected both keen argument and a lively performance. Such preachers as 'silver-tongued Smith' at St Clement Danes and Clappam of Foster Lane with his 'sour look, but a good spirit, bold, and sometimes bluntly witty', or Egerton at Blackfriars with his great congregation 'specially of women', were popular London figures. Resounding sermons had made reputations. Jewel, Hooker's first patron, had a famous success at St Paul's Cross in 1560. The appointment of Hooker indicated that the eye of the church hierarchy was upon him. When he came down from Oxford for the sermon he lodged at the house of John Churchman in Watling Street and there met the family which was to become so important in his life, providing him with his future wife and the home in which to begin his great labour.

With the mark of favour upon him Hooker returned to Oxford while his friends, chief among whom were the Sandys, father and son, looked for his preferment. Church affairs move at a leisurely pace; in December 1584 Hooker was given the benefice of Drayton Beauchamp, near Aylesbury, but this was only a temporary appointment before he took up the Mastership of the Temple in February 1585. It is likely that Hooker was an absentee vicar of Drayton Beauchamp. The practice was a common abuse of the time. 'What do you patrons?' Latimer had complained as early as 1550. 'Sell your benefices, or give them to your servants for their service, for keeping of hounds or hawks, for making of your gardens.' Hooker's friend and pupil Edwin Sandys was absentee prebend of Wetwang in Yorkshire for twenty years while he was a lawyer at the Middle Temple and then M.P. for Plympton in

Devon. Hooker himself defended the practice on the grounds that servants of the Church who were scholars or writers could not continue their work without an income, which they would not have without a benefice. And this was exactly the kind of church service which the authorities had marked out for Richard Hooker. He was to become a controversialist for the Anglican Church.

When Elizabeth came to the throne her first concern was to restore the absolute authority of the Tudor State which Mary's Catholicism had lessened to some degree. She herself was naturally a Protestant; to be otherwise would have been an admission of illegitimacy. But though she made a certain show of religion, suiting her action to the company, most observers thought her either sceptical or indifferent. At the end of her reign one of her countrymen boldly declared that she was 'an atheist and a maintainer of atheism'. The most unfanatical and cautious of women, she was not intolerant, and the religious changes she made were done steadily and slowly. Her instinct was to take the middle course. 'There are three notable differences of religion in the land, the two extremes whereof are the Papist, and the Puritan, and the religious Protestant obtaining the mean.'

But theological questions were of little importance to Elizabeth. Her chief aim was to follow the path found out by her father and make the English Church solely responsible for its own faith, ritual and organization. A national Church was but a part of the commonwealth, and the only legislator for the commonwealth was the Crown acting through Parliament. Parliament became the only true interpreter of the Scriptures and the religious duty of the subject was to obey or be convicted of treason. The faith which Queen and Parliament ordained for the people in 1559 was rather more Protestant than the settlement of Henry VIII. The Mass was called a 'blasphemous fable and dangerous deceit'; transubstantiation, which Henry's Parliament of 1539 had defended even unto the death penalty, was 'repugnant to the plain words of Scripture'; and purgatory and the cult of the saints were now 'fond things, vainly invented'. Elizabeth's Act of Supremacy asserted the jurisdiction of the Crown in spiritual matters and put the Bishop of Rome firmly in his place as 'bishop of that one see and diocese and never yet well able to govern the same'. The same Act reminded the clergy that they ought, 'specially and before others', to be

9 SIR HUMPHREY GILBERT

10 RICHARD HOOKER

obedient to their sovereign. The English hierarchy learnt the lesson well. 'For this is our doctrine', declared Bishop Jewel, 'that every soul of what calling soever he be—be he monk, be he preacher, be he prophet, be he apostle—ought to be subject to Kings and magistrates.' And Aylmer, Bishop of London, wrote to Sir Christopher Hatton that 'I trust not of God but of my sovereign which is God's lieutenant and so another God unto me'. With this submission, Elizabeth was content.

Queen and Parliament were satisfied, but fervent men were not. Elizabeth's settlement was so obviously a part of social policy, to secure the power of the monarchy and to prevent unrest, that no man possessed by true religious enthusiasm could be satisfied with it. At Mary's death the Catholic opposition diminished. Many Catholics went abroad and those who remained at home were caught between their loyalty to the Queen, which as patriotic Englishmen they felt most strongly, and their loyalty to the Pope who in 1570 excommunicated Elizabeth and released her subjects from their allegiance. The hapless Edmund Campion, a Jesuit missioner executed for treason in 1581, cried from the scaffold that 'your queen is my queen'. It gradually appeared to Englishmen that Catholicism was not so much a religion as a treasonable activity intent on deposing the Queen and setting up in her stead a sinister continental tyranny.

The greatest challege to Elizabeth's settlement came not from the discomforted Catholics, but from those on the left wing of the Reformation—Anabaptists, Calvinists and the like—generally known in England under the collective title of 'Puritans', a group angrily divided among themselves but united in thinking that Elizabeth's faith was too secular and not radically different from Catholicism. John Knox had spurned the settlement of 1559, and had denounced Cecil's 'carnal wisdom and worldly policy'. The thoroughgoing doctrine of Knox was equally repugnant to Elizabeth's accommodating bishops who supported the authority of the Crown. 'God save us', wrote Archbishop Parker, 'from such a visitation as Knox has attempted in Scotland; the people to be the orderers of things!' The Puritans retorted by rejecting the episcopacy itself as unlicensed by Scripture and as actually anti-Christian. From there they went on to attack most of the outward signs of worship, the ritual of the service, the dress of the clergy, the fast-days and holidays, the use of choirs and organs—all these

L

were marks of idolatry. They condemned as 'things stained with superstition', Hooker wrote, 'our prayers, our sacraments, our times and places of public meeting together for the worship and service of God, our marriages, our burials, our functions, elections and ordinations ecclesiastical, almost whatever we do in the exercise of our religion according to laws for that purpose established'. Most worrying of all to Elizabeth and the supporters of her settlement, the Puritans, like the Catholics, denied the royal supremacy. Though they claimed to be loyal subjects, they could not understand how laws devised in Parliament should make them go against their clear reading of the Bible.

The English Church was a child of the Reformation and so there were many among the English clergy who held Puritan or non-conformist views. Archbishop Grindal was easy on nonconforming ministers so that his successor, Whitgift, complained to Lord Burghley that the bishops, instead of turning them out, 'offend rather, the most of them, on the contrary part'. Puritans were also well entrenched in the universities, particularly at Cambridge where Cartwright and Travers stirred up the people to establish a blessed church republic such as Calvin had built in Geneva and Knox in Scotland. Two Puritan *Admonitions* in 1571 called the attention of Parliament to the faults of the church system which Parliament itself had devised in 1559. Soon Puritan opinions had infiltrated even into Parliament and the attack on the bishops was delivered from the floor of the House. The royal supremacy, the whole edifice of the English Church, was shaken. 'To which end', wrote pious Izaak Walton in his life of Hooker, 'there were many that wandered up and down and were active in sowing discontents and seditions, by venomous and secret murmurings, and a dispersion of scurrilous pamphlets against the Church and State; but especially against the Bishops; by which means, together with venomous and indiscreet sermons, the common people become so fanatic, as to believe the Bishops to be Anti-Christ, and the only obstructers of God's discipline!'

The task of repelling the Puritan's persistent attacks rested largely on John Whitgift, at first Bishop of Worcester and after 1583 Archbishop of Canterbury. He was such a stout defender of the Elizabethan orthodoxy that the Queen called him 'her little black husband'. His position was that the English Church contained 'all points of religion necessary to salvation', and that matters beyond these essentials of faith, such as forms and ceremonies, were 'things indifferent' which a national Church had the right to determine. And this determination should be done by the governors of the State, for Church and State were one. 'I perceived no such distinction', he wrote in his *Defence of the Answer,* 'of the commonwealth and the Church that they should be counted as it were two several bodies governed with divers laws and divers magistrates.' Since he thus assumed what the Puritans vehemently denied, his arguments were not convincing to them. Nor were the writings of other Anglican apologists such as Bancroft and Bilson any more persuasive. When Whitgift became archbishop in 1583 he took energetic practical measures against the nonconformists. Licenses to preach were withheld from those who would not conform; commissions in London and under Sandys, by now Archbishop of York, in the North examined the beliefs of the ministers; and, at the orders of the Privy Council, a censorship was put on Puritan propaganda, and illicit presses were suppressed. But censorship rarely works, then as now; the Puritan printers, driven underground, soon showered the bishops with the fierce, joyous vituperation of the Marprelate Tracts. The Puritans could only be beaten down by a cool, learned, authoritative defence of the English Church, and in search of this the bishops came to Richard Hooker.

The chance to recruit Hooker to the fray against the Puritans came in 1585 when Dr Alvey, the Master of the Temple, died and left the succession likely to fall upon Walter Travers, one of the most vehement Puritans who was already a lecturer at the Temple. Archbishop Sandys, always the good friend and patron, immediately proposed Hooker for the Mastership, a suggestion taken up by Archbishop Whitgift. And these two powerful ecclesiastics easily overrode the objections of Travers's supporters, even though they had gained the ear of Burghley. The objections of Hooker himself had also to be overcome, the extent of whose gentle ambition it was to live and study in the country and 'eat that bread which he might more properly call his own, in privacy and quietness'. Finally, he gave way and was installed in the Mastership in February 1585.

The theological battle was now joined between Hooker and Travers, between the Anglican and Puritan, so that it was said at the Temple that 'the forenoon sermon spake Canterbury, and the afternoon Geneva'. Travers was a formidable, and courteous, opponent who made his reputation some years before with his *Book of Discipline*. He had entered the controversy at about the time that Whitgift had left it; and since that time the Anglican argument had languished for want of a champion. The controversial debates between the two preachers at the Temple marked the arrival of the new champion, the successor to Jewel and Whitgift. Within two years Hooker had triumphed over his rival. Travers was sent to Trinity College, Dublin, where his Puritan views did not bar him from an academic position.

The defeat of Travers was only the beginning of Hooker's great work for the Church. The leaders of the Church, both among the clergy and the laymen, had decided on a comprehensive attack against the Puritans. A campaign was started in the House of Commons to harry nonconformists by law, a campaign which culminated in the Conventicle Act of 1593 and the execution of Barrow, Greenwood and Penry in the same year. This legislation was to be accompanied by a grand defence of the English Church, and Hooker, his arguments sharpened by the match with Travers, was given the task of writing this. Perhaps he began the task as early as 1585. The witty and lively scorn with which the Puritan pamphleteer who went under the name of Martin Marprelate had dismissed Dr Bridges's huge, worthy and unreadable *Defence of the Church of England* in 1588 made a more satisfactory defence essential. The preparation of the Conventicle Act made publication necessary by 1593. Hooker set about the composition of the *Laws of Ecclesiastical Polity.*

When Hooker came to the Temple in 1585, a learned scholar in his early thirties with a shy and gentle disposition, he settled immediately into the solid comfort of John Churchman's house in Watling Street. Churchman was a prosperous member of the Merchant Taylors' Company, and in his house Hooker found the small considerations that eased his scholarly and withdrawn life. The Churchman servants saw to his wants, and the Churchman ladies kept a tender eye on the quiet bachelor to such good effect that Hooker married the daughter, Joan, in February 1588. She brought him a dowry of £700 and bore him four daughters. In spite of the recriminations heaped upon Joan by Hooker's early biographers, the marriage seems to have been tranquil and happy. When his duties at the Temple were done, well cared for in the quietness of his wife's home, with the active assistance of Edwin Sandys and his friends, Hooker had the first four books of *Ecclesiastical Polity* ready for publication in 1593.

'Hooker would not have been', Cardinal Newman wrote, 'but for the existence of Catholics and Puritans, the defeat of the former and the rise of the latter.' *Ecclesiastical Polity* was written to answer the Puritan criticism of the English Church and to show that the Puritan refusal to conform to the church laws of the land was rationally unjustified. The first four books were published in 1593, the fifth in 1597; the sixth, seventh and eighth books were roughly completed before Hooker's death in 1600, but may not have come down to us as Hooker wrote them.

Hooker's work is marked with the modesty, reason and judiciousness of the man. The tone is always sweet and calm : 'I am not hasty', he wrote, 'to apply sentences of condemnation.' And the easy, flowing writing is a model of Elizabethan prose, one of the few books that can be read with pleasure despite its portentous subject. In his English way he was cautious and practical, looking not for the ideal, but for what was possible. 'In polity', he wrote, 'as well ecclesiastical as civil, there are and will be always evils which no art of man can cure, breaches and leaks more than man's wits hath hands to stop.' He distrusted large generalities and sought exact cases, for 'they that walk in darkness know not whither they go'.

Hooker was not primarily a theologian; as the title of his book implies, his work had as much to do with politics as with faith. He was concerned with reason, human nature and law. After considering the ecclesiastical laws of England, he found them not inconsistent with the law of God revealed in the Scriptures. It was part of his task to show that in England commonwealth and Church were one. After a full and steady examination he reached the required conclusion : 'We hold, that seeing there is not any man of the Church of England, but the same man is also a member of the commonwealth; nor any man a member of the commonwealth which is not also of the Church of England . . . no person appertaining to the one can be denied to be also of the other.' And again, more succinctly, 'with us one society is both Church and commonwealth'. If the validity of the argument be admitted, then it follows inescapably that Parliament, the governor of the commonwealth, has the right to govern the Church : 'to define of our church's regiment, the parliament of England hath competent authority'.

The work, which made no money, brought Hooker fame instead. At the request of Clement VIII the first book was turned into Latin, and when the Pope had read it he was amazed : 'There is no learning', he is reported to have said, 'that this man hath not searched into, nothing too hard for his understanding : this man indeed deserves the name of an author.' Alas, the Puritans were less impressed; for Hooker was talking about politics and they were talking about faith, and the two never met. Despite the stately elegance of the exposition, the *Ecclesiastical Polity* showed the same flaw as the works of Jewel, Whitgift and all those apologists who put the stability of the commonwealth above the calls of faith. In asserting the right of Parliament to legislate for the Church, Hooker, like the others, assumed what he had to prove. But the very reasonableness of Hooker's writing echoed the reasonableness and political good sense of Elizabeth's religious compromise. While the countries on the continent were engaged in the ferocious battles of the Wars of Religion, comparatively few people died for their faith in England. After the revolt of the northern Earls in 1569, many Catholics were executed, but the Tudors had always used a heavy hand against rebellion. Jesuit missioners were caught and condemned for treason, and several Puritans died under the penal laws. The Elizabethan State was sacrosanct and beyond criticism, and this was perceived even by those Englishmen who suffered for their opposition to the state religion. They went to the scaffold declaring themselves patriotic Englishmen and loyal subjects of the Queen.

In 1591 Hooker gave up the Mastership of the Temple. He exchanged benefices with Nicholas Baldgay, rector of Boscombe in Wiltshire, and was also made prebend of Netheravon. Once more it seems he held these positions *in absentia,* for there is no record of his attendance at either place. And at this time he most needed to be free in London; his great book was coming into shape, and his counsellors and advisers among the church leaders were daily at his apartments pressing the work forward. When the first four books of *Ecclesiastical Polity* were ready and printed, Hooker was at last allowed to retire to the country quietness that he had always wanted, and there to finish his work at a more leisurely pace. In 1595 he became parson of Bishopsbourne, and spent the rest of his short life among the pleasant Kentish fields, three miles from Canterbury.

The shy scholar was an exemplary priest. He had not been at Bishopsbourne a year, Walton wrote, 'but his books, and the innocency and sanctity of his life became so remarkable, that many turned out of the road, and others—scholarly especially—went purposely to see the man'. They saw an obscure, harmless man in a coarse gown, small and stooped with 'his face full of heat-pimples, begot by his inactivity and sedentary life'. His uneventful life was not without its small tragedies; both his sons, Richard and Edwin, died in infancy. But in the handsome parsonage at Bishopsbourne he wrote and studied and went the placid rounds of the country parish priest.

'The life of a pious clergyman', Hooker used to say, 'was visible rhetoric; and so convincing, that the most godless men did yet secretly wish themselves like those of the strictest lives.' The duties of the parish priest were fully and clearly laid down in the new ordinances of the Anglican Church. On Sunday, Morning Prayer was at 7 a.m., followed by Communion, and in the early evening before the light failed, there was Evening Prayer. The priest wore 'a comely surplice with sleeves' and was to possess a cover for the paten and a communion cup, both of silver. He needed also certain books, in particular 'the Book of Common Prayer with the new Kalendar, a Psalter, the English Bible in the largest volume, the two tomes of the Homilies, and the Paraphrases of Erasmus translated into English'. The priest had a duty to preach, and Hooker did so every Sunday. 'His sermons were neither long nor earnest, but uttered with a grave zeal and an humble voice : his eyes always fixed on one place, to prevent imagination from wandering; insomuch, that he seemed to study as he spake.' With careful attention, he taught the catechism, watched the attendance at communion, regulated the singing (avoiding overuse of the organ which was considered too Catholic), warned the slack and irreverent, and tolled the bell for the dead. He saw that unmarried mothers made a public confession of their fault before the congregation, he supervised the churchwardens, and on Rogation Days walked the bounds of his parish with his parishioners; 'in which perambulation he would usually express more pleasant discourse than at other times, and would then always drop some loving and facetious observations to be remembered against the next year, especially by the boys and young people.'

And the duties of the priest extended beyond the church and into every corner of the parish. Education and charity were in the care of the church. Priest and churchwardens were responsible for schoolmasters : were they licensed, loyal and well-behaved? Did they have the grammar book of Henry VIII, and the Latin catechism of Elizabeth? Priest and churchwardens were also the supervisors of hospitals and almshouses, and Hooker, as Walton relates, was 'diligent to enquire who of his parish were sick, or any ways distressed, and would often visit them, unsent for'. He reconciled quarrels and prevented law-suits; he gave advice and consolation, 'insomuch, that as he seemed in his youth to be taught of God, so he seemed in this place to teach his precepts as Enoch did, by walking with him in all holiness and humility, making each day a step towards a blessed eternity'. His own conduct was austere and self-denying. He observed the fast days strictly, and in Ember Week took the key of the church door and locked himself in for several hours a day.

In the winter of 1600, after about five years in his parish, Hooker caught a cold journeying by water from London to Gravesend. Though he was not yet old, being only forty-six, his health did not recover. He could not sleep and then lost his appetite so that 'he seemed to live some intermitted weeks by the smell of meat only'. Feeling that his end was near, he gave all his time to the still incomplete *Ecclesiastical Polity*; in his last sickness his constant enquiry was whether his books and papers were safe. When he was assured that they were, he replied, 'Then it matters not; for no other loss can trouble me.' He knew very well that his book was the unique achievement of his quiet, orderly and obscure life. He died on 2nd November 1600.

It has been said that, from the point of view of religion, the Elizabethan settlement settled nothing. 'Now and ever', wrote Cardinal Allen in 1584, 'when the superiority temporal hath the pre-eminence and the spiritual is but accessory, dependent and wholly upholden of the other, error in faith is little accounted of.' The Queen wished it that way. Knowing the wide divergence of religious opinion among her subjects, buffeted by half a century of controversy, she cast the net as wide as possible. The state Church had no distinctive doctrine or theology, unclear laws and little order. It was designed this way so as to catch as many different views as possible. For a clergyman to conform to it was not difficult; one must sign certain papers when compelled to do so by the bishop, read parts of the prayer-book, wear a surplice occasionally, and say nothing out loud against the royal supremacy. Indeed, the doctrine of the royal supremacy was the one certain doctrine of the English Church.

Such a scheme could never satisfy religious temperaments for long, and by the end of Elizabeth's reign men of strong faith were already in revolt, moving towards either the Protestantism of Calvin or Knox, or a kind of Anglican Catholicism. But in the early days of the Queen's reign, the reasonable Elizabethan compromise had the admirable effect of keeping fierce religious passions damped down, and so England avoided the horrific religious bloodshed which the continent of Europe witnessed in these years. The Tudors, in particular Henry VIII and Elizabeth, had given England nationalism as its new religion, and in this patriotic age when England at last blossomed into a land whose enterprise and spirit matched any in Europe, most Englishmen were content with the new Tudor faith.

And it may also be said that Hooker's *Ecclesiastical Polity*, as a religious document, was as unsatisfactory as the religious settlement. But it had the same reasonable virtues. In his easy, lucid way, Hooker pointed out that the beliefs of the English Church were not inconsistent with primitive Christianity, and that the good man was as likely to be saved there as anywhere. He also pointed out that, for better or worse, there was a particular relationship between Church and State in England, and that this was not to the disadvantage of the Church. His examination of this aspect, practical, shrewd and sympathetic, was the part of his work that his successors turned to. His mark is upon most later thinkers who consider the English polity and the bond between citizen and State. To have been forerunner and teacher to Hobbes, Locke and Hume is one part of his fame; to have been an ideal example of the Elizabethan clergyman is the other, and quieter part.

9
Sir Philip Sidney

THE DAWN OF a new age breaks with grief and questionings. The sixteenth century in England saw civil disturbance and religious strife, bodies at the gallows, the axe ringing on the block; violence on the roads, thriving crime, the towns bursting and pestilent; the poor dispossessed, the rising gentry rapacious, the great consumed by greed and ambition. 'I set this down', wrote the priest John Gerard after the torture inflicted on him in 1597, 'in this last age of a dying and a despairing world.' Geoffrey Fenton lived his life in 'seasons so perilous and conspiring'. Men blind to everything but the pain of the present lamented the passing of a golden antiquity. 'We have fallen into the barren age of the world', wrote a contemporary of Shakespeare, Bacon and Raleigh; 'there is general sterility.' A few of deeper judgment saw the real virtues of the time. Gabriel Harvey in a letter to Edmund Spenser spoke truly of the past 'when all things were rude and imperfect in comparison of the exquisite finesses and delicacy that we are grown into at these days'. And he continued: 'England never had more honourable minds, more adventurous hearts, more valorous heads or more excellent wits than of late.' Nothing bore out his thesis so well as the life of Sir Philip Sidney.

Sidney felt the uneasiness of the age; it was, he said, one 'that resembles a bow too long bent, it must be unstrung or it will break'. But the task he imposed upon himself was affirmation of life. He would have wished for no better epitaph than the words taken from his own *Arcadia*: 'We have lived, and loved to be good to ourselves and others: our souls, which are put into the stirring earth of our bodies, have achieved the cause of their hither coming. They have known, and honoured with knowledge, the cause of their creation, and to many men (for in this time, place and fortune, it is lawful for us to speak gloriously) it hath been behoveful that we should live.' Many, from the greatest to the poorest, felt justified and enheartened by the example of Sidney's life—from William the Silent to the thirsty wounded soldier at Zutphen, from the unlucky poet Edmund Spenser to the least citizen that bowed the head to Sidney's funeral procession.

Philip Sidney was born at Penshurst on 30th November 1554. His ancestry was one of mixed fortunes; for while his father Sir Henry was a favoured courtier whom Holinshed commended for 'his forwardness in all good actions', his mother Mary was a Dudley, a member of a family noted for greed and ambition. Her grandfather, the most hated minister of Henry VII, had been executed by Henry VIII; her father, the Duke of Northumberland, had in the year before Philip's birth tried to steal the throne from Mary Tudor and had in his turn been executed for it. It is a mark of Philip's hopeful acceptance of his lot that he gloried in his blood. Though he was by his father's side 'of ancient and well-esteemed and well-matched gentry', he wrote that his 'chiefest honour is to be a Dudley'. His godparents were the Duchess of Northumberland and the Queen's new husband, Philip of Spain, for whom the child was named. Watched over by a traitor's widow and a cold alien prince, the boy was given an equivocal introduction to the world.

In the gentle Kentish land at Penshurst, later celebrated by Ben Jonson, young Philip spent his first years with his mother :

> Thou hast thy orchard fruit, thy garden flowers
> Fresh as the air, and new as are thy hours.

His father, who in the reigns of Edward and Mary was 'the paragon of the Court by reason of the many good gifts God had bestowed on him', in the new reign of Elizabeth was still employed by the government, because of his honesty and diligence, though the Queen never showed him any personal favour. Between two terms of administration in Ireland, Sir Henry became in 1560 Lord President of the Welsh Marches and governed his territory from Ludlow Castle. Philip came from Kent to join his father and was sent to the nearby free grammar school at Shrewsbury. The boy was fortunate in his schooling, for when he entered Shrewsbury in 1564 the headmaster was Thomas Ashton, a scholar of reputation from Trinity College, Cambridge. And the headmaster was fortunate to receive such an apt pupil. Fulke Greville, Philip's lifelong friend and later his biographer, who entered Shrewsbury on the same day, gave an account of the studious young Sidney : 'His talk ever of knowledge, and his very play tending to enrich his mind, so as even his teachers found something in him to observe and learn above that which they had usually read or taught. Which eminence by nature and industry made his worthy father style Sir Philip in my hearing (though I unseen) *lumen familiae suae.*'

It was apparent at an early age that Philip had great ability; at the age of twelve he was writing to his father in both Latin and French. But Sir Henry demanded more than mere book learning in his eldest child. Like most cultivated men of his time, he had before him an ideal of courtly behaviour which he had pieced together out of Castiglione's famous *Il Cortegiano,* out of various courtesy books, and from Renaissance works written as far apart as Spain and Poland. Like many of his time, he knew the general aim of this education, but was not very explicit on the actual elements to be taught. In a letter to his son in 1566 he recommended diligence, obedience, humility, and a care for health and fitness; he gave little practical advice except to exercise 'without peril to your bones or joints', and to learn how to take wine 'lest being enforced to drink upon the sudden you should find yourself inflamed'. But the first principle of education, as the authorities conventionally agreed, was a due reverence and humility before God. 'From God only', said Sir Thomas Elyot, one of the first Englishmen to write on the training of gentlemen, 'proceedeth all honour'.

No doubt Philip Sidney took his father's admonition to heart and accomplished what Sir Henry had hoped for. With his fine critical intelligence, he judged his progress as he went along; and when, years later, his younger brother Robert in his turn asked Philip for advice on education, he was able to amplify for the young man the ideal which Sir Henry had set for him. 'Your purpose is', he wrote, 'being a gentleman born, to furnish yourself with the knowledge of such things as may be serviceable to your country and fit for your calling.' In particular, he advised Robert to study arithmetic and geometry, to acquire an easy but not pedantic command of Latin, take a delight in music and practise it often, to exercise horsemanship, to learn to write a better hand, and lastly to 'take care of your diet, and consequently of your complexion'.

In his fourteenth year Philip Sidney went to Christ Church, Oxford, a precocious, sober young Protestant. At university, he continued his easy academic triumphs and gave much time to the study of Aristotle. 'For though translations are made almost daily', he explained later to Hubert Languet, 'still I suspect they do not declare the meaning of the author plainly or aptly enough.' At this time also he came to the attention of William Cecil, and the Queen's first minister was duly impressed. 'Your Philip is here', he wrote to Sir Henry in January 1569, 'in whom I take more comfort than I do openly utter for avoiding of wrong interpretation. He is worthy to be loved, and so I do love him as he were my son.' Emboldened by this, Sir Henry proposed a marriage between his son and Cecil's daughter, Anne. But the Sidneys were poor and the Cecils never allowed affection to stand in the way of their ambition; Anne was married to the unruly but rich Earl of Oxford. Sidney did not stay long at Oxford and left without a degree. Perhaps it was the taste of life about the court which pulled him away; in any case his aristocratic temperament could not have liked the old-fashioned, provincial world of dusty books at Oxford, which the famous Italian philosopher Giordano Bruno condemned for its pedantic ignorance and conceit joined to rustic rudeness. To continue his education, Sidney wished to see something of the world outside England, and in May 1572 the Queen granted him a licence to go abroad for two years 'for his attaining the knowledge of foreign languages'.

Schoolboy brilliance counted for little in the great world; to men of affairs Sidney was still a callow youth. His uncle, the Earl of Leicester, sent him to Walsingham in Paris with a recommendation and an explanation : 'He is young and raw, and no doubt shall find those countries and the demeanours of the people somewhat strange unto him; and therefore your good advice and counsel shall greatly behove him for his better direction.' But the qualities of his mind joined to the charm of his youth, his debonair manner and athletic presence, soon captivated the French. He had a natural feeling for languages (except for German whose rough inelegance offended his ear); his friend Languet could find no fault in his French, and his companion Bryskett noted that the French courtiers liked both the wit and the fluency of his conversation. For the aristocratic young Englishman foreign travel served a double purpose : he looked at governments and met politicians as a preparation for public service in his own land; and he studied Renaissance thought and literature in the countries of their birth, for the full development of his own mind. In Paris, in the summer of 1572, Sidney met such men as Henry of Navarre, the future king of France, and de l'Hôpital, the tolerant and judicious *politique*; he also sought out the Protestant culture of the French Reformation, and talked with Ramus, the philosopher, du Bartas, the dullest of poets, and Hubert Languet, humanist and scholar. Languet was particularly drawn to Sidney and made himself the mentor of the dashing youth. In August Sidney witnessed in Paris the slaughter of St Bartholomew, and this massacre of the Huguenots impressed on Sidney's young mind the value of Languet's sober Protestant morality. In his later verse he acknowledged the debt to his master, praising Languet for :

> faithful heart, clean hands, and mouth as true :
> With his sweet skill my skilless youth he drew,
> To have a feeling taste of Him that sits
> Beyond the heaven, far more beyond our wits.

In the lurid days after St Bartholomew, Walsingham sent Sidney out of France. He went to join Languet in Frankfurt and then followed the Huguenot to the Imperial Court in Vienna. For some months Sidney travelled in Germany, Austria and Hungary, confirming at each step his detestation of Catholicism, meeting scholars, improving his command of classical literature, and learning Protestant ethics from the high-minded correspondence of Languet. The journeys were pleasant, the company distinguished —he met, among others, the man who first brought tulips to Europe from Constantinople, and the man who established the text of Aristotle—but for the young Englishman something was missing in the austere northern airs. The wicked vitality, the resplendent history, the pure art of Italy summoned him; and despite the protests of worthy Languet, who feared for his Protestant virtue, at the end of 1573 Sidney set out for Venice.

Venice did not please him and nor, entirely, did the Italians. 'For the men you shall have there,' he later warned his brother, 'although some indeed are excellently learned, yet are they all given to so counterfeit learning, as a man shall learn of them more false grounds of things, than in any place else that I do know.' Some things, he admitted, they did well, such as fencing and horsemanship; and since these were among the attributes of a gentleman Sidney studied them. To the relief of Languet, Sidney moved from the decadence of Venice to the sobriety of Padua, to study moral philosophy and politics at the famous university. These serious matters took most of his time; at least he has left few opinions on lighter subjects. He deprecated the opulent architecture, but was silent on the other arts. The evidence of profound Italian influence is only apparent in his writings, in *Astrophel and Stella* and in *Arcadia*. In 1574, just before his twentieth birthday, he rejoined Languet in Vienna; and in the spring of the next year returned to England.

Sidney came back, said Thomas Drant in a poem to Leicester, 'praised by all the world'. He was something new in cultured English society—the Protestant chevalier. Grace and good looks he already had, with auburn hair and delicate features resembling his sister's. 'If I were to find a fault in it,' wrote Aubrey, 'methinks 'tis not masculine enough.' Yet Aubrey added that 'he was a person of great courage'. Fulke Greville said that Sidney was from his earliest years grave and composed, sound masters at Shrewsbury and Oxford had made him learned; manners and social graces he had learnt from Castiglione, his athletic body had been trained on horse and in the tiltyard by Pugliano. And he had taken his ideals of morality and justice from Languet and other Protestant mentors. He was, as the famous Dutch jurist Lipsius later said, 'the flower of England'.

His birth, his training, his Protestant idealism, his instruction abroad, all naturally inclined him to seek service at court. His chief ends, wrote Greville, were 'above all things the honour of his Maker, and the service of his prince or country'. His ambition was encouraged by Languet who knew that Sidney at court would be a firm opponent of Catholicism and Spanish power. Languet advised him to cultivate Lord Burghley : 'he is fond of you, and will make everything easier for you.' But despite the affection of Burghley, and despite the support of his uncle Leicester, Sidney was sharply checked by the realities of Elizabeth's rule. His handsome and gallant presence was welcomed for the lighter business at court. Soon after his return he accompanied the Queen on one of her stately progresses, to his uncle's castle at Kenilworth and then to Lichfield where his father, Sir Henry, was admitted to the Privy Council before being hastened away for another barren and impoverishing tour of duty in Ireland. But Sidney found no immediate favour from the Queen. Elizabeth did everything by calculation, and the young man, for all his brilliance, did not fit her requirements. He was very inexperienced in the faithless affairs of princes, and perhaps too obdurate a Protestant : she always put flexibility and cunning before high principle. He was also Leicester's nephew and she had no wish to strengthen the faction of the earl who was proud enough already : Leicester was a Dudley and the Queen knew from the history of her dynasty that it was wise to keep a tight rein on the house of Dudley. And perhaps Sidney's qualities told against him. For public service, Elizabeth preferred plain worth to glitter; her most trusted servants were quiet, laborious men like Burghley, Walsingham and Hatton. Young Sidney was extravagant, impatient, hot-blooded—on one occasion he threatened the life of a secretary whom he suspected of intercepting letters to his father. Lastly, and most damning, Sidney was poor and had no fortune to squander on the Queen's behalf. The modest sinecure of royal cup-bearer was the only fruit of his first attendance at court.

The ambition to do great things in the world of affairs is not easily given up and for the next eighteen months Sidney served the nation where he could. He accompanied his father to Ireland and generally approved of his country's barbarous behaviour in that wretched land. He had a sympathy for the poor 'who may groan, for their cry cannot be heard', but in a *Discourse on Ireland* he made the characteristic English claim that lenience was no use in Ireland because the people hated their conquerors and were papists besides. In February 1577 he found more congenial employment when he was sent on a formal embassy to the Emperor Rudolph, and to the Counts Palatine, Lewis and Casimir, condoling all these men on recent family losses. He went with his friends Fulke Greville and Edward Dyer, and he proved once again his high European reputation. He captivated in turn three most dissimilar men. In Louvain he met the Catholic Don Juan of Austria, the victor of Lepanto, and the onlookers were astonished, said Greville, 'to see what ingenuous tribute that brave and high-minded Prince' paid Sidney. In Prague he had long talks with another earnest Catholic, the Jesuit Edmund Campion, later captured and executed in England. And on the way back, at the Queen's command he turned aside to see William the Silent, the most resolute Protestant leader in Europe. William saw in Sidney a champion of the revolt against Spain, and offered his sister in

11 SIR PHILIP SIDNEY

12a ROBERT
GREENE

12b CHRISTOPHER
MARLOWE

marriage; but Elizabeth did not intend to make Sidney an instrument of destiny and forbade the match. Leicester and Walsingham, the leaders of the aggressive faction, were pleased with the embassy. 'The honourable opinion he hath left behind him with all the Princes with whom he had to negotiate', wrote Walsingham, 'hath left a most sweet savour and grateful remembrance of his name in those parts.' This young man had become a sharp tool for their purpose.

And Sidney was theirs to use. His Protestant sympathy was not in doubt. He had travelled up and down Europe and was admired by all who knew him. He was beginning to show powers of persuasion, able to put a blunt argument in elegant forms. He was bound to Leicester by ties of blood, and cut off from peaceful Burghley through dislike for the Earl of Oxford, Burghley's son-in-law, who had insulted Sidney on the tennis court. He was the upright, outspoken innocent ready to be employed by the wiles of politicians. When Leicester needed a forceful argument against the proposed match between Elizabeth and the Duke of Anjou, he came to Sidney who willingly complied.

The declaration he sent to the Queen was very bold indeed. He spoke of Anjou in most contemptuous terms as the 'son of that Jezebel of our age'[1] and a party to the St Bartholomew Massacre. He warned that Englishmen 'will be galled, if not alienated, when they shall see you take to husband a Frenchman and a Papist'. He showed Elizabeth the duty of a Protestant sovereign. To send such a document was hazardous; the sturdy nationalist John Stubbs, who had written against the marriage in a pamphlet, had his right hand chopped off for his temerity. Sidney escaped punishment because of his birth and position, and because the Queen herself had no intention of marrying. But the presumption, even though the advice was good, was too great for any Tudor to bear. Sidney could now expect no advancement to great office.

The act that was the ruin of the politician was the making of the poet. In the ideal courtier all graces and talents were bound up. He was expected to have skill in diplomacy, administration, arms and arts. Earlier Tudor courts had been served by Wyatt, Sackville, Surrey, labouring for the commonwealth of the realm

---

[1] Catherine de Medici, the dowager Queen of France, whose compromising policies were generally held to have aggravated the religious troubles of the land.

and the commonwealth of letters with equal distinction. At the court, more than anywhere else, there was the learning, wealth, leisure and interest to make the arts flourish under the encouragement of sympathetic sovereigns. Manuals on arms were written by courtiers, but so too were manuals on poetry; George Puttenham wrote his *Art of English Poesy* (1589) for 'young gentlemen or idle courtiers' and his intention was 'to make a rude rimer, a learned and a courtly poet'. But the noble ideal of service to the two realms no longer applied in Elizabeth's reign. The gifted amateur was excluded from government, as Sidney discovered. The English courtier, without responsibility, became an affected butterfly; Languet found the life of the English court effeminate and artificial.

Sidney agreed with his moral tutor. The mark of his mind, wrote Greville, was 'lovely and familiar gravity as carried grace and reverence above greater years', and such a nature, denied a place in government, could not be content with the parcel of idle, decadent loiterers about the court. He retired from court and gave himself up to the second part of his courtly endowment, the service of English letters.

In 1577 Philip's sister Mary had married the Earl of Pembroke whose house was at Wilton near Salisbury. The house was comfortable, the countryside lovely, the company congenial; Sidney was happy to be there when he could, and he and his friends were always welcome. When he retired from court at the beginning of 1580 he went to Wilton where the pleasures of enquiry among a company of friends awaited him. He considered, wrote Dr Moffett, the doctor at Wilton, 'that day most propitious to him upon which he might withdraw for a time from the noisy squabbles at court' and 'might read and dispute with a few university men, in some place where he was made welcome'. Chief among the young disputants—Sidney was in his mid-twenties and his friends not much older—were Fulke Greville, his companion from childhood, Sir Edward Dyer, who had travelled with him to the Emperor Rudolph, and Edmund Spenser, an aspiring courtier whom he had met in 1578 at Leicester's house in London. All these young men were devoted followers of Renaissance learning, all were jealous for the dignity of English writing, and all were budding authors. The meetings of this little group were begun in London and continued at Wilton, and when they were apart their common ideals and extensive arguments were carried on, in many a letter.

Sidney's first piece of writing was a dramatic trifle called the *Lady of May,* performed for Elizabeth at Wanstead in 1578, and now only remembered because it may have suggested to Shakespeare the character of Holofernes in *Love's Labour's Lost.* Though this drama was only a small achievement and Sidney was the youngest of the group, he was looked on as the moving spirit; his reputation had gone before him, and older men gladly acknowledged his qualities. When Spenser published his *Shepherd's Calendar* in 1579 he dedicated it to 'the noble and virtuous gentleman and worthy of all titles both of learning and chivalry, Mr Philip Sidney'. Sidney beat the critical hares out of the tangle of English poetic practice, and led his companions in pursuit; he knew, said Nashe, 'what belonged to a scholar', and knew 'what pains, what toils, what travail conduct to perfection'.

The investigations of Sidney and his friends were carried on with more energy than success. They recognized problems but their theories provided few answers. Noting the uncertainty of English metrics, they tried to discipline English verse to classical measures, and they experimented with hexameters, sapphics and other awkward, un-English shapes. Sidney was no pedantic classicist—he called 'Ciceronianism' the 'chief abuse' at Oxford— but the Renaissance mind, when it was puzzled, loved to start at classical principles. Whatever his debt to the classics, Sidney was never one to doubt his own language. At a time when many were gloomy about the chances of English as a literary language, unfavourably contrasting its rugged changeability with the chaste permanence of Greek and Latin, he insisted on its eloquence and power. Bacon might write that 'these modern languages will play the bankrupt with books' and put his major works of philosophy into Latin; but Sidney agreed with Richard Mulcaster, the old master of his friend Spenser, who boldly stated 'I love Rome, but London better; I favour Italy, but England more; I honour the Latin, but I worship the English.' And Mulcaster would not admit that Latin, though a fine and elegant tongue, was in any way superior to English for any kind of writing. 'But why not all in English,' he wrote in his *Elementary,* published in 1582, 'a tongue of itself both deep in conceit, and frank in delivery? I do not think that any language, be it whatsoever, is better able to utter all arguments, either with more pith, or greater plainness than our English tongue is.' The writings of Sidney and his friends, especially Spenser's *Shepherd's Calendar* and Sidney's own *Arcadia,* were in part attempts to vindicate the opinion of Mulcaster and demonstrate the various and eloquent resources of English. And the virtues of the language appeared not only in the careful rhetoric of an elevated style; Sidney also recognized the glory of traditional forms. He wrote on the old ballads : 'I never heard the old song of Percy and Douglas that I found not my heart moved more than with a trumpet, and yet it is sung by some blind crowder with no rougher voice than rude style.'

In his own tongue Sidney saw a true language of poetry worthy of the best writers; and the purpose of his studies and his practice was always to prove to his countrymen the true dignity of poetry. Only the poet perfects nature : 'her world is brazen, the poets only deliver a golden.' The poet's power to catch, hold and fire the imagination is worth all the wearisome logic of the philosophers. The poet 'cometh to you with words set in delightful proportion, either accompanied with, or prepared for, the well enchanting skill of music; and with a tale forsooth he cometh unto you, with a tale which holdeth children from play, and old men from the chimney corner'. When the Puritan critic Stephen Gosson wrote an attack on poetry called *The School of Abuse,* and had the gall to dedicate it to Sidney—relying on Sidney's well-known Protestant sympathies—he found that he had badly misjudged his man; Sidney was quickly in the field with a resounding defence.

The *Defence of Poesie* was possibly written about 1580 though not published until fifteen years later. It is a curious work of criticism in that it is more notable as an affirmation of the poet's dignity than as an example of critical acuteness. Gosson had particularly attacked the theatre and Sidney had, on the whole, agreed with him. In a lengthy consideration of his contemporary drama Sidney quite failed to see that, even though in many ways preposterous, it still contained vigorous elements which in a few short years would lead to the overwhelming triumph of English letters—the plays of Kyd, Marlowe, Shakespeare and their many followers. But the *Defence of Poesie* deserves its fame, for in the characteristic manner of Sidney its clarity and charm more than make up for the fallibility of the criticism.

It was a strange and fortunate case with Sidney and his friends that the actual practice of their writing proved what their theories could not. The arguments and theoretical attempts to reform English prosody on classical principles failed; but what did that matter when the actual poems scattered through *Arcadia* successfully demonstrated a wonderful variety of English verse forms? *Arcadia* was written at Wilton for the entertainment of his sister, the Countess of Pembroke, 'at his vacant and spare times of leisure (for he could endure at no time to be idle and void of action)'. It was written on odd sheets which were taken to his sister as they were done, one by one, for her to keep or to show 'to such friends as will weigh errors in the balance of good will'. The first version was finished by 1580, but a year or two later Sidney began to re-cast it. It was not published at all until after his death; a small part was published in 1590, and an amplified version in 1593. *Arcadia* was a startling light piercing clear through the general artistic muddle of the time. It reconciled in an English book various Renaissance and medieval influences and devised a golden prose to celebrate the reconciliation. *Arcadia* is often called a romance, but it is a work that does not fall easily into any class. Sidney took the romance of *Amadis de Gaul,* the pastoral of Sannazaro, the prose epic of Heliodorus and combined them in a work where narrative, moral lesson and poetry are nicely blended. It is certainly not a novel in the modern sense (though perhaps a forebear of the novel); it is rather the expression in art of Sidney's courtly ideal, a picture of virtuous living. The style of *Arcadia* is no longer to the taste of many readers; it is too high-flown, too rhetorical, too mellifluous. But in its day the style was no less remarkable than the matter of the book. It was an appropriate and disciplined prose, clear in syntax and vivid in language; it was a style that for elegance and ease surpassed what had been written before in English, a prose that caused Ben Jonson to name Sidney, together with Richard Hooker, the masters of good writing.

To be an historical master of prose would be enough for any man; but Sidney also became an historical master of English poetry. He had first met Penelope Devereux, daughter of the Earl of Essex, when he was twenty and she a girl of twelve. Sidney had been with Essex in Ireland and the earl formed such a good opinion of the young man that he wished on his death bed to give Sidney his daughter in marriage. Philip was serious and high-minded; Penelope much younger, wayward and something of a coquette. There is no knowing what was between the two : true friendship, passion, or merely an expectation of marrying? It never came to that, for Penelope's family did not favour Sidney (possibly on account of his poverty) and hurried Penelope in 1581, at the age of eighteen, into a marriage with a wealthy and well-named Lord Rich. Sidney, however, immortalized her as the 'Stella' of his *Astrophel and Stella,* the first English sonnet sequence.

For the purpose of the poems the true relationship between the young people does not matter. The sonnet sequence is not a narrative history of an affair, but a long lyrical reflection, chiefly on the nature of love. *Astrophel and Stella* was written at about the same time as *Arcadia,* and like *Arcadia* was not published till after the poet's death. The sonnet sequence was imported from Italy and Sidney stayed very close both to the Italian form of the sonnet and to the Italian idea of the sonnet. Some of the poems are carelessly written and the quality is uneven; but the whole was an extraordinary achievement which impressed his contemporaries more than any other poetry of the century. Sidney gave to Stella the same unearthly fame that Petrarch, his Italian master, had given to Laura. The sequence was an inspiration to later Elizabethans and brought forth in time Spenser's *Amoretti* and Shakespeare's own sonnet sequence. The form was wonderfully suited to the Elizabethan sensibility—a lyrical outpouring that permitted passion, reflection and criticism of life in a form that tightly curbed the notorious rambling exuberance which Elizabethan writing was prone to. It would be hard to say which aspect of *Astrophel and Stella* was the more valuable for English letters : the regularity of the metrics and the precision of the form which helped to tame the wilderness of English prosody; or the beauty of the expression which encouraged the lyricism that is now, and always has been, the particular excellence of English poetry.

The contemplative life was never the aim of Sidney's courtly ideal; 'for as Aristotle sayeth, it is not Gnosis, but Praxis must be the fruit'. The retirement to Wilton was but a pleasant episode in a life devoted to service. And for Sidney, service of the arts demanded that he become an active patron, a helper not only of the great poet Edmund Spenser, whom he guided to a post in Ireland, but also of modest scholars like William Temple, who became his secretary, and Abraham Fraunce, who was directed by

Sidney to study Ramus and Aristotle and who replied with an endearing dedication 'to the right Worshipful his very good Mr and Patron, Mr P Sidney'. The correspondence with the learned men of the continent continued. His old mentor Languet died in 1581, but other famous scholars, French, Italian, German and Dutch, were anxious to share their thoughts with the Englishman. They were captivated by the qualities which Giordano Bruno perceived. 'The poetry in the book', he wrote in the dedication to his *De gli Eroici Furori,* 'is under the criticism and protection of a poet; the philosophy is nakedly revealed to so clear an intellect as yours; and the heroic matters are directed to a heroic and noble mind, with which you have shown yourself to be endowed.'

Service to the arts and service to the State were but two kinds of action, different expressions of the whole man. By the spring of 1581 Sidney was back in London. He sat in Parliament and took his place on two committees for the suppression of papists and for the control of sedition against the crown. He attended once agan at court and indulged his love of ceremony at the royal entertainments. In April, at a show for the French ambassador, he appeared in 'armour part blue and the rest gilt and engraven, with four spare horses having caparisons and furniture very rich and costly, as some of cloth of gold embroidered with pearl, and some embroidered with gold and silver feathers very richly and cunningly wrought'. He was attended by four pages, thirty gentlemen and four trumpeters. This extravagance, in a sense the natural outpouring of a generous mind, was extremly unwise, for Sidney was not rich; and all his life his striving towards a noble and grand ideal was checked by the crude realities of finance. His father, Sir Henry, had nearly ruined the family by his efforts on the Queen's behalf in Ireland. Sidney had returned to court partly in an attempt to find employment, and therefore income. At this time he was reduced to some undignified shifts in his search for money. Elizabeth had promised to do something for him but, as usual, was slow in keeping her word. Sidney wrote several times to Hatton begging him to give the Queen a tactful reminder, or he would have to petition Elizabeth directly, for 'need obeys no laws and forgets blushing'. At last Elizabeth, with what seems like cynical ingenuity, offered Sidney a sum taken from recusant fines and from the sale of forfeited Catholic goods. Sidney had scruples about accepting—'I like not their persons and much worse their religions, but I think my fortunes very hard that my reward must be built upon other men's punishments'—nonetheless to his discredit he did accept and received £3,000. His poverty was also eased by the sprinkling of official positions that at last began to come his way. He was Steward to the Bishop of Winchester, joint Master of the Ordnance with his uncle Warwick, and in 1583 General of Horse. In the same year he was knighted so that he could represent John Casimir at the installation of the German prince as a Knight of the Garter. And in the same year again his financial problems were finally solved by marriage to the daughter of Sir Francis Walsingham. The Queen's secretary agreed to pay the debts of his son-in-law to the extent of £1,500, and to lodge the young couple in his house at his expense. The acquisition of such a brilliant son-in-law was an expensive honour for Walsingham. When Sidney was killed three years later, Walsingham very honourably cleared up the huge debts left behind.

Perhaps it was the need for money that first turned Sidney's eyes toward maritime exploration; for nearly every Elizabethan of rank at one time or another looked on England's sea voyages as a means to riches. He had contributed £25 to Frobisher's first journey in 1576, £50 to the second voyage and £67 10s. to the third. The money was all wasted, for Frobisher made no profit. But the search for wealth was not his only interest in exploration. Drake's circumnavigation had caught his imagination, as it had that of all England; in 1580 he wrote to his brother Robert that the return of Drake was the only talk of the town. The success of Drake altered the balance of sea power in the Americas and Sidney, like his political tutors Leicester and Walsingham, was quick to see the favourable implications for England and for the Protestant alliance against Spain. Walsingham and Sidney were the chief promoters of Sir Humphrey Gilbert's plans for colonization, attracted especially by the proposal to encourage English Catholics to emigrate, thus ridding the country of their objectionable influence. Sidney purchased from Gilbert the rights to three million acres of land which he then assigned to the Catholic Sir George Peckham. These plans foundered and sank on 9th September 1583, when the *Squirrel* carried its bold captain Sir Humphrey Gilbert beneath the ocean.

The failure of Gilbert did not end Sidney's interest in the New World. When Parliament met in November 1584, Sir Philip served with Drake on the committee which confirmed the grant of lands in what became Virginia to Sir Walter Raleigh. With Drake, he also planned an expedition to the West Indies, which came to nothing, and then another expedition to join Ralph Lane in Virginia. Sidney and Fulke Greville were eager for the voyage. In August 1585 they arrived at Plymouth with high hopes and were received 'with a great deal of outward pomp and compliment'. But the Queen's permission had not been obtained. To Sidney's great disappointment he was summoned back to London, and his discontent was only eased by the thought that at last Elizabeth had a task for him worthy of his powers: he was appointed Governor of Flushing.

For the last act in this short life Sir Philip Sydney returned to the Netherlands where some years before he had been acclaimed by William the Silent, and where his reputation for Protestant chivalry stood as high as anywhere in Europe. Sidney's heart was entirely with the Dutch in the fight against their Spanish overlords, but the signs were ominous when he entered his new command. He took the oath at Flushing on 21st November 1585. 'I find the people very glad of me', he immediately wrote to his uncle Leicester, but 'the garrison is far too weak to command by authority.' Elizabeth in her usual way had failed to make proper provision for the garrison; the numbers were too few and two hundred of them were sick; they were ill paid, ill housed, ill fed, and the fortifications of the town were in disrepair. Sidney was forced to do what his father had done in Ireland—find his own money to finance the Queen's campaign. He borrowed £300 at high rate of interest for the poor soldiers who were 'scarce able to keep life with their entire pay'. This debt was one of many which his father-in-law inherited. Leicester was the aggresive voice that had persuaded the Queen to wage a limited war in the Low Countries, and he was given command of all the English forces. But matters did not improve when he arrived in the Netherlands. He was a poor general and Elizabeth distrusted his ambition; the suspicion of the Queen naturally undermined Leicester's influence with the Dutch.

Some of the displeasure with Leicester fell also on the head of Sidney, his nephew, especially as Sir Philip was outspoken against the Queen's meanness: 'If the Queen pay not her soldiers', he wrote, 'she must lose her garrisons, there is no doubt thereof.' The fighting in the Netherlands, being in the cause of both religion and nationalism, was notoriously brutal and Sidney could find no honour in the exchange of atrocities. Long ago Languet had written to him of the ferocious madness in the Low Countries, and condemned those who looked for reputation in bloodshed. He begged Sidney to use his humanity 'for the preservation and not the destruction of man'. Now that he was drawn into the terrible affair, with his usual high purpose he determined to look beyond the slaughter, the misery and Elizabeth's mean calculations, to see the task as God's holy work in the Protestant cause which could go on despite the Queen. 'For methinks I see', he wrote to Walsingham in March 1586, 'the great work indeed in hand against the abusers of the world.' And he continued : 'I know there is a higher power that must uphold me or else I shall fall.'

He was trying to reconcile himself to the pain of being there, to the pain of seeing men die miserably neglected in a squalid war. He was anxious to bear his part in the fighting. When Leicester finally decided to face the Spanish at Zutphen, having spent the summer avoiding them, Sidney left his own troops safely at Deventer and joined Leicester. When the attack of the Spaniards came on 22nd September, Sydney with the same intrepidity went out without the thigh-pieces of his armour; for he had seen his colleague Sir William Pelham go out without his, and he would not take the advantage over an old man. One horse was shot under him. He mounted again and at the second charge a shot penetrated his unprotected thigh, smashing the bone. He was carried off bleeding profusely and called for a drink; then, in the famous scene made immortal by Greville's account, 'as he was putting the bottle to his mouth he saw a poor soldier carried along, who had eaten his last at the same feast, ghastly casting up his eyes at the bottle. Which Sir Philip perceiving, took it from his head before he drank, and delivered it to the poor man with these words, "Thy necessity is yet greater than mine".' For twenty-five days he endured, but mortification had set in; he died in his thirty-first year on 17th October 1586.

Before Sidney left England to take up his post in Flushing, he had written to the Queen asking her 'legibly to read my heart in the course of my life, and though itself be but of a mean worth, yet to esteem it like a poor house well set'. England judged him in this sense. The funeral, which was long delayed while Walsingham settled the complicated debts of the estate, took place on 16th February 1587 with solemn majesty and before a huge crowd. Seven hundred mourners followed the coffin and they could hardly pass through the streets to St Paul's because of the press of the London populace. After the service in the black-hung cathedral, the body was buried by the choir while a double volley echoed in the churchyard. The respects, the lamentations, the memorials came from all over Europe, even from Philip of Spain who remembered that the younger Philip was his godson. The most affecting of the tributes very fittingly came from his friend and fellow-poet Edmund Spenser :

> He grew up fast in goodness and in grace,
> And doubly fair wox both in mind and face.
>
> Which daily more and more he did augment,
> With gentle usage, and demeanour mild;
> That all men's hearts with secret ravishment
> He stole away, and wittingly beguiled.

At the distance of time, history judges him more severely. Gabriel Harvey declared that 'his sovereign profession was arms'; but his experience of war was extremely limited and he had no success on the battlefield. He had the gallantry of a good soldier, but not the prudence of a good general. In the arts, though his achievements are important as the first of their kind in England, he was soon overtaken. *Astrophel and Stella* was certainly an extraordinary work, for though Wyatt and Surrey in the reign of Henry VIII had assimilated Italian forms and set the poetry of the English Renaissance on its way, Sidney had refined and disciplined their somewhat uncertain attempts. That Spenser and Shakespeare built grander edifices on the foundation he had laid is a part of his credit. But the *Arcadia,* with too much sentiment and too little characterization, has been taken as a mistake—a wrong direction—in English prose fiction. Milton called it 'a vain and amatorious poem'. He wrote fine, musical songs and dignified translations of the Psalms; but Thomas Campion was soon to write better songs, and his Psalms would not displace those of the Authorized Version.

His contemporaries, however, could not look at him in this critical way. For them, Sidney was an extraordinary manifestation of an Elizabethan ideal, greatness in action, putting virtue and talent disinterestedly to the benefit of the community. That was how his oldest and best friend Fulke Greville saw him. 'The truth is', he wrote, 'his end was not writing, even while he wrote; nor his knowledge moulded for tables, or schools; but both his wit and understanding bent upon his heart, to make himself and others, not in words or opinion, but in life and action, good and great. In which architectural art he was such a Master, with so commanding and yet equal ways amongst men, that wheresoever he went he was beloved and obeyed.' And this, it seems, was how Sidney saw himself. 'I would rather be charged', he once said, 'with lack of wisdom than of patriotism.' He was merely an instrument for the good of England, and to inspire goodness in her countrymen. Even Elizabeth, in his view, was only an agent in a great Protestant cause which would well continue without her. He wrote to Walsingham from Utrecht shortly before his death : 'If her Majesty were the fountain I would fear, considering what I daily find, that we would wax dry but she is but a means whom God useth.' Though from time to time, especially in letters to Languet, Sidney admitted self doubt, and though in his poems he sometimes put on the fashionable dress of melancholy, the whole of his life gave evidence of a great hope for humanity, and a confidence in the working out of God's will.

Many regarded Sidney as the exemplar of an English gentleman, but even in his own time there were signs that his life was far out of touch with reality. Ideals must be paid for; Sidney's were expensive ones, and he could not have pursued his grand design, in an inflationary age, without the support of his unlucky father-in-law who was left debts amounting to £6,000. His impatience with the intrigues and subtleties of government disqualified him from important office. The Queen grieved at his death but in his life showed him no favour. No man seemed to have more talent or a better preparation to serve the State. His father Sir Henry, as honest an official as the Tudors ever had, trained him well. His own brilliance and integrity were without question; his love of his country was profound. But no worthwhile employment came his way. Elizabeth, offended by his unyielding and impractical spirit, seemed deliberately cold to him. When the Earl of Oxford insulted him on the tennis court in front of the French envoy, Sidney challenged the nobleman to a duel. The Queen prevented this, pointing out that it was not for a gentleman to challenge an earl; such a disregard for the nobility, she said, taught the peasants the spirit of revolt. It is one of the little ironies of history that Philip Sidney, the chevalier par excellence, was only knighted so that he could stand substitute for a German prince in the ceremony of the Garter.

Elizabeth and Sidney were far opposed, representatives of contrary tendencies of the age. She was the voice of experience, he the voice of innocence. They became united in the affection of their countrymen who forgave the Queen her faults and remembered Sidney only for his virtues :

> Sidney, as he fought
> And as he fell, and as he lived and loved,
> Sublimely mild, a spirit without spot.

To live in the national imagination is a fame reserved for few.

10
Robert Greene

His name was notorious. 'I know you are not unacquainted with the death of Robert Greene', his printer wrote to his readers, 'whose pen in his lifetime pleased you as well on the stage, as in the stationers' shops.' His work was prolific, his death sad and edifying; but his origins were obscure, and his conduct a scandalous enigma. In troubled times he came to London, a provincial youth of bright attainments whose feckless and indulgent life challenged the old order of society. Like a little meteor he blazed for a while, and died suddenly.

Greene was born in 1558, in Norwich, where his parents, as he wrote in his *Repentance,* 'for their gravity and honest life were well known and esteemed amongst their neighbours'. His father was not rich; when Robert went to university he was a poor sizar, a scholar who waited at table in return for his tuition. But the family did their best, as the son admitted : 'My father had care to have me in my nonage brought up at school, that I might through the study of good letters grow to be a friend to myself, a profitable member to the commonwealth, and a comfort to him in his age.' Greene became none of these things.

In November 1575 Greene went to St John's College, Cambridge. The Reformation in England had severely damaged Oxford and Cambridge, since both had been intimately connected with the Church, and when Greene arrived at St John's his university was in the process of recovering and changing. Oxford, with its Catholic sympathies, had suffered the more, and now Cambridge was rivalling the reputation and achievements of the older institution. The new colleges, Queens', Christ's, St John's, were founts of the New Learning of the Renaissance, being particularly strong on Greek studies. Sir John Cheke, the greatest Greek scholar of the day, Roger Ascham, Elizabeth's tutor, and William Cecil, her great minister, had all been at St John's; no wonder the Queen looked favourably on Cambridge. She visited it first, in 1564, and Cecil—Lord Burghley—was the chancellor of the university. Elizabeth's government was also pleased that the religion of Cambridge was distinctly Protestant, though later the university fell somewhat from grace when it became the breeding place for Puritans. But in the first days of the reign, when the Queen was anxious to assert her mastery over all aspects of national life, the Reformed faith of Cambridge enabled the university to accept the secular spirit of the new reign. The government could rest easy that the sons of Cambridge were being prepared to become good servants of the State.

Other changes were afoot. The colleges 'were erected by their founders', William Harrison wrote in the *Description of England,* 'at the first only for poor men's sons, whose parents were not able to bring them up unto learning; but now they have the least benefit of them, by reason the rich do so encroach upon them'. In the Middle Ages the universities had provided the poor, diligent clerics that the vast organization of the Church required; now the university was becoming the place where the gentleman completed his education, perhaps with no thought at all of a life in the Church. There was now some competition for preferment in which the poor student was at a disadvantage : 'it is in my time', wrote Harrison, 'an hard matter for a poor man's child to come by a fellowship (though he be never so good a scholar and worthy of that room).' And the new wealthy students brought a new attitude to their studies, a casual approach of those who knew that their prospects in life, because of their birth and connections, did not desperately depend on a university degree. 'I would I had bestowed', lamented Sir Andrew Aguecheek in *Twelfth Night,* 'that time in the tongues that I have in fencing, dancing and bear-baiting. O had I but followed the arts.'

In 1575 there were temptations enough to distract the poor, young student. 'Such playing at dice,' Lyly wrote of the Oxford of the time, 'such quaffing of drink, such daliance with women, such dancing, that in my opinion there is no quaffer in Flanders so given to tippling, no courtier in Italy so given to riot, no creature in the world so misled as a student.' The student was becoming better known for his style than his study; in the manner of the country gentleman he played when he could, and when he could not play he idled. John Earle, in the elegant portraits of his *Micro-*

cosmography (1628), gave him this character: 'The two marks of his seniority are the bare velvet of his gown and his proficiency at tennis, where when he can once play a set, he is a fresh-man no more. His study has commonly handsome shelves, his books neat silk strings, which he shews to his father's man, and is loathe to untie or take down, for fear of misplacing.'

Some, of course, worked amid temptations; and Greene, a poor scholar, needed his degree. In 1578 he graduated from St John's and passed on to Clare Hall where he became, in 1583, Master of Arts. He had studied the philosophy of Aristotle and perhaps flirted with the Protestant logic of Ramus fashionable at Cambridge. He had looked into the works of Cardano for arithmetic, Euclid for geometry, and Ptolemy for astronomy. Cicero and Quintilian had taught him rhetoric. He knew the Latin poets well, and the plays of Seneca; he was likely to have some knowledge of Greek and French. His learning was sufficiently solid for Oxford also to grant him a degree. After 1588 he proudly announced himself as *Academiae Utriusque Magister in Artibus*—'Master of Arts in both Universities'. But his studies did not prevent him from tasting the pleasures of the place. The poor young man plunged happily into the world of the idle wits. 'At the University of Cambridge', he wrote in his *Repentance,* 'I light amongst wags as lewd as myself, with whom I consumed the flower of my youth.'

After university, foreign travel was a usual course for young gentlemen. 'Travel, in the younger sort,' said Francis Bacon, 'is a part of education.' And Greene was drawn to Italy and Spain by his wealthy friends at Cambridge. For Bacon, the travels of the student were to be a sober and diligent time: he was to keep a diary; observe architecture, harbours, fortifications; attend the courts of justice and church consistories; visit libraries and colleges; listen to disputations and lectures; look at comedies, pageants and fairs; and enquire into the business of governments, armies and merchants. And most of all he was to remain modest and English; 'let it appear that he doth not change his country manners for those of foreign parts, but only prick in some flowers of that he hath learned abroad into the customs of his own country.'

But many of the young travellers were rich, idle and wilful; and the wonders of their voyages spun their giddy heads. 'Farewell, Monsieur Traveller,' says Rosalind to the affected and melancholy Jaques in *As You Like It*: 'look you lisp, and wear strange suits, disable all the benefits of your own country, be out of love with your nativity, and almost chide God for making you that countenance you are; or I will scarce think you have swam in a gondola.' Italy, indeed, the home of notorious Machiavelli where Renaissance princes luxuriated in sin and wealth, was thought particularly dangerous to unsophisticated English lads. 'Italy now is not that Italy, that it was wont to be', Ascham wrote in *The Scholemaster* (1570): 'and therefore now not so fit a place, as some do count it, for young men to fetch either wisdom or honesty from thence.' Alas, he admitted, the very reputation of the place made the young eager to try its charms; 'many of our travellers into Italy do not eschew the way to Circe's court, but go, and ride, and run, and fly thither.' Greene and his companions were of this kind. In Italy and Spain, he wrote, 'I saw and practised such villany as is abominable to declare.'

For his friends, the case was perhaps not serious, for they had money to squander and secure places to return to at home. But Greene was from a poor family living beyond his means in spendthrift company. He became proud and touchy, and the expenses of his life led him into deceit. He sponged on his family, tricking his father and playing on the tender heart of his mother, 'so that being then conversant with notable braggarts, boon companions and ordinary spend-thrifts, that practised sundry superficial studies, I became a sien grafted into the same stock, whereby I did absolutely participate of their nature and qualities'. Everything joined to divorce him from family and home—his education, his new luxurious habits, his pride, his dishonesty. He could not go back to Norwich and the provincial life. 'At my return into England, I ruffled out my silks, in the habit of *Malcontent,* and seemed so discontent, that no place would please me to abide in, nor no vocation cause me to stay myself in.' He had become the displaced man.

The social changes of the sixteenth century made it the century of the dispossessed. Agrarian reform, enclosures, the advent of capitalism, wide-spread inflation, the Reformation and the dissolution of the monasteries—all shook the social fabric. Vagrancy and lawlessness were the preoccupation of Tudor government. Numberless measures for their control were passed, but the country still seemed overburdened with turbulent men, thrown out of their accustomed order and living on their wits. All observers remarked on the extraordinary dislocation of everyday life. 'There is no country in the world', an Italian visitor wrote around 1500, 'where there are so many thieves and robbers as in England; insomuch that few venture to go alone in the country, excepting in the middle of the day, and fewer still in the towns at night, and least of all in London.' Harrison, writing in about 1577, dated the increase in vagabondage from the first decade of the century. 'It is not yet full threescore years since this trade began,' said his *Description of England* : 'but how it has prospered since that time it is easy to judge, for they are now supposed, of one sex and another, to amount unto above 10,000 persons.' In 1594 Sir John Spenser, Lord Mayor of London, estimated the number of begging poor in London alone at 12,000. In England, three to four hundred vagrant rogues were hanged each year; according to Strype's *Annals,* the searches of 1569 caught some 13,000 masterless men.

The ranks of the vagabonds included all sorts of men and women. Very many were peasants turned off the land by enclosures. Others, particularly at the beginning of the century, were disbanded retainers from the feudal armies. Later, soldiers discharged at Plymouth, Dover or Southampton after a foreign expedition were reluctant to go home; used to a riotous, brutal life of arms, they took their pay and formed robber gangs. In 1589 the remnants of an unsuccessful expedition to Portugal, which had been led by Drake and Norris, drifted up to London and threatened the city so that martial law was proclaimed and 2,000 militiamen called out. Other vagabonds were servants of aristocrats, perhaps dismissed for bad service, or perhaps let go because inflation caused the lord to cut back his expenses. And yet others were churchmen and monastic servitors cast adrift by the Reformation —former monks and friars, pardoners and proctors, monastic butlers, valets, cellarmen, gardeners, etc. And last of all there were the gypsies, known to the Elizabethans as 'Egyptians'. The gypsies had first come to England in the middle of the fifteenth century, and their strange appearance and wandering ways were immediately suspicious. 'They be swart and do go disguised in their apparel contrary to other nations', Andrew Borde wrote in 1547. 'They be light-fingered and use picking; they have little manner and evil lodging, and yet they be pleasant dancers.' As early as 1530 Parliament began to legislate against them; in 1562 it was enacted that anyone consorting with Egyptians and counterfeiting their speech and behaviour would be apprehended as a felon.

The placeless man, especially if he had some skill or education, would make for London. There, in the huts, hovels and brothels of the liberties on the edge of the city, he could escape detection, avoiding the expulsion, branding or execution that Tudor justice had in store for him. In London he found a flourishing underworld, the despair of the city fathers, which derided the good order beloved of the Tudor governments. The cheat found his mark, the libertine his women, the gambler his dice, the drunkard his taverns, the idler his scraps of charity; all who wished to pit their wits against fortune found a great public to be gulled. A young man such as Greene, by turns angry, discontented, proud and ashamed, was inevitably drawn to the capital city. He returned from Italy and completed his studies for the M.A. degree at Clare Hall. But academic life was not for one who had tasted sweeter joys; 'being new come from Italy (where I learned all the villanies under the heavens) I was drowned in pride, whoredom was my daily exercise, and gluttony with drunkenness was my only delight'. He was also a budding author, his romance *Mamillia* having been written in 1580. He wandered like a distracted dog between Cambridge, London and Norwich. He married a gentleman's daughter, had a child by her, and left her. That event seemed to have decided him; his wife left for Lincolnshire and he for London, there to win his bread as a hack author.

In London, Greene became 'a penner of Love Pamphlets, so that I soon grew famous in that quality'. When he began to write fiction, the art was under the influence of Lyly's *Euphues* (1578). That famous work was ornate, rhetorical, didactic, and Greene deliberately incorporated these qualities into his own work. The rambling, digressive, unlikely stories he told were tales of the European romances set in Italy, Spain, Arcadia—anywhere but England. And to these accounts of broken hearts, true love, lovers' sacrifice, lust, fortitude, he added the little moral lesson. He would speak of wifely obedience, he wrote in *Penelopes Web*, 'that both we may beguile the night with prattle, and profit our minds with some good and virtuous precepts'. He had stories to illustrate chastity, to show the evil influence of love, to praise silence in women, to condemn adultery, to glorify country life, and many others of a similar kind. His high-flown prattle and his virtuous sentiments pleased the ladies; his friend Thomas Nashe called him 'the Homer of women'.

These tales were undistinguished examples of an art that we now find insufferable. Prose fiction was new to England, and the writers had an unsure command of narrative. They put all their labour into the sentiment and especially into the affected 'beauties' of the euphuistic style while the narrative slumped along painfully, slow, weary and laiden down with huge grandiloquent speeches, tedious interjections that deprived the action of all point and drama. But in the course of time Greene's well-practised hand began to learn the elements of narrative construction: he was among the first in England to do so. In the long 'romance' *Pandosto* (1588) the moral lesson of the tale is not obtrusive, if it exists at all. The hero is a tyrant at the start, bloody and violent, and remains a tyrant to the end. The story is powerful, cold and cruel, well suited to Greene's sombre imagination. And at last the narrative is compact and progressive, the euphuistic language changed for a plain factual style, and the people characterized by their conversation. With *Pandosto* the English novel was at last hesitantly on its way, but still with far to go. And the good advance made by this book was continued in *Menaphon* (1589), a work that added a little subtlety and wit to the plain style of its predecessor.

After two or three years in London, Greene was a great success. He was wonderfully versatile; plays, poems, stories, romances flowed from his pen, even a little ranting propaganda against the Spanish in 1588, the year of the Armada, 'least I might be thought to tie myself wholly to amorous conceits'. With his long red beard —'like the spire of a steeple', said Nashe, 'whereat a man might hang a jewel, it was so sharp and pendant'—he cut an elegant figure in the company of the wits. Such great lords as Leicester, Arundel and Essex were his patrons, to whom he dedicated his works. He was now 'famozed for an arch-playmaking-poet, his purse like the sea sometime swelled, anon like the sea fell to a low ebb; yet seldom he wanted, his labours were so well esteemed'.

In his success he indulged the wildness of his youth. 'I was beloved of the more vainer sort of people, who being my continual companions, came still to my lodging, and there would continue quaffing, carousing, and surfeiting with me all the day long.' Kyd, Peele, Lodge, Nashe, Marlowe and other wits were his acquaintances; he shared their desperate ways and their exuberant discovery of a new age of English letters; collaborating, quarrelling, drinking, they saw the sun up on many mornings. 'A good fellow he was', wrote Nashe defending Greene against the censorious Cambridge scholar, Gabriel Harvey, 'and in one year he pissed as much against the walls, as thou and thy two brothers spent in three.' But he was still the malcontent, subject to melancholy and remorse. Once, in Norwich, he heard a sermon which made him hate his life. Then his companions teased him, calling him 'puritan' and 'precisian', 'so that I fell again with the dog to my old vomit, and put my wicked life in practice, and that so thoroughly as ever I did before'.

He had other grounds for dissatisfaction. His riotous life and carelessness about money made the funds fly. 'He had no account of winning credit by his works', said Nashe; 'his only care was to have a spell in his purse to conjure up a good cup of wine with at all times.' Moreover, he was beginning to face professional competition which worried him. Perhaps he was tired of his 'love pamphlets'—in any case he saw a new generation of playwrights growing in success, cutting into his income and, what was more, stealing many of their plots from the novels written by Greene and his friends. In his *Groatsworth of Wit* he warned his good companions Marlowe, Nashe and Peele to beware particularly of young William Shakespeare, 'an upstart crow, beautified with our feathers, that with his *Tigers heart wrapt in a Players hide,* supposes he is as well able to bombast out a blank verse as the best of you : and being an absolute *Johannes fac totum,* is in his own conceit the only Shake-scene in a country'. At a later date Shakespeare took the story of *Winter's Tale* from Greene's *Pandosto*.

'Many things I have wrote to get money', Greene said at the end of his life. He was a hack with a living to earn and a fickle public to please. The attention of his audience was no longer so easily caught by romances and he saw the necessity to find new subjects, new styles. Fortunately, the very disorder of his life gave him the opportunity to change. The hard-living writers, like Marlowe and Greene, spent a large part of their time in the shadows. They were the darlings of literary society and of the frivolous young gentlemen, but they also knew very well the underside of the town, the world of taverns, brothels, spies, informers, cheats and rogues of all kinds. Greene had gradually reformed his prose from the flights of euphuism to a more simple, colloquial style; he decided to use this new manner to portray the disreputable life of London.

The city of London, still standing within its medieval walls, made a great impression on Englishman and foreigner alike. 'London is a large, excellent and mighty city of business', the Duke of Wurtemberg wrote after his visit in 1592. 'The inhabitants are magnificently apparelled, and are extremely proud and overbearing.' And the citizens had much to be proud of. Observers such as William Harrison and Fynes Moryson spoke of the commodious luxury of the houses (though the streets themselves were narrow and dirty); the dignity of old St Paul's, longer than the present church and with a spire one hundred and fifty feet taller than the present dome; the life and bustle of the Thames; and the stately aristocratic palaces that led away from the gates of the city, through Whitehall to Westminster with its great Abbey and long, low Norman Hall. London Bridge was considered 'among the miracles of the world' with its twenty arches built over with houses, leading to the scattered houses, fields, vegetable-gardens, pleasure-grounds and newly erected theatres of the south bank. The grand congregation of buildings and men was presided over with fitting pomp and dignity by the city government. 'There is no subject upon earth', the playwright Middleton wrote in his *Triumphs of Truth,* 'received into the place of government with the like state and magnificence as is the Lord Mayor of the City of London.'

But the Lord Mayor governed a city that had grown so fast from the commercial expansion of the Tudor age that it was almost out of control, always verging on the edge of lawlessness. Thomas Dekker, a poor citizen born and raised in London, gave this picture of his city in a book persuasively titled *The Seven Deadly Sins of London* (1606): 'In every street, carts and coaches make such a thundering as if the world ran upon wheels : at every corner, men, women and children meet in such shoals, that posts are set up of purpose to strengthen the houses, lest with jostling one another they should shoulder them down. Besides, hammers are beating in one place, tubs hooping in another, pots clinking in a third, water-tankards running at tilt in a fourth. Here are porters sweating under burdens, there merchant's men bearing bags of money. Chapman skip out of one shop into another. Tradesmen are lusty at legs and never stand still. All are as busy as country attorneys at an assizes.' Such a pressure and overcrowding led inevitably to brawls, riots, threats, duels and all kinds of debauchery which the inadequate constables and watchmen were powerless to stop.

And unruly as the life was within the city walls, outside in the suburbs, all agreed that wickedness itself reigned. 'And what saw he there?' asked Dekker in *Lanthorne and Candlelight.* 'More alehouses than there are taverns in all Spain and France! Are they so dry in the suburbs? Yes, pockily dry.' In the garden alleys of the suburbs the brothels thrived. Stow mentioned them in his *Survey;* Stubbes, the Puritan, railed against them, and Dekker described them : 'The doors of notorious carted bawds like Hell-gates stand night and day wide open, with a pair of harlots in taffeta gowns, like two painted posts, garnishing out those doors, being better to the house than a double sign.' Here the plague bred and other diseases, and here came the 'masterless men, needy shifters, thieves, cutpurses, unthrifty servants', Whetstone complained. 'Here a man may pick out mates for all purposes, save such as are good.' This was the playground of the London rogues, Greene's uneasy acquaintances. The city rogue lived as a gallant, haunted taverns and theatres, bantered with wits and actors, played the roaring boy, beat the watchmen, cut purses and lived on his wits. Though he sometimes sank to ruffian and murderer, as he was shown in *Arden of Faversham* or *Macbeth,* his real business was cozening, cheating by the nimbleness of his wits and the quickness of his hand. And it was these tricks that Greene now decided to expose to the public for their entertainment and his profit.

'Rogue' literature, the vein which Greene now set out to explore, had already been mined in a desultory way for several centuries. The Middle Ages had seen various complications of *Merrie Tales;* writers such as Barclay and Skelton had written social satires, partly fiction and partly everyday stories of low life. Towards the middle of the sixteenth century several pamphlets by different authors began to expose the tricks, habits and cant language of the rogues. These works, the most important of which were *A Manifest Detection* (1552) by Gilbert Walker, *The Fraternity of Vagabonds* (1561) by John Awdeley and *A Caveat for Commen Cursetors* (1566) by Thomas Harman, were not fiction, being aids towards reform rather than entertainment. Harman, a prosperous country gentlemen, told his readers that he wrote for 'the utility and profit of his natural country', and regretted that he had to present his facts in a plain style, without much artistry : 'Eloquence have I none', he wrote; 'I never was acquainted with the muses.' The hidden lore and strange lives contained in these works caught the fancy of the people; Harman's little book went to four editions in a short time. Seeing the popularity of these stories, Greene decided that the London rogue was as apt a subject as Harman's country vagabond.

In 1591 Greene began to write a series of pamphlets which exposed the tricks of the town to the public. The first piece, *A Notable Discovery of Coosnage,* was licensed in December 1591, and the last, the *Blacke Bookes Messenger,* in August 1592. In between came four pamphlets on *Conny-catching.* Because he wished to profit from a popular work, Greene very artfully took over entirely the conventions of Harman's work. He, too, would write for the good of the country. He had *Nascimur pro patria* boldly printed on the title page of his first pamphlet, and informed his readers that his aim was to preserve 'young gentlemen, merchants, apprentices, farmers, and plain countrymen' from the card-sharpers and cheats of London. Like Harman, he would write in a racy, colloquial style, not because he was incapable of fine phrases, but because a 'certain decorum is to be kept in everything, and not to apply a high style in a base subject'. Like Harman, he would write from his own intimate knowledge; he had mixed with 'those mad fellows' whom he learned 'at last to loath'. And to spice his expositions with the salt of danger, he warned his readers that his old criminal companions were out to get him : 'yet gentlemen am I sore threatened by the hacksters of that filthy faculty, that if I set their practices in print, they will cut off that hand that writes the pamphlet.' All this was merely self-advertisement. Perhaps Greene did have some intention of remedying the evils of life, for he was a person subject to remorse and repentance. But first of all he was a working writer with a living to make; he took Harman's worthy social observation and turned it into popular journalism. And he quickly perceived that what the public in all ages likes best is a scandalous tale, told in the greatest and most lively detail by a writer who claims his purpose is purely moral and patriotic.

The arts of 'cozenage' and 'conny-catching' were arts of cheating, especially cheating at gambling and card playing. And if we are to believe the literature, the amount of gambling that went on in London was very great indeed. The fleecing of the citizens went on the year round in taverns, cheap ordinaries, dicing houses and bowling alleys. The law forbade gaming, but the royal patents overrode the law, licensed gaming houses and so protected the sport that the citizens loved. To the taverns and dicing houses came 'your gallant extraordinary thief that keeps his college of good fellows'; to the ordinaries came 'your London usurer, your stale batchelor, and your thrifty attorney' so that the room became as crowded as a jail; and to the disreputable alleys of the suburbs came the riff-raff 'that have yet hands to filch, heads to deceive, and friends to receive'. All times were good for cheating, but the best time was during the court terms when the dull countrymen came to London either on business or to taste the pleasures of the town, with their purses well stuffed. 'What whispering is there in Term times', wrote the knowledgeable Dekker, 'how by some slight to cheat the poor country clients of his full purse that is stuck under his girdle?' The ways of parting the gull from his purse were many and highly developed. In the crowded paths round St Paul's, at Westminster in term time, at the Tyburn executions, at the theatres and at the bear garden, the skilled pickpocket waited. In the evenings, the 'cross-biter' flourished—a whore who tempted the gull into her room and then had a roaring bully interrupt the proceedings in the character of her brother and demand satisfaction from the craven victim.

But the prince of deceivers, the man most likely to spirit money out of simple purses, was the one Greene called the conny-catcher, the dishonest gambler. His boldness, his sleight-of-hand, his ingenuity with marked cards, loaded dice and the like made him something of an artist; his various 'laws'—or cheating devices—were fully expounded in Greene's pamphlets. 'Though I have not practised their deceits', he wrote, 'yet conversing by fortune, and talking upon purpose with such copes-mates, hath given me light into their conceits, and I can decipher their qualities, though I utterly mislike of their practices.' Greene's investigations were perhaps not quite as original as he pretended : much of his material had appeared in the *Manifest Detection* of forty years before. 'I have shot at many abuses,' Greene said in his *Vision*, 'over shot myself in describing of some; where truth failed, my invention hath stood my friend.' But his stories, some in the form of conversations between rascals, and other in the form of 'merry tales' illustrating the tricks of the cheats, gave a surprising view of the London underworld. Honest citizens were not to know that the Elizabethan rogue often regarded gaol as a refuge and could not be persuaded to leave. Prison was the university of their profession. In the King's Bench gaol and in the Marshalsea there were workshops for the manufacture of false dice. Friends, confederates and mistresses were allowed in, and when the rogue had perfected his tricks in gaol, he was allowed out at so much a day to practise them on the outside. When he had made his mark he bolted back to the comparative safety of the wards; even highwaymen returned to the anonymity of the Counters after their robberies.

These social pamphlets of Greene are among the first examples of the now universal popular journalism. They have too much imagination to be quite 'news' reports in the modern sense, but they gave the appreciative public an entertaining prose picture, based on fact, of the London world, and this had hardly been attempted before in England. But for all their original virtues they were not great art. Greene wrote too fast and, as the popularity of his subject overtook him, too carelessly. 'In a night and a day', said Thomas Nashe, 'would he have yarkt up a pamphlet as well as in seven years, and glad was that printer that he might be so blest to pay him dear for the very dregs of his wit.' Also he had but a year to live. The riot of his life was catching up with him and his name was on every censorious tongue as an example of bad living. Gabriel Harvey, the Cambridge scholar who attacked him violently after his death, though he did not know Greene personally, had heard all about his ways : the debts he left at every lodgings; the meetings with criminals at Bankside, Shoreditch and Southwark; the libelling and the cheating; the desertion of his wife and the seduction of the sister of a rogue called 'Cutting' Ball by whom he had an illegitimate son; and the 'contemning of superiors, deriding of others, and defying of all good order'.

As Greene's body was undermined by excess, so his art was undermined by success. In 1592, in the last year of his life, he tried to marry the good qualities of the conny-catching pamphlets to a better sense of form. The results are three wistful works of varying success. The *Quip for an Upstart Courtier* showed what might be done. It is subtitled 'a quaint dispute between velvet breeches and cloth breeches' and is a lament for a lost age of simplicity, written in a lively controlled style that owed something to the early graces of his novels, and something to the direct plainness of his pamphlets. The note of regret is what one might expect from a sick and disappointed man, but it seems that his despair was too much for him. In *Greene's Vision* he declares that his work was in vain and worthless, and in his *Repentance,* the last confession of a sinful man, he damns his life entirely.

Greene's sad end was related in picturesque detail by his enemy Harvey. After a 'fatal banquet of pickle herring' he lay amid his lice and begged for a penny-pot of malmsey. His friends and fellow writers deserted him, and his only companions were his mistress, his landlady and her husband. He was down to one shirt, his doublet, hose and sword being sold for three shillings; he owed his landlord £10. Here Greene's printer took up the story. On the last night he heard that his deserted wife was well and sent him good wishes; he was glad, confessed that he had wronged her, and, knowing that his time was short, wrote her a letter : 'Sweet wife, as ever there was any good will or friendship between thee and me see this bearer (my Host) satisfied of his debt : I owe him ten pound, and but for him I had perished in the streets. Forget and forgive my wrongs done unto thee, and Almight God have mercy on my soul. Farewell till we meet in heaven, for on earth thou shalt never see me more.' He died on 3rd September 1592. His kind hostess crowned him with a garland of bay leaves and buried him in New Churchyard, near Bedlam.

'He inherited more virtues than vices', Nashe wrote in defence of his friend against the sour criticisms of Harvey. 'Debt and deadly sin, who is not subject to? With any notorious crime I never knew him tainted.' Unlucky, weak and wilful rather than bad, Greene might have passed unnoticed in a more forgiving time. Nor was he a rebel against society and country. To him, 'fair England' was the 'flower of Europe'; London, with its vigorous trade, was equal to the 'strongest city in the world'; and even English courtesans, he wrote in his *Never Too Late,* 'are far superior in artificial allurement to them of all the world'—their looks 'contain modesty, mirth, chastity, wantonness and what not'. Indeed, so far as he had political views, he regarded England as 'this glorious Island' corrupted from ideal simplicity by foreign, especially Italian, ways. Like many wild, indulgent men, he was a natural conservative and moralist. The pastoral sentiments of one of his gentle, conventional poems expressed well enough the world he could not find :

Sweet are the thoughts that savour of content,
　The quiet mind is richer than a crown,
Sweet are the nights in careless slumber spent,
　The poor estate scorn fortune's angry frown,
Such sweet content, such mind, such sleep, such bliss
　Beggars enjoy when princes oft do miss.

When Greene came to manhood, there was no room already prepared for him in the English scheme of things. The universities,
in their new secular life after the Reformation, were turning out
young scholars at a great rate. By the middle of Elizabeth's reign
there were already too many of them, as the famous schoolmaster
Richard Mulcaster pointed out. Living high at university, and
having a good opinion of their abilities, these young men were then
put out in the world and found nothing for them to do. They
drifted to London looking for patrons and jobs, and they tried their
hand at writing, for that was one task they were qualified to do.
But the profession of hack writer as yet hardly existed. In former
ages the writer had been an amateur, one who combined a love of
literature with a place that paid his wages—in the Church, in the
government, in trade, or in the nobleman's household. Or the
writer had been a man of independent means himself. Now, in the
late sixteenth century, there was at last a growing public in London that would make commercial writing a possibility. But the
market was difficult and badly organized, and the young learned
wits, haughty and privileged until then, had to grub for their
living, they had the difficult task of reconciling their pretensions
with their needs. It is no wonder that many went astray.

In the *Quip for an Upstart Courtier,* Greene has left an excellent portrait of the Elizabethan author : 'I espied far off a certain
kind of an overworn gentleman, attired in velvet and satin; but it
was somewhat dropped and greasy, and boots on his legs, whose
soles waxed thin and seemed to complain of their master, which
treading thrift under his feet, had brought them into that con-
sumption. He walked not as other men in the common beaten way,
but came compassing *circumcirca,* as if we had been devils and
he would draw a circle about us, and at every third step he looked
back as if he were afraid of a bailiff or a serjeant.' Greene himself was such a figure, and he was put to many questionable shifts
to keep alive. 'Poverty is the father of innumerable infirmities',

he complained. Certainly it made him write too much and too quickly; even Nashe admitted that 'Greene came oftener in print than men of judgement allowed of'. And the same cause made him resort to a little 'conny-catching' on his own. Once he sold the same play to two companies; the Queen's Players bought *Orlando Furioso* for 20 nobles,[1] and when they were out of London Greene resold the play to the Lord Admiral's men for the same amount.

Drinking, whoring, a little cheating, a lot of irresponsibility—it is not a great catalogue of crime. Many of Greene's literary companions were involved in more desperate scrapes than he was. The poet Thomas Watson and the famous playwright Christopher Marlowe were arrested for homicide in 1589, and so too was Ben Jonson in 1598. The tragic dramatist Thomas Kyd was arrested for atheism in 1593; he was imprisoned and tortured, and tried to shift the blame onto Marlowe. Marlowe was a government agent of some kind, and was killed in an obscure brawl at Deptford. Anthony Munday was a paid informer and delivered up to the government Jesuits and Puritans alike. The attractive Thomas Lodge, being the son of a bankrupt, a prodigal and a Catholic, was forced to become an adventurer; he sailed on a couple of piratical expeditions, and afterwards, driven by need to all kinds of writing, showed as good a knowledge of low life as Greene. The equally attractive and brilliantly versatile Thomas Nashe was more than once in trouble with authority. In 1594 he was prosecuted by city fathers, and in 1597 his lodgings were searched by order of the Privy Council. It is no wonder that Greene, knowing the violence and despair of his colleagues, should have warned them, in one of his reforming moods, to note his bad life and mend theirs. 'Look unto me', he said in *Groatsworth of Wit,* addressed especially to Marlowe, 'and thou shalt find it an infernal bondage. I know the least of my demerits merit this miserable death, but wilful striving against known truth, exceedeth all the terrors of my soul. Defer not (with me) till this last point of extremity; for little knowest thou how in the end thou shalt be visited.' Less than a year later, Marlowe was dead, stabbed above the right eye at Eleanor Bull's tavern on Deptford Strand.

In his penitent mood Greene was hard on his friends and very severe on himself. The picture he gives of himself in *Groatsworth*

---

[1] The noble was a gold coin worth 6s. 8d.

of Wit, his *Repentance* and his *Vision* is altogether too black and
dramatic to be taken as the whole truth. Obviously there were
men, and some in high places, far more evil than he was. But the
English public, it seems, judged Greene to be as bad as he sometimes thought he was; for both the writer and his countrymen used
the same standard of judgment. What worried respectable opinion
about Greene and his fellow hacks was their rootlessness, their
lack of a place in the scheme of things. The Elizabethans believed
in order: the famous passage in Shakespeare's *Troilus and
Cressida* put this belief best:

> The heavens themselves, and planets, and this centre
> Observe degree, priority, and place,
> Insisture, course, proportion, season, form,
> Office, and custom, in all line of order:

and the speech goes on:

> How could communities,
> Degrees in schools, and brotherhoods in cities,
> Peaceful commerce from dividable shores,
> The primogenitive and due of birth,
> Prerogative of age, crowns, sceptres, laurels,
> But by degree, stand in authentic place?
> Take but degree away, untune that string,
> And hark! what discord follows.

But who were these turbulent hacks? Greene was a poor man's
son, Marlowe was the son of a shoemaker, Nashe, Dekker and
many another were born poor. They were educated, yet they had
no profession (for hack author was not recognized as a proper vocation); they lived as gentlemen and consorted with rabble; they
wrote on all topics, even society and government, in a way that
authority found suspicious. In a word, they were disorderly themselves, and a force for disorder in others. Gabriel Harvey, himself
a ropemaker's son and a scholar, but acceptably placed as a university tutor, voiced the conventional view when he accused Greene
for the 'contemning of superiors, deriding of others, and defying
of all good order'; and in another place he prayed that Greene's
works 'have not done more harm by corruption of manners, than
by quickening of wit'. Greene in his remorse accepted this criticism, for he was at heart a patriotic Englishman. He accused

himself and Marlowe of 'atheism', though by this he meant not so much religious unbelief, but bad living, questioning of authority, and acts against the well-being of the State.

Greene no doubt longed for the place that Elizabethan society was not yet ready to accord to the hack writer. Perhaps part of his animosity against the actors and the playwrights attached to the theatrical companies was because they had achieved an acceptance, almost a respectability, that the hack prose writer had not. In Elizabeth's time, the theatre, like gambling, was a suspicious business; but again like gambling, the royal patents given to the various theatrical companies protected the stage and gave its servants a certain place in society.

But insecurity made Greene the writer he was. Because he had no settled place he sank; and because he needed to live by his pen he wrote about the world he knew. With him and a few others of his kind a note of common reality enters into English literature that had hardly existed before. And though this kind of writing was not always very accomplished, literature gained, for a large part at the bottom end of society that had been hidden before was suddenly illuminated. The conny-catchers, the rogues, the cheats, the cross biters and the bullies were not just types as they sometimes had appeared in the medieval 'merrie tales'. They were figures taken from close observation who talked and swore and tricked in the pamphlets as they did in life. Greene's experience in the shadows affected his art. He was one of those who helped to bring English fiction out of the foolish, artificial country of romance and to root it firmly in the ground of ordinary life. He became also, because he was one of them, the chronicler of the dispossessed, the portraitist of a sombre society that lay beneath the glittering successes of Elizabeth's reign. Injustice and cruelty walked in the world he pictured, where too rapid social changes had left so many wandering, lawless and in despair.

11
Tudor Playwrights

WHEN THOMAS MORE was a boy serving in the household of Cardinal Morton he took part in the dramatic interludes presented in the winter for the great man and his guests. These entertainments in the hall at Lambeth were at first a kind of morality play, simple allegories bringing home religious and moral lessons. Then, as repetition weakened the moral and wearied the onlookers with the dull formality of the drama, Henry Medwall, the Cardinal's chaplain and resident playwright, tried to enliven the performance, having in mind pleasure rather than instruction. In *Fulgens and Lucrece,* written around 1497, he suppressed the allegory and told a secular tale of a wooing with plenty of incident and some characterization joined to a sub-plot of coarse rustic humour. The result was not a great play, but the audience found it 'right honest solace' for leisurely gentlemen in the contented hour after dinner. Since 1485 the times had been peaceful, and the country was becoming prosperous. Men were ready for whatever ingenious and attractive tales the playwright could devise for them.

A few years later when the poet John Skelton began his brave campaign against the rising churchman Thomas Wolsey, he framed his first condemnation in the form of a morality. The cumbersome *Magnificence,* a monument to the eccentric garrulity of the poet, is more static preaching than lively drama, but the author perceived that the stage was a good place for an attack on a public figure and his policy; a play was as useful for satire, criticism or denunciation as it was for moral instruction.

Drama in England began in the Church and most dramatic performances in the Middle Ages were connected with religion. Theatre was a part of religious instruction. Mystery, or miracle, plays, such as the cycles presented in York, Chester and Wakefield, were based on biblical stories and given by the guilds of the town. Later, the morality play reflected the favourite medieval habit of allegorizing, putting in simple dramatic form the struggle of the virtues and the vices for the soul. Performances of the mystery cycles continued even into the seventeenth century, and moralities were still written in the reign of Elizabeth, but slowly drama began to lose its intimate connection with religion.

Secular plays were not unknown in the Middle Ages. Travelling minstrels and players went their rounds, as Shakespeare has pictured them in *Hamlet;* by 1469 they had formed their own guild with a charter granted by Edward IV. In the countryside, folk festivals and holidays were enlivened by mummery and simple plays. In the towns, expensive pageants, often on mythological or historical themes, were devised for great occasions such as the entertainment of an ambassador or a royal wedding. In the houses of the rich, the lordly amateurs had a passion for the new 'interlude', or short play. Special servants were hired whose duties included acting; in 1473 Sir John Paston spoke of one employed 'to play Saint George and Robin Hood and the Sheriff of Nottingham'. The plays themselves have largely disappeared, but some of the subjects have been recorded. Many interludes were about the popular heroes of the romances—Sir Guy, Sir Eglamour, Robert of Sicily and the like. Others were about St George, or Robin Hood —'very proper to be played in May games'. Sometimes fragments of a play have been preserved, and these show a variety of topics from the bawdy *Interludium de Clerico et Puella* to the incestuous *Dux Moraud.*

Performances of secular interludes were occasional and haphazard. But as settled times came with the reign of Henry VII men began to think more of ease and entertainment, and drama was looked at with new eyes. Since aristocratic patrons—Cardinal Morton and the Earl of Northumberland for example—wanted interludes, writers began to consider the form; they discovered with Medwall and Skelton that the drama had unsuspected virtues. Renaissance scholarship helped by unearthing new sources, new examples, new stories, and new uses for plays. The introduction of printing into England spread this new knowledge. A renewed interest in plays flourished among those who loved the arts, and foremost among the new enthusiasts was Sir Thomas More, so that the beginnings of Tudor drama seemed a family affair, centred round his fine intelligence and genial personality.

The fascination of the theatre had caught More early. As a boy

o   *209*

in Morton's house he would 'suddenly sometimes slip in among the players and make a part of his own there presently among them'. He met Henry Medwall and saw the new art Medwall had given to the interlude; perhaps he had acted under the direction of the playwright. In his youth, said his contemporary John Bale, More was a writer of comedies. Although none have survived one may guess at their virtues, for the English works of More abound in both humour and dramatic conversations. Soon More had no time to spend on comedies, and having led by example he was later content to encourage others. His practical interest in drama was taken up first by his brother-in-law John Rastell, and then by his nephew John Heywood.

Rastell was a lawyer from Coventry who eventually became a printer in St Paul's Churchyard. Law books and plays were the specialities of his press; of the eighteen plays printed before 1534 no less than twelve were printed by him and his son William. From his press came plays by Medwall, Heywood, possibly Skelton, and of course those by Rastell himself. Without the efforts of Rastell and his son the early Tudor drama might have disappeared like that of the Middle Ages. It was natural for a lawyer to print law books, but for the Rastells the printing of plays was a duty of love. John Rastell, despite a busy career as lawyer, printer, then M.P. and later agent for Thomas Cromwell, was active in all kinds of dramatic ventures. He was a deviser and producer of pageants, being entrusted with some of the design for the Field of Cloth of Gold at Guisnes in 1520. When he built a new house in Finsbury Fields, in 1524, he erected a stage in the garden; with the help of his wife and a tailor he designed and made costumes, curtains and hangings which he hired out. And he was a playwright himself, perhaps producing his own pieces on his own stage.

Rastell was not the most skilful writer, but his interludes showed the way drama was going. *The Four Elements* was on the thoroughly secular subjects of astronomy and geography, and included some far-sighted, patriotic remarks on the need for English voyages to the New World. In this interlude the old medieval allegory was still used, but in *Calisto and Melibea*[1] (taken from the famous novel *La Celestina* by Fernando de Rojas) individual characters take the place of the old personifications. While Rastell's

[1] There is some doubt about the authorship of this piece. It is possible that only the conclusion is by Rastell.

interludes were rather stiff and, in their desire to teach a lesson, not far from the medieval moralities, the plays of his son-in-law John Heywood were a great advance. With Heywood, pleasure came before instruction and natural events drove out the artifices of allegory. He was among the first, wrote Thomas Warton, who 'introduced representations of familiar life and popular manners'.

In the course of a long life devoted to drama Heywood suffered many misfortunes, most of them caused by his Catholicism. He was in danger under Henry VIII, prospered under Mary, and fled the country under Elizabeth. He died in exile around 1579, over eighty years old, with his 'mad merry wit' intact to the end. Like his father-in-law, he was prepared for any theatrical task, and was actor, orator, pageant-maker and playwright; he was as happy with a rustic farce as with a masque at court. His plays seem to have been written in his middle years. Although he lived forty more years, into another and golden age of literature, his plays are his memorial. In these interludes of limited stage technique (all his pieces are in the medieval form of a debate), he established a strong line of realistic satire and farce; hypocritical rogues, roaring bullies, snivelling priests, termagant wives and hen-pecked husbands were his stock in trade. The anti-clerical satire of *The Pardoner and the Friar* and the domestic discord of *Johan Johan* would amuse today as they did then.

By the middle of the 1530s the early group of Tudor playwrights, from Medwall to Heywood, had given the idea of the new drama. In many ways it was tied to the past. The plays were short, the characters were few, stage business was at a minimum, and there was little action; allegory was still used, moral lessons were still attached, and the characters tended to declaim. In other respects there had been some remarkable changes. Drama was now finally out of the hands of the Church. The new playwrights, even those who were churchmen such as Medwall and Skelton, were writing on secular subjects, and their intention was to amuse as much as to instruct. Instead of the formal interchange between vices and virtues, as in the old morality, a wealth of new matter appeared in the interludes. Sharp details begin to portray contemporary life; a play will show a prisoner in Newgate, give the names of wines available in London, describe games of chance and ways of cheating, or give the news of shipping and the state of the tide. Social commentary and criticism appeared. Rastell in particular had an inquiring and reforming mind. He was interested in language and thought 'our tongue maternal' was sufficient 'to expound any hard sentence'. He was a patriot and chided his country for lack of interest in exploration. He scattered his plays with criticisms of education, government and law; he thought that judges should be appointed for short periods and examined for partiality before reappointment. Indeed, the tone of this early drama, not only in plays by known writers but also in anonymous pieces like *Youth, The Holy War* and *Hickscorner,* was pessimistic. The comedy, which often appeared in a sub-plot, was rough and unkind; the drama reflected a time of change when England was worried by the social and religious troubles which More's *Utopia* set out so poignantly.

> A mirror uncleared is this interlude,
> This life inconstant for to behold and see

wrote Skelton in *Magnificence.* 'The weeds overgrow the corn' was the message of the plays.

Secular drama for a fairly wide public had begun. Many different things influenced its development. Education both at school and university, the rediscovery of ancient literature by the humanists, the practice of the fashionable young men at the Inns of Court, and the life at the king's court, all had a part to play in forming Elizabethan drama.

The Tudor schoolboy was something of an actor. Schooling was largely an education in Latin and much of the instruction, for want of text-books, was by repetition and practice. The staging of Latin plays, in which the boys took the parts, improved the command of the language and helped to keep the scholars interested. The comedies of Terence and Plautus were particularly recommended; they were good entertainment and they had the approval of the humanists for their elegant Latin. Terence was the first classical dramatist printed in England, just before the turn of the sixteenth century, and thirty years later Rastell published a translation of one of his plays under the title *Terens in English.* The acting that the boys learnt in school made them in demand outside the schoolroom. Courtesy insisted that great visitors to England should be entertained with interludes, naturally given in Latin which was the international language. But Latin was beyond the powers of the professional players and so the boys were called out to perform. The young players, possibly of St Paul's, acted a 'goodly comedy of Plautus' before Henry VIII at Greenwich in 1519. Under their High Master, John Ritwise, the boys of St Paul's in 1528 played Terence's *Phormio* for Cardinal Wolsey and his guests. By the middle of the century most of the famous schools were taking their plays into the houses of the great. The boys of Eton played for Cromwell in 1538; thirty-five years later they were acting for Elizabeth at Hampton Court. At Westminster, the duties of performing were written into the statutes. The students of Merchant Taylors', under their famous headmaster Richard Mulcaster, were very active. An old pupil of Mulcaster recalled that 'yearly he presented some players to the court, in which his scholars were only actors, and I one among them, and by that means taught them good behaviour and audacity'. Nor was it only the London schoolboys who acted. There are records of plays by students at Canterbury, Shrewsbury, Beverley and elsewhere.

After their success in Latin, the boys were soon giving performances in English also. At first they gave translations of the classical plays, in particular Terence and Plautus; then they began to act original plays in English, usually comedies influenced by the classics they knew so well. To provide this English fare, schoolmasters turned playwright, and the most famous of these was Nicholas Udall, one time headmaster of Eton, from where he was dismissed for theft and vice, and later headmaster at Westminster. Udall's best known comedy, *Ralph Roister Doister* (c. 1553), showed the good influence of Terence and Plautus. At last the native play was given a clear structure; following the classical models, *Roister Doister* was divided into acts and scenes; the comic business was well organized; and the characters, sturdy English versions of the Roman types, had strong personalities. To the broad humour of Heywood's comedy, Udall added better form, better logic, more ingenuity in plotting and greater variety in handling. Classical principles had aided English humour to good effect.

When Tudor boys turned to youths and went from school to university, they still continued their acting. Oxford and Cambridge had always liked drama. Records of the late Middle Ages reveal plenty of activity. There were Christmas plays, and liturgical dramas; there were pageants and mummeries. The Boy-Bishop held his mock rule on the Feast of the Innocents; Christmas Lords directed the merry-making at many colleges; at Merton College,

Oxford, the *Rex Fabarum*—'the King of Beans'—was the Lord of Misrule from 19th November until Candlemas on 2nd February. With the coming of the 'new learning' of the Renaissance, classical drama was taken up, as it was in the grammar schools, and for the same reason. University men acted, wrote the academic playwright William Gager, 'to practise our own style in prose or verse; to be well acquainted with Seneca or Plautus; honestly to embolden our path'. Seneca was the master for tragedy, and Plautus the master for comedy. And as the schoolboys often played for the court in London, so the undergraduates played for the royal visits to the university.

The academic playwrights usually wrote in Latin, as befitting the dignity of a scholar. But the most delightful and surprising of the university plays was an English comedy called *Gammer Gurton's Needle*, acted at Christ's College, Cambridge around 1563, and written by a certain 'Mr S. Mr. of Art'. This play was the confirmation that the native comedy first seen in *Ralph Roister Doister* had taken firm root. Though written by an academic playwright for a learned audience, *Gammer Gurton's Needle* was boisterous village comedy, all entertainment and no moral. The tidy influence of the classical drama was there, but well hidden. It was a confident work, rougher than Udall's earlier play, but better because closer to English life and character. English comedy had come of age.

Education was the nurse of comedy; tragedy was fostered at the Inns of Court. The Inns were not merely places for the training of lawyers. They were the university for the prosperous young gentleman who aimed to make a place in the world rather than in the Church. And like their fellows at Oxford and Cambridge the young students of London had a taste for all kinds of revels, masques and dramas. As the colleges had their Lords of Misrule, so Gray's Inn enacted the mock reign of the Prince of Purpoole. As the boys of the grammar schools and the undergraduates of the colleges entertained the court on occasions, so the young men of Gray's Inn and the Inner Temple welcomed the monarch to their revels. Elizabeth pronounced herself 'very much beholden' to Gray's Inn, 'for that it did always study for some sports to present unto her'.

When they turned from the fun of the revels and the formal elegance of the masque to more extended drama, the lawyers preferred the austerity of tragedy. Seneca had long been a favourite of scholars. His melodramatic violence and dark imagination made him a more appropriate master for the worldly young Londoners, who were soon to know the pains of society as they took up their places in Tudor government, than Terence with his lighter talent. The authors of *Gorboduc,* acted for the Christmas revels of the Inner Temple in 1561–62 and the first blank verse tragedy on a London stage, were Thomas Sackville and Thomas Norton, two men of affairs who rose high in the country's service. To a legendary story of English history they added the structure and the gloomy conventions of Senecan drama, and gave it topicality for the England of the Virgin Queen by making the play bear on the question of royal succession. Here were the elements for future success—noble characters falling to violent tragedy seen as a mirror of the contemporary world, and expressed in the flexible poetry of blank verse given form by the Senecan model. This pattern, more or less, was followed in the future productions of the Inns of Court, in *Jocasta,* mainly by the versatile George Gascoigne, in *Gismond of Salern,* by various hands, and in *The Misfortunes of Arthur,* by Thomas Hughes. But by the time this last play was acted, on 28th February 1588, by the men of Gray's Inn for the Queen at Greenwich, tragedy had passed from lawyers to professionals and was being developed on the public stage.

The changes in comedy and tragedy were done with the encouragement of the court. The development of Tudor drama could hardly have gone on without the active interest of the court. Scholars and lawyers alike entertained the courtiers; the court was the fountain that nourished the popular pageants and masques which taught a later age so much about stage production, about effects, scenery and costume, about music, song and dance. By the reign of Henry VII, the Gentlemen and Children of the Chapel Royal already existed. These were primarily musicians and choristers for religious celebrations who were gradually given the task of organizing the royal entertainments. William Cornish, the Master of the Children from 1509 to 1523, greatly extended the dramatic activities of the Children and was a composer of interludes and masques himself. It seems that John Heywood had begun as one of the Children and no doubt learnt the rudiments of the theatre here. Henry VII was too cold to care for expensive entertainments; he was, wrote Bacon, 'rather a princely and gentle spectator than seemed much to be delighted'. But when the gallant young Henry VIII and the ingenious Cornish came together in the first year of the new reign, pleasure was the business of the court so that ceremonious revels, interludes, pageants, masques, dumb-shows, dances, theatrical performances of all kinds, were the delight of all the later Tudors. Such was their liking for these entertainments that they were prepared to overlook remarkable failings in those who amused them. Nicholas Udall was a vehement Reformer, a thief and a lecher, yet he still devised shows for the pious and moral Queen Mary; the well-known papist Sebastian Westcott, master of the choir school at St Paul's Cathedral, produced with his company of boys some twenty-seven plays for Elizabeth. When a professional public theatre at last emerged in the reign of Elizabeth, it did so protected by the crown against the law which frowned upon it; the dramatic companies were licensed by the Queen and supervised by her official, the Master of the Revels.

Public theatre was slow to come. A hopeful start had been made in the first thirty years of the sixteenth century, when Rastell and Heywood were writing their secular interludes, and Rastell set up a stage in his own garden and got together costumes and props to hire to other professionals. In the play *Sir Thomas More* there is a picture of these early professionals presenting an interlude in More's house before an audience of burgesses. Strype noted that companies of actors, some amateur and some professional, 'played at certain festival times, and in private houses at weddings, or other splendid entertainments, for their own profit'. Then, with the coming of the religious troubles, the public theatre made little advance for many years. Secular drama was not in favour with the religious controversialists of the Reformation. The economic and social troubles of the mid-century disrupted the players. Though money could be found for the entertainments and shows of the court, the reliable *Discourse of the Common Weal,* published about 1549, said that popular 'stage plays, interludes, May games' and the like were abandoned because of 'much expenses'.

The public theatre, when it did arrive, benefited from the pause. Following after Rastell and Heywood, it might have produced little except their old-fashioned secular moralities. As it was, in the long interval of disquiet, amateur players made experiments which later invigorated the public stage. The efforts of the schoolboys, the scholars, the lawyers and the courtiers reformed the drama. *Gorboduc* became a model for verse tragedy, *Gammer Gurton's Needle* for verse comedy, and Gascoigne's *Supposes* (1566) for prose comedy. Historical and biographical plays had been written, chiefly by the industrious John Bale, who died in 1563. Stage production and the art of blending music and song with drama had been fostered by the entertainments of the court. All the elements out of which Shakespeare was later to construct his magic were present : they only awaited the men to use them.

By 1557 the churchwardens of St Botolph, in London, were renting their parish hall to players, and they continued to do this regularly for the next eleven years. Nor were they alone. The stability that Elizabeth slowly gave to the country brought the actors back before the public. Small ventures were tried here and there. Elizabeth liked the court revels, though her well-known parsimony prevented her from supporting them with the lavish generosity of her father. Westcott and his company of children from St Paul's choir school acted for her in 1560, and then every year except one until his death in 1582. The Children of the Chapels Royal were also active under William Hunnis and Richard Farrant. In 1576 Farrant took a lease on some old buildings in Blackfriars, converted them to a theatre for the Children of the Chapel, and began to give performances to a courtly audience. The great men of the kingdom were encouraged to re-form their 'servants' into companies of actors. In 1574 the Earl of Leicester, an enthusiastic patron, persuaded the Queen to grant his company a licence under royal patent. This was a wise precaution, for Elizabeth's government was even then enacting strict laws against vagrancy, and wandering players were liable to severe penalties unless well organized and well protected. Even a royal patent was no absolute safeguard against the enmity of city fathers. In London, the Common Council banned performances within the city limits.[2] James Burbage, the first of the famous family, was forced to take his players in Leicester's Company to the liberties outside the walls. In 1576 he built the *Theatre* in Shoreditch, the first playhouse designed and built for public performances.

[2] Blackfriars, though within the city walls, claimed to be outside city jurisdiction. The theatre thus avoided the ban of the Common Council. Though the *Blackfriars* was known as a 'private' theatre, the performances were public in the sense that the aristocratic audience paid to come in.

Soon the *Curtain* arose nearby; then, in 1587, Philip Henslowe went south of the Thames and built the *Rose* on Bankside which became the centre of popular theatrical activity. The *Swan* appeared in 1594; four years later Richard and Cuthbert Burbage, the sons of James, pulled down the old *Theatre* and took the timber across the river to build the famous *Globe*. While the theatres were going up, the lordly companies were more and more in demand. They played by the command of the Queen at court, acting in banqueting halls and presence chambers; they played in the public theatres at Holywell, Moorfields, Newington Butts and Bankside; they went on country tours, playing in churches, parish halls, inn-yards, schoolrooms, 'upon boards, and barrel-heads, to an old crackt trumpet'. Leicester, Pembroke, Lord Strange, the Lord Admiral, and the Lord Chamberlain were the patrons of the most notable companies; by the end of the century the last two companies were the most famous. The Admiral's Men were led by Henslowe and Edward Alleyn, and the Chamberlain's Men were under Richard Burbage with William Shakespeare as playwright.

The public was eager, stages were available, actors had a new-found confidence : only playwrights were lacking. Sentimental or lascivious stories from Heliodorus and Apuleius, or weak versions of the old chivalrous romances, seem to have made up the bulk of the popular fare offered to the public in the first half of Elizabeth's reign. 'I may boldly say it, because I have seen it', the Puritan critic Stephen Gosson wrote in 1579, 'that the *Palace of Pleasure,* the *Golden Ass,* the *Æthiopian History, Amadis of France,* the *Round Table,* bawdy comedies in Latin, French, Italian and Spanish, have been thoroughly ransacked to furnish the playhouses in London.' Gosson was chiefly concerned with public morals, one of the first of the carping Puritans who later utterly condemned the theatre. But Philip Sidney, the upholder of poetry and the opponent of Gosson, also severely criticized the drama, even the more imaginative pieces that came from the academies and the Inns of Court. Writing his *Defence of Poesie* within a year or two of Gosson's attack, Sidney could find nothing to praise in comedy, and only *Gorboduc*—with reservations—in tragedy. Luckily, better times were ahead.

The first notable development came about through the happy conjunction of a new writer, John Lyly, with a new theatre, that of the Children at Blackfriars. Lyly, a young man just down from Oxford, had a staggering success with *Euphues* in 1578, and confirmed that triumph with the sequel *Euphues and his England* two years later. These works of prose fiction were a new blend of careful rhetoric, romantic interest, and lively conversation. These qualities were as suitable for drama as they were for prose fiction, and since Lyly's patron was the Earl of Oxford, a man who had both a company of children and a company of adult actors in his service, Lyly soon turned his hand to drama. On New Year's Day 1584 his play *Campaspe* was given at Blackfriars, and then repeated at court before the Queen, by a company of children drawn from the Chapel Royal, the St Paul's choir school and Lord Oxford's own company. Lyly's second play, *Sapho and Phao,* appeared at Blackfriars on 3rd March 1584, and for the next six years he continued to write plays for the children which were also seen at court. All his plays, except the *Woman in the Moon,* were in prose, owing something to *Supposes,* the prose-comedy Gascoigne wrote for the Inns of Court in 1566. But in all other respects Lyly was a true pioneer. His plays were the first successful romantic comedies. He wrote for an aristocratic audience, and his plays reflected the society of the court: the classical background of the plots complimented the learning of the Queen and her courtiers; the sparkling dialogue was taught to Lyly by the conversation in ante-room and presence chamber; the gallantry, the witty interchange between the sexes was modelled on the graces of courtly behaviour. Heywood's rough farces and Udall's country humour seemed now the product of dark ages. Lyly's sun rose on a new world fashioned by knowledge, leisure and wealth. His characters in *Midas* greeted the dawn:

> Sing to Apollo, god of day,
> Whose golden beams with morning play,
> And make her eyes so brightly shine,
> Aurora's face is called divine.
> Sing to Phoebus and that throne
> Of diamonds which he sits upon.

Lyly's comedies depended largely on children's companies for their acting and on the favour of the court for their success. Yet even while Lyly was writing for the children, their importance in the theatre was declining. The lease of the first *Blackfriars* ended in

1586, and the second theatre at Blackfriars did not open until 1600. The boys of St Paul's were inactive between 1590 and 1600. At the same time the adult companies under the patronage of such noblemen as Leicester, Warwick and Suffolk were preferred at court. The adult companies could, and did, act romantic comedies, and they still retained youths to play the women's parts. But most of their work was for a grosser public outside the court who were not very interested in the polite world of manners of the court comedies. This public, making for the new playhouses of Shoreditch and later Bankside, wanted the sterner drama of tragedy, or history plays, or boisterous comedy, which the adult companies studied to provide. As the men drove the boys from the stage, so tragedy began to advance; and the first popular writer of tragedies for the public theatres was Thomas Kyd.

Born in 1558, the son of a London scrivener, Kyd went to the newly-founded Merchant Taylors' School where he was a contemporary of Edmund Spenser. Under the headmaster, Richard Mulcaster, he had his first taste of plays and acting. He missed university, joining his father's trade instead, but the loss to his education was no great matter for a future writer of tragedies. The interesting developments in tragedy—*Gorboduc, Jocasta, Gismond*—took place in London, at the Inns of Court. Kyd knew Seneca well from his schooling; coming from a prosperous family, he was likely to know also what was happening on the private and public stages of London. When he began to write for the public stage Kyd took the structure and the machinery of Senecan drama, which *Gorboduc* had made familiar, but added modifications out of his own originality. He was a masterly plotter with an instinctive sense of the theatre, holding his audience by surprise and expectation. The formal elements of Senecan drama—the typed characters, the action related at secondhand, the rhetorical moralizing—were cut as far as possible. Kyd liked swift action and characters who displayed their all-too-human virtues and frailties.

Kyd demonstrated his new tragic art in *The Spanish Tragedy*, which may have appeared on the London stage as early as 1585. Here was a tale of blood, using the 'revenge' motive beloved by the Senecan dramatists. Here were the Senecan ghosts and chorus, but now revitalized by Kyd's technical skill so that they inspired fear and wonder in the groundlings. Here, in rapid action, were lives of nobility, pathos, cruelty. His blank verse was not great poetry,

but he had a rugged power and an ear for the sharp phrase. The
themes that start out of his play go running on through the drama
for years to come:

> What out-cries pluck me from my naked bed,
> And chill my throbbing heart with trembling fear?

And:

> what murderous spectacle is this?
> A man hanged up and all the murderers gone.
> And in my bower, to lay the guilt on me.

These were the dire questions that kept the audience hurrying back
to Shoreditch and Bankside. Kyd inaugurated 'the tragedy of
blood' and other dramatists quickly followed him. 'Yet English
Seneca read by candle-light', Nashe wrote in 1589, scoffing at the
influence of Kyd, 'yields many good sentences as *blood is a beggar*
and so forth: and if you entreat him fair in a frosty morning, he
will afford you whole *Hamlets*,[3] I should say handfulls of tragical
speeches. . . . The sea exhaled by drops will in continuance be
dry, and Seneca let blood line by line, and page by page, at length
must needs die on our stage.' That death did not come until the
Senecan blood had flowed through Marlowe, Chapman, Shakespeare, and into the next century to Webster, Tourneur and
Middleton.

The liveliness of the stage, both at the 'private house' of Blackfriars and in the public theatres, attracted a new generation of
young playwrights. These men, of whom Lyly and Kyd were
among the first, were all born about the time, or shortly after,
Elizabeth's accession to the throne in 1558. They had the Elizabethan view, unaffected by the harsh events which had so depressed
the drama and the actors in the last years of Henry VIII and in
the reigns of Edward and Mary. They came to the drama as a
fresh art which they approached not so much through the English theatrical tradition, a tradition grown weak from the knocks
of the mid-century, but rather by way of their classical training at
school and university and their readings in Renaissance literature.
For most of the new playwrights were learned young men, the 'university wits', who had taken up writing as a way to earn a living.

[3] This is a reference to an early *Hamlet* which Shakespeare most likely
used for his play. It is a matter of argument whether or not this *Hamlet*
was by Kyd.

They wrote both prose and poetry, ready to turn out by order a romance, a pastoral, a satire, a controversial pamphlet, or a flattering dedication. They were the first hacks of writing, professionals made possible by the spread of printing and the growth of public literacy. They wrote plays because the theatre was flourishing and there was money to be made on the stage. Robert Greene, who was one of them, related in his *Groatsworth of Wit* how he met an actor by the roadside, when his fortunes were low, who advised him to make plays 'for which you will be well paid, if you will take the pains'. Greene, 'perceiving no remedy, thought best in respect of his present necessity to try his wit and went with him willingly'.

When the university wits took to plays, most of them had behind them some success in other forms of writing. In pursuit of income, they were prepared to try all types of drama; but being inexperienced they found it best to experiment with plays that would owe something to their former successes in fiction or verse. So Lyly's court comedy took the notable features of *Euphues* and cast them into dramatic form.

Of this group of new young playwrights, none was more versatile than George Peele. He had been to Oxford where he had made a reputation as a poet, and where he had run into expense through an early marriage. In 1581 he came to London looking for work, and was drawn, like Lyly, to write plays for the children and the court. And his *Arraignment of Paris,* published in 1584, was very close to Lyly's comedy, with a plot from classical mythology embroidered in the elegant manner of the pastoral romance. Peele, however, wrote his play in verse, in a wide variety of metres—old, lumbering 'fourteeners' and new flexible blank verse, rhymed couplets and short lyrics—which tested the possibilities of all kinds of dramatic poetic diction. If Peele was never a master of dramatic construction, he was at least a writer of masterly poetry, and his experiments in beautiful verse pleased greatly. Nashe commended him 'as the chief supporter of pleasaunce now living' and praised the *Arraignment of Paris* for 'present dexterity of wit and manifold variety of invention'.

Peele went on to prove his 'manifold variety of invention'. Before his early death in 1596, he had produced many pageants for the court and the city. He had written a burlesque of the supernatural in his *Old Wives' Tale.* He had written a history play on *Edward I,* and another historical chronicle, *The Battle of Alcazar,* based on the swashbuckling life of the famous Devonshire adventurer Thomas Stukeley. And he had even written a biblical play, *King David and Fair Bethsabe,* making an Elizabethan revenge tragedy out of the second Book of Samuel.

Robert Greene, infamous in his day for bad living, was less experimental than Peele, not such a good poet but a better dramatist. He began his writing career with prose romances, particularly pleasing to the female readers. He, too, was driven to the theatre by the sad state of his purse. *Alphonsus,* produced about 1588, was a perfunctory, ranting imitation of Marlowe's *Tamburlaine,* which also influenced the later and better *Orlando Furioso,* with a plot taken from Ariosto's epic poem. Greene had little luck competing with the bombast of *Tamburlaine*; he had more success with *Friar Bacon and Friar Bungay,* written to benefit from the resounding triumph of Marlowe's *Doctor Faustus. Friar Bacon* also dabbled in the supernatural, but the most notable part of the play was the picture of romantic love in a pastoral setting which Greene added. In the days of his prose fiction Greene had been called 'the Homer of women', and his great strength in drama was in sympathetic portraits of his heroines. Margaret in *Friar Bacon* and Ida and Dorothea in his Scottish historical play *James IV,* moving in ideal pastoral worlds, where sentiment puts reason to flight, are the ancestors of Viola, Perdita, Rosalind and the other gracious, spirited women that Shakespeare loved to write about.

These 'wits' were the best of the experimenters. Other busy writers, sometimes alone and sometimes in collaboration, threw off a play for the money from time to time in the midst of their fiction and controversy. Munday, Chettle and Nashe had a hand in several kinds of drama; Nashe, in *Summer's Last Will and Testament,* even gave a fresh turn to allegory. Besides the work of the known writers, many anonymous plays were acted, especially those based on history, legend or biography. An old *King John,* an old *King Henry V* and an old *King Leir* appeared on the London stage before Shakespeare took up the same subjects. There were plays on *Sir Thomas More, Thomas Lord Cromwell* and *Robert Earl of Huntingdon,* alias 'Robin Hood'. All these plays had serious defects : the comedies were too often ill-constructed, things of awkward parts and more froth than substance; the tragedies were full of weary noise; and the histories disjointed and episodic, improbable where they weren't downright impossible.

But remarkable things had been done. The young writers from university had brought their education, their taste and their wide knowledge of European literature to bear upon the drama. They broadened the scope of both comedy and tragedy. Older academic playwrights at the colleges and the Inns had given the English play a sense of classical form. The new men breathed into this form the sentiment and feeling of contemporary Europe. And because they were writing for the public rather than scholars, in theatres where success was measured by vulgar applause, their plays, though full of faults, were more active, better characterized, more 'theatrical' than the old dramas. They set out to please a wayward audience and in doing so accurately reflected the world of those who watched the plays. The grace of Lyly and Peele was a grace learnt from the Queen's court; their fulsome praise of Elizabeth echoed the general opinion of the country as the power and reputation of England increased under her guidance. Greene's attractive heroines were women taken from experience, tributes to the place that women had in England where, foreigners agreed, they had a freedom almost unknown on the continent. The female influence was felt particularly in literature. The writers of pastorals and romances discovered that they had, in the sixteenth-century woman, a new audience for their wares, which they steadily cultivated. In the Dedication of *Euphues and his England,* Lyly commended his work to the ladies, saying that '*Euphues* had rather lie shut in a lady's casket than open in a scholar's study'. The refinement that Lyly introduced to please the ladies was carried over into the court comedy. The lyrical songs of Peele were another compliment to the cultivation and taste of the audience at Blackfriars. His lyrical experiments were part of the general attempt by English poets, Sidney and Spenser amongst them, to give a new Renaissance form to the native music of English poetry. And Peele succeeded as well as any. He ranged widely, using many different forms, portraying subtle feelings. He was capable of both the pastoral gaiety of :

> Fair and fair and twice as fair,
>   As fair as any may be :
> The fairest shepherd on our green,
>   A love for any lady.
>   (*The Arraignment of Paris*)

and the intricate evocation of passion and sensuous feeling that would do credit to John Donne :

> Hot sun, cool fire, tempered with sweet air,
> Black shade, fair nurse, shadow my white hair :
> Shine, sun; burn, fire; breathe, air, and ease me;
> Black shade, fair nurse, shroud me, and please me :
> Shadow, my sweet nurse, keep me from burning,
> Make not my glad cause cause of mourning.
>
> (King David and Fair Bethsabe)

The comedies, for the court audience, reflected the light of society; the tragedies, and sometimes the histories, for the rougher public stage, showed the dark side of the contemporary portrait. The intrigue, treachery and ferocious bloodletting in the plays was an image of part of polity. With good reason the name of Machiavelli was invoked again and again in the drama. As Marlowe wrote in the Introduction to his *Jew of Malta* :

> Albeit the world think Machiavel is dead,
> Yet was his soul but flown beyond the Alps,
> And now the Guise is dead, is come from France
> To view this land, and frolic with his friends.

The remorseless men of the plays—Lorenzo in Kyd's *Spanish Tragedy,* Tamburlaine, Mortimer and the Duke of Guise in Marlowe's *Edward II* and *Massacre at Paris*—had traits which were to be seen clearly in the high-flying ambitions of great men— Leicester, Raleigh, Essex in England, the hated Guise and the Duke of Anjou in France, Alva and William the Silent in the Netherlands, Philip II, and many another. Persecution, torture, murder on the stage mirrored the use of these same horrors in the State. The consuming selfish greed of Marlowe's Barabas was hardly greater than that of an Elizabethan financier, a Palavicino, a Stoddart, a Gresham. The ruthless pursuit of power of Tamburlaine was but one aspect of Renaissance individualism.

The production of Lyly's *Campaspe,* at Blackfriars on New Year's Day 1584, announced the great age of English drama. Kyd and the university wits made the plantation and nourished the shoots. The flowering was delayed a short while, until 1587, when the young graduate Christopher Marlowe astonished the town with his *Tamburlaine.* Marlowe, son of a Canterbury shoemaker, was born on 6th February 1564. He went to King's School in his home town, where it is known that plays were performed, and passed on to Corpus Christi College, Cambridge, in 1581. He was thus representative of the kind of student who made up the company of the 'university wits' : he was of humble family and had risen to university by his own brilliance; he was ambitious and wished to make a place in the world, but his lowly position and lack of money stood in his way; his talent had made him a poet, and he took to literature to advance his fame and to make a living. Starting so low and with so far to climb, Marlowe was reckless even by the standards of his fellows. By the time he came down from Cambridge with his M.A. in July 1587, he had already been employed by the secret service of the government. In the rest of his very short life he played out his dreams of power, beauty and grandeur against the reality of his poor existence, scheming, threatening, plotting, drinking, brawling until, in 1593, amid spies and informers, the random thrust of a dagger killed him in a Deptford tavern.

Yet Marlowe's tempestuous youth and grandiose dreams were the making of the dramatist. Tamburlaine, the 'Scythian shepherd' who conquered the world, was an emblem of Marlowe's own ambition. And when the Lord Admiral's Men acted the two parts of *Tamburlaine* in 1587 the London stage had never seen such energy, such power and such poetry. The theme was terrific, a running war that leapt across expanses of geography and dazzled the home-bound heads of insular Englishmen so that the hero could exult :

> The god of war resigns his room to me,
> Meaning to make me general of the world;
> Jove viewing me in arms looks pale and wan,
> Fearing my power should pull him from his throne.

This is the man who annihilates armies, massacres virgins and keeps the Turkish sultan in a cage, who harnesses captured kings to his chariot, and hangs the Governor of Babylon from the walls for his soldiers to shoot at.[4] Marlowe was infatuated by the almost superhuman destiny of his hero, and the play irresistibly piled

[4] According to a contemporary letter, when this scene was played in the theatre the stage effect misfired, killing a child and a pregnant woman in the audience.

triumph on triumph. No such portrait of Renaissance 'virtù', of the power-in-action which the Elizabethan world so greatly admired, had ever been seen before. Nor was that all. The grandeur of the vision was matched by the grandeur of the poetry. Kyd had used blank verse for the effective tragedy of his revenge play, but Marlowe went far beyond this rugged verse. His line, which was able to convey the overwhelming drive of ambition :

> Nature that framed us of four elements,
> Warring within our breasts for regiment,
> Doth teach us all to have aspiring minds :
> Our souls　　.　　　.　　　.　　　.
> Will us to wear ourselves and never rest,
> Until we reach the ripest fruit of all,
> That perfect bliss and sole felicity,
> The sweet fruition of an earthly crown—

was also capable of the beautiful lament for Queen Zenocrate :

> Now walk the angels on the walls of heaven,
> As sentinels to warn th' immortal souls
> To entertain divine Zenocrate.

In the plays that followed, the fascination of power still held. Marlowe's mind dwelt on Barabas, the Jew of Malta, amassing huge wealth, devising faithless stratagems, his every breath an act of treachery; on Warwick and Mortimer plotting against and bringing down Edward II; on the monstrous Duke of Guise, causing the massacre at Paris to secure the Catholic power; and on Faustus bartering his soul to the devil in return for all knowledge. As in *Tamburlaine*, the later plays had the same wide-ranging curiosity, the spectacular and horrific elements, that so delighted the public. The professional actors vied for his dramas. Performances of *The Jew of Malta*, *The Massacre at Paris* and *Doctor Faustus* helped to ensure the success of the *Rose*, Henslowe's new theatre on Bankside, and gave the great actor Edward Alleyn outstanding parts. And as Marlowe's stage skill increased, so the verse became more varied, more subtle. Glittering images suggested the wealth of the Jew; exact observation and swifter verse gave the characters of *Edward II* a new depth; and at last Faustus, deceived by the devil and awaiting death, called out with the startled vision and broken lines of true tragic poetry :

The stars move still, time runs, the clock will strike,
The devil will come, and Faustus must be damned.
O I'll leap up to my God : who pulls me down?
See see where Christ's blood streams in the firmament.
One drop would save my soul, half a drop, ah my Christ.

When the precocious Marlowe died at the age of twenty-nine, William Shakespeare, younger by a few weeks, was still learning the craft of the dramatist. He had already several plays behind him—*Love's Labour's Lost* and the *Comedy of Errors*, the three parts of the history play *Henry VI*, and perhaps one or two others—but his development was slow and steady, and his best work was to be done in the next century. As he wrote, however, nearly all he touched—comedy, romance, pastoral, tragedy, history, biography—had been tried already, and in many cases given some degree of polish. The experiments had been done, the forms were established, the actors were gathered, and the stages were being built. The genius of Marlowe had put the stamp of maturity on the English theatre, and his triumphs found an enthusiastic, paying audience. The way was open for Shakespeare and his notable fellow dramatists, at the turn of the century and in the next reign, to make English verse drama the astonishing thing it became.

A SHORT BIBLIOGRAPHY

1. Bibliography:

Read, Conyers. *Bibliography of British History: Tudor Period, 1485–1603* (1959)

2. General Works:

(a) Contemporary

Hall, Edward. *Chronicle*; ed. H. Ellis (1809)
Harrison, William. *Description of England* (1577–87)
Holinshed, Raphael. *Chronicles*; ed. H. Ellis (1808)
Old English Ballads, 1553–1605; ed. H. E. Rollins (1920)
Stow, John. *Chronicles & Annals* (1580–1605)

(b) Later Studies

Bindoff, S. T. *Tudor England* (1950)
Black, J. B. *The Reign of Elizabeth* (1936)
Einstein, L. *Tudor Ideals* (1921)
Elton, G. R. *England under the Tudors* (1955)
Garvin, Katherine. *The Great Tudors* (1935)
Hall, H. *Society in the Elizabethan Age* (1902)
Mackie, J. D. *The Earlier Tudors, 1485–1558* (1952)
Pollard, A. F. *History of England, 1547–1603* (1910)
Rye, W. B. *England as Seen by Foreigners* (1865)
Shakespeare's England; 2 vols. (1926)

3. Tudor Monarchs:

(a) Contemporary

A Relation of the Island of England, 1498; ed. C. A. Sneyd (1847)
Bacon, Francis. *History of the Reign of Henry VII* (1622)
Literary Remains of Edward VI; ed. J. G. Nichols (1857)

(b) Later Studies

Elton, G. R. *England under the Tudors* (1955)
Neale, J. *Queen Elizabeth* (1958)
Pollard, A. F. *Henry VIII* (1913)
Scarisbrick, J. J. *Henry VIII* (1968)

4. Thomas More:

(a) Contemporary

Harpsfield, Nicholas. *Life of Sir Thomas More* (Everyman 1963)

More, Sir Thomas. *Utopia* [in Latin and English]; ed. J. H. Lupton (1895)

More, Sir Thomas. *Works*; ed. W. E. Campbell (1927)

Roper, William. *Life of Sir Thomas More* (Everyman 1963)

(b) Later Studies

Allen, J. W. *History of Political Thought in the Sixteenth Century* (1951)

Chambers, R. W. *Thomas More* (1945)

Pollard, A. F. *Henry VIII* (1913)

5. Robert Kett:

(a) Contemporary

Hales, John. *A Discourse of the Common Weal*; ed. E. Lamond (1929)

Tawney, R. H. and Power, Eileen. *Tudor Economic Documents*; 3 vols. (1924)

(b) Later Studies

Clayton, J. *Robert Kett and the Norfolk Rising* (1911)

Lipson, E. *Economic History of England*; v. 1 (1945)

Russell, F. W. *Kett's Rebellion in Norfolk* (1859)

Tawney, R. H. *The Agrarian Problem in the Sixteenth Century* (1912)

6. Mary Tudor:

Pollard, A. F. *History of England, 1547-1603* (1910)

Prescott, H. F. M. *Mary Tudor* (1953)

Waldman, Milton. *The Lady Mary* (1972)

7. Thomas Gresham:

(a) Contemporary

Tawney, R. H. and Power, Eileen. *Tudor Economic Documents*; 3 vols. (1924)

Wilson, Thomas. *Discourse upon Usury*; introduction by R. H. Tawney (1925)

(b) Later Studies

Burgon, J. W. *Life and Times of Sir Thomas Gresham*; 2 vols. (1839)

Clapham, J. H. *Concise Economic History of Britain* (1949)

Cunningham, W. *Growth of English Industry*; 3 vols. (1903)
Lipson, E. *Economic History of England*; v. 1–2 (1945)

8. Francis Walsingham:

(a) Contemporary
Smith, Sir Thomas. *De Republica Anglorum* [in English];
ed. L. Alston (1906)

(b) Later Studies
Black, J. B. *The Reign of Elizabeth* (1936)
Neale, J. *Elizabethan Government and Society* (1961)
Read, Conyers. *Mr. Secretary Walsingham*; 3 vols. (1925)

9. Humphrey Gilbert:

(a) Contemporary
Gilbert, Sir Humphrey. *Queene Elizabethes Achademy*; ed.
F. J. Furnivall (EETS 1869)
Hakluyt, Richard. *Principal Navigations*; v. 7–8 (1903)
Quinn, D. B. *Voyages and Colonizing Enterprises of Sir
Humphrey Gilbert;* 2 vols. (Hakluyt Soc. 1940)

(b) Later Studies
Gosling, W. G. *Life of Sir Humphrey Gilbert* (1911)
Raleigh, Walter. *English Voyages of the Sixteenth century*
(1906)

10. Richard Hooker:

(a) Contemporary
Hooker, Richard. *Laws of Ecclesiastical Polity*; ed. J. Keble
(1888)
Walton, Izaak. *Life of Richard Hooker* (World Classics 1927)

(b) Later Studies
Allen, J. W. *History of Political Thought in the Sixteenth
Century* (1951)
Frere, W. H. *The English Church, 1558–1625* (1904)
Gairdner, J. *The English Church in the Sixteenth Century* (1902)
Sisson, C. J. *The Judicious Marriage of Mr. Hooker* (1940)

11. Philip Sidney:

(a) Contemporary
Correspondence of Sir Philip Sidney and Hubert Languet; trans.
& ed. S. A. Pears (1845)
Greville, Fulke. *Life of Sir Philip Sidney* (1652)
Sidney, Sir Philip. *Works*; ed. A. Feuillerat (1922–26)

(b) Later Studies
Boas, F. S. *Sir Philip Sidney* (1955)
Fox-Bourne, H. R. *Sir Philip Sidney* (1891)
Lewis, C. S. *English Literature in the Sixteenth Century* (1954)

12. Robert Greene:

(a) Contemporary
Greene, Robert. *Complete Works*; ed. A. B. Grosart (1881–86)
Judges, A. V. *Elizabethan Underworld* (1930)
(b) Later Studies
Aydelotte, F. *Elizabethan Rogues and Vagabonds* (1913)
Jordan, J. C. *Robert Greene* (1915)
Jusserand, J. J. *English Novel in the Time of Shakespeare* (1890)
Lewis, C. S. *English Literature in the Sixteenth Century* (1954)

13. Tudor Playwrights:

(a) Contemporary
Adams, J. Q. *Chief Pre-Shakespearean Drama* (1924)
Armstrong, W. A. *Elizabethan History Plays* (1965)
Cunliffe, J. W. *Early English Classical Tragedies* (1912)
Dodsley, R. *Old Plays*; 15 vols. ed. W. C. Hazlitt (1874–76)
Marlowe, Christopher. *Works*; ed. C. F. T. Brooke (1910)
(b) Later Studies
Boas, F. S. *Introduction to Tudor Drama* (1933)
Cambridge History of English Literature; v. 5 (1907–15)
Wilson, F. P. *The English Drama, 1485–1585* (1969)

INDEX